WALT DISNEY WORLD® with Kids

2007

KIM WRIGHT WILEY

Seventeenth Edition

To my children,
Leigh and Jordan,
the best ride-testers in the business.

Published by Fodor's Travel, a division of Random House, Inc.

Fodor's is a registered trademark of Random House, Inc.

www.fodors.com

Every effort has been made to make this book complete and accurate as of the date of publication. In a time of rapid change, however, it is difficult to ensure that all information is entirely up-to-date. Although the publisher and authors cannot be liable for any inaccuracies or omissions in this book, they are always grateful for corrections and suggestions for improvement.

All products mentioned in this book are trademarks of their respective companies.

This book is available for special discounts for bulk purchases for sales promotions or premiums. Special editions, including personalized covers, excerpts of existing books, and corporate imprints, can be created in large quantities for special needs. For more information, write to Special Markets/Premium Sales, 1745 Broadway, MD 6-2, New York, New York 10019, or e-mail specialmarkets@randomhouse.com.

Seventeenth Edition

ISBN: 1–4000–1694–0

ISBN-13: 978–1–4000–1694–5

PRINTED IN THE UNITED STATES OF AMERICA
10 9 8 7 6 5 4 3 2 1

Contents

Chapter 3 Once You Get There   85

Chapter 4 Touring Tips and Plans   101

Chapter 5 The Magic Kingdom   129

Chapter 6   Epcot   171

Chapter 7   Disney-MGM Studios   201

HELPFUL PHONE NUMBERS

All Orlando numbers have a 407 area code. Be sure to make all Disney hotel reservations by calling 934–7639 (W–DISNEY), and use the resorts' direct lines only to report a delayed check-in, call Guest Services, or reach a registered guest.

General Walt Disney World Information Phone Numbers

General Information	824–4321
WDW Resort Information	934–7639 (W–DISNEY)
WDW Dining Information and Advance Reservations	939–3463 (WDW–DINE)
WDW Recreational Information	939–7529 (WDW–PLAY)
WDW Golf Information	939–4653 (WDW–GOLF)
WDW Tour Information	939–8687 (WDW–TOUR)
Disney Cruise Line	800/951–3532
Disney Travel Company	800/828–0228
Blizzard Beach	824–4321
Typhoon Lagoon	560–4141
Pleasure Island	939–2648
Wide World of Sports	828–3267

Walt Disney World Resort Phone Numbers

All-Star Movies	939–7000
All-Star Music	939–6000
All-Star Sports	939–5000
Animal Kingdom Lodge	938–3000
Beach Club Resort	934–8000
Beach Club Villas	934–2175
BoardWalk Resort	939–5100
BoardWalk Villas	939–5100
Caribbean Beach Resort	939–3400
Contemporary Resort	824–1000
Coronado Springs Resort	939–1000
Dolphin Resort	934–4000
Fort Wilderness Campground	824–2900

Grand Floridian Resort	824–3000
Old Key West Resort	827–1198
Polynesian Resort	824–2000
Pop Century	938–4000
Port Orleans Resort	934–5000/6000
Saratoga Springs	827–1100
Swan Resort	934–3000
Wilderness Lodge	824–3200
Wilderness Lodge Villas	824–3200
Yacht Club	934–7000

Universal Orlando Phone Numbers

General Information	363–8000
Universal Orlando Resort Information	888/273–1311
Universal Studios	837–2273

SeaWorld & Discovery Cove Phone Numbers

SeaWorld	351–3600
Camp SeaWorld	800/406–2244
Discovery Cove	351–3600

Other Helpful Phone Numbers

Alamo Car Rental	800/462–5266
American Airlines	800/433–7300
Avis Car Rental	800/331–1212
Budget Car Rental	800/527–0700
Delta Airlines	800/221–1212
Dollar Car Rental	800/800–4000
Hertz Car Rental	800/654–3131
Islands of Adventure	363–8000
Mears Shuttle Service	423–5566
National Car Rental	800/227–7368
Orlando Visitors Bureau	800/255–5786
Ticketmaster	839–3900
US Airways	800/428–4322

HELPFUL WEB SITES

Walt Disney World	www.disneyworld.com
The Disney Corporation	www.disney.com
The Disney Cruise Line	www.disneycruise.com
Universal Orlando	www.universalorlando.com
SeaWorld	www.seaworld.com
Discovery Cove	www.discoverycove.com

LIST OF MAPS

LIST OF QUICK-GUIDE REFERENCE TABLES

ABBREVIATIONS, TERMS, AND ICONS

Abbreviations and Terms

Downtown Disney	A shopping, dining, and entertainment complex composed of Pleasure Island, the Marketplace, and the West Side
MGM	The Disney–MGM Studios Theme Park
Minor parks	Typhoon Lagoon, River Country, Pleasure Island, and Blizzard Beach
Major parks	The Magic Kingdom, Epcot, Disney–MGM Studios, and the Animal Kingdom
Off-season	The less crowded times of the year—specifically those weeks between September and May that do not flank major holidays
On-season	The most crowded times of the year—specifically summers, holidays, and spring break
Off-site	Any resort or hotel not owned by Disney
On-site	A Disney-owned resort
TTC	Ticket and Transportation Center: The monorail version of a train station, where riders can transfer to monorails bound for Epcot, the Magic Kingdom, or monorail-line hotels. You can also catch buses at the TTC bound for the parks, the on-site hotels, and Downtown Disney.

Icons

 Helpful Hint

 Hidden Mickey

 Insider's Secret

 Money-Saving Tip

 Scare Factor

 Time-Saving Tip

PREFACE

How Has Walt Disney World Changed?

The simple answer is, it's gotten bigger. And they're still building.

In the 17 years since I first began researching this guide, Disney has added one major park, three minor ones, six hotels, a cruise line, and more attractions and restaurants than I can count. It was once possible for a fleet-footed and well-prepared family to see most of Walt Disney World in a four-day stay. But that is no longer true. As the Disney complex expands, it's more vital than ever that you target what you want to see, work these priorities into your schedule, and then relax. Anything beyond that is pure gravy.

Sometimes I'm asked if the prevalence of travel guides makes them less useful to their readers. After all, if everyone knows about a "secret tip," is it still a secret?

Good question, but even with all those books on the market, a relatively small number of WDW visitors actually make advance preparations. Most people still show up late and wander around aimlessly, so anyone with any sort of touring plan at all is automatically a step ahead of the crowd.

It's tempting to treat Orlando as if it were a kiddie version of Las Vegas—you go there to play the numbers, and a family that hits 24 attractions in a day must, by definition, be having twice as much fun as a family that sees 12. Not so.

You'll find a lot of crying kids and exasperated parents by mid-afternoon, largely because everyone is frantic with the idea that this trip is so expensive they darn well better squeeze the most out of every minute. Actually, the most successful touring plans boil down to a few simple guidelines:

1. Plan your trip for times of year when the parks are less crowded. When people write to me about having bad experiences at Disney World, it seems that about 90% of the disasters happen in July.

2. Order maps and tickets and arrange all hotel and dining reservations well in advance. Every phone call you make from home is a line you won't have to stand in later.

3. Read up on attractions and let each family member choose three or four must-see attractions per park. An amazing number of parents plan this trip for their kids without really consulting them about what they'd most like to do.

4. Accept your differences and be willing to split up occasionally. Forcing a sullen 13-year-old onto It's A Small World or strapping a terrified 5-year-old into Rock 'n' Roller Coaster in the interest of family togetherness will guarantee at least one tantrum per hour.

5. Arrive at the parks early, rest in the afternoon, and return to the parks at night. Walt Disney World can be very tiring and regular rest stops are key.

What hasn't changed in 17 years is my belief that Walt Disney World is the best family travel destination on the planet. There is truly something for everyone within these gates, and the spectacular, awe-inspiring rides are counterbalanced with sweet, small moments of joy. When you check into your room the first night and discover that you can see the fireworks of *IllumiNations* from your balcony . . . when your toddler first spots Mickey . . . when they release the doves at the end of the Beauty and the Beast show . . . or when your 13-year-old actually smiles—then, trust me, you'll forget about the crowds and the heat and the expense and you'll remember why you came to Disney.

For this edition, I've added comments from Disney visitors who've written to me to share their best tips and "never again" stories. I'd love to hear how your trip went and any feedback you have about this book. If you'd like to share your travel experiences with me, please take a few minutes to respond to my survey online at www.fodors.com/disneysurvey, e-mail me at kwwiley@fodors.com, or write to me at Fodor's, 1745 Broadway, New York, NY 10019. Thanks for your time, and have a great trip!

— Kim

CHAPTER

1

Before You Leave Home

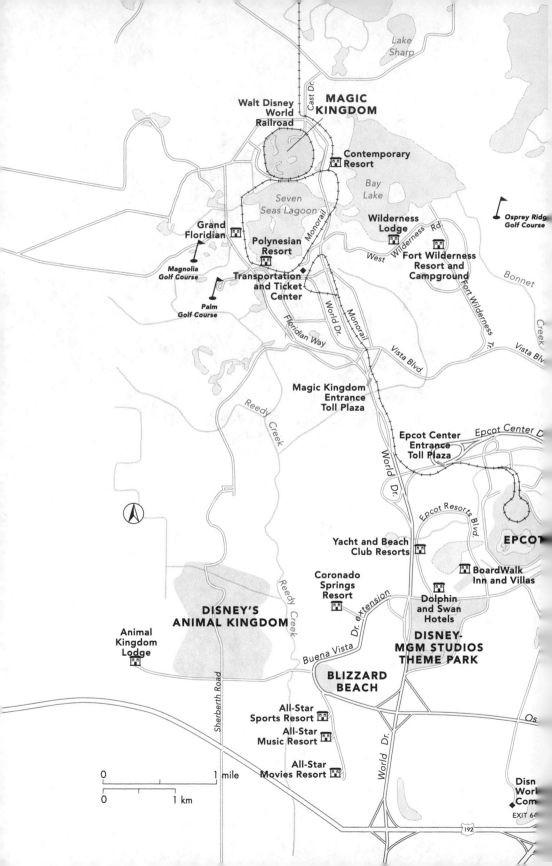

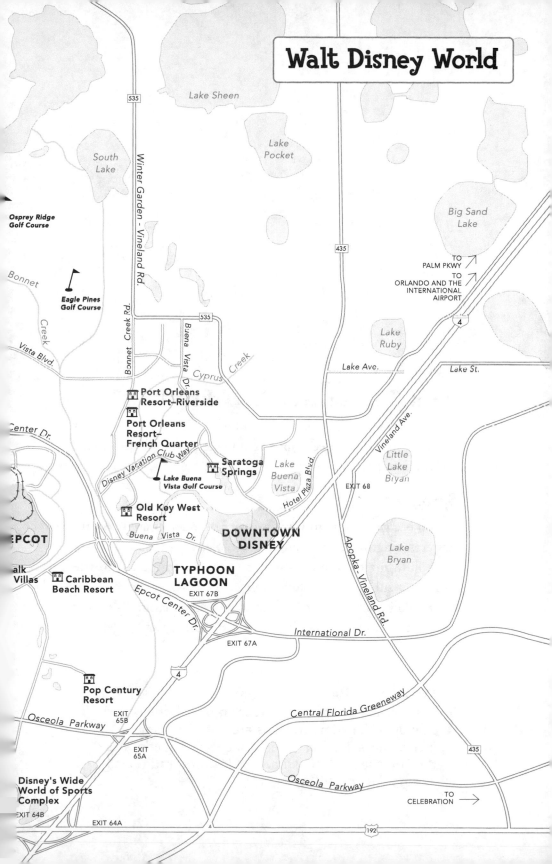

Sunglasses ✓
Camera ✓
Tickets ✓
Flip-Flops
Swimsuits
Beach Bag
Sunscreen ✓
Guidebook ✓
Travel Games
Snacks ✓

What Time of Year Should We Visit?

Crowd levels at Walt Disney World vary seasonally, so one of the most important decisions you'll make as you plan is deciding when to go.

Spring

Spring is a great time to visit. Except around spring break and Easter, springtime crowds are manageable. They're not as sparse as in fall, but they're far smaller than in summer. And the weather is sublime, with highs in the 70s, lows in the 60s, and less rainfall than in any other season. Disney maintains longer park hours in spring than in fall, but schedules vary widely. To

Helpful Hint

The size of the crowds corresponds with the school schedule. Any time the kids are out of school (i.e., summers, spring break, and major holidays) is the "on-season." Any time children are traditionally in school is the "off-season."

check projected hours of operation visit www.disneyworld.com or call 407/824-4321.

Summer

The good news about summer is that everything is open and operational, and the parks run very long hours. The bad news is that it's hot and crowded—so crowded that the wait for many rides can be as long as 90 minutes.

If your children's school schedule dictates that you must visit in summer, the first two weeks of June and the last two weeks of August are your best bets.

Helpful Hint

If you have preschoolers, babies, or senior citizens in the party, avoid summers like the plague.

Insider's Secret

Certain annual events—most notably the marathon in January, College Week in April, Gay Day in June, and various press events scattered throughout the year—bring large groups into the parks. Ask about events or groups before you book your reservations so you'll know what to expect.

Fall

Fall has lighter crowds than any other season and the weather is usually great. There are, however, disadvantages to a fall visit. You have to work around the fact that older children are in school. The parks run shorter hours in fall; the Magic Kingdom, Animal Kingdom, and MGM may close as early as 5 PM, although Epcot always remains open later. Earlier closings mean that some of the special evening presentations, such as the evening parade in the Magic Kingdom, are scheduled only on the weekends.

Fall is also hurricane season in Florida, so there is some risk that you'll schedule your trip for the exact week that hurricane Laluna pounds the coast. (In terms of tropical storms, September and October are riskier than November.) Fortunately, Orlando is an hour inland, meaning that coastal storms usually only yield rain. Furthermore, there are more rainy days in the summer months than there are in the fall, so in general the advantages of autumn touring far outweigh the disadvantages.

Helpful Hint

Don't underestimate the holiday crowds. In the weeks flanking Easter and Christmas, Disney World is mobbed, and any holiday when the kids are out of school—such as Presidents' Day weekend—will draw larger-than-average crowds.

Winter

Winter is a mixed bag. The absolute worst times are holidays. Christmas and New Year's can pull in as many as 80,000 visitors per day, and even extended hours can't compensate for crowds of this size. But if you avoid the holiday weeks, winter

Insider's Secret

Winter can be a great time to visit Walt Disney World, but water babies take note: pools may be closed for refurbishing on certain days in January and February. Generally, only one water park is open at a time in winter, and both may close if the temperature dips below 55 degrees.

can be an ideal time to visit. With the exception of the week-ends around Martin Luther King Jr. Day and Presidents' Day, January and February are relatively uncrowded—and pleasantly cool. The first two weeks of December, when the Christmas decorations are already up but the crowds have not yet arrived, are another good option. The parks run the same shortened hours in winter that they run in fall, but since the crowds are so much lighter, you'll still have time to see everything you want.

Insider's Secret

One caveat to winter touring: Mickey's Very Merry Christmas Party, held each year on several evenings throughout December, is madly popular and the party dates are especially crowded. If you want to attend the party, get tickets early—they sell out months in advance. If you don't want to attend, avoid the party days. Dates for each year's parties are listed on www.disneyworld.com.

Off-Season Touring Caveat

Some parents have written in to say that they like the idea of taking the kids to Orlando during the off-season, but that they've heard this is when Disney is most apt to close attractions for refurbishing. It's a valid point. On a recent trip in January, I found five attractions closed for refurbishing, including Big Thunder Mountain in the Magic Kingdom and Star Tours at MGM. But I still believe it is better to tour during the off-season, especially if you've been to Disney World before or plan to return. Here's why: during that same January week, the most popular Magic Kingdom attractions, such as the Many Adventures of Winnie the Pooh and Splash Mountain, were posting wait times as short as 20 minutes, about a third of what they normally are. You're still more likely to see more and wait less when it's less crowded. If you do decide to visit during the off-season, you can avoid last-minute disappointments by checking www.disneyworld.com to see what is scheduled to be closed during your trip.

How Long Should We Stay?

It will take at least four days for a family to tour the major parks. If you also want to visit the water parks and Downtown Disney, make that five days. Six days are best for families who'd like to work in sporting options like boating or golf, or those who would like to tour at a more leisurely pace.

If you plan on visiting other area attractions, such as Sea-World or Universal Orlando, allow a week.

Should We Take the Kids out of School?

Even if you're sold on the advantages of off-season touring, you may be reluctant to take your children out of school. However, there are ways to highlight the educational aspects of a trip to Disney World; some suggestions are listed at the end of this section.

If you're considering pulling your child out of school for a couple of days, work together with his or her teacher to create a plan that keeps him or her from falling behind. Ideally, half of the makeup work should be done before you leave—the posttrip blues are bad enough without facing three hours of homework each night. Also, timing is everything. Don't plan your trip for the week the school is administering exams or standardized testing. Check with the teacher about the best times for your child to be absent.

In addition, help your child create a project that's related to the trip. Your child might want to make a scrapbook. The mother of one first grader helped him design an "ABC" book

Epcot Projects

- The greenhouse tour in the Land is full of information on space-age farming.

- Marine biology is the theme of the Living Seas pavilion.

- Missing health class? The Wonders of Life pavilion is devoted to that greatest of all machines, the human body.

- Report on the culture of a country represented in the World Showcase, highlighting the music, architecture, food, and history.

- Innoventions, although often described as the world's hippest arcade, is also a preview of technological advances.

before he left home, and he spent his week at Disney World collecting souvenirs for each page—Goofy's autograph on the "G" page, a postcard of a Japanese pagoda on the "P" page, and so on. An older child might gather leaves from the various trees and shrubs that were imported to landscape the countries in the World Showcase. Or a young photographer could demonstrate her proficiency with various lighting techniques by photographing Cinderella Castle in early morning, high noon, sunset, and after dark.

You can even work on math. If a car containing six people departs from the Test Track loading area every 20 seconds, how many riders go through in an hour? A day? If the monorail averages 32 mph how long does it take it to travel the 7 miles from the Magic Kingdom to Epcot? Once you get going on these sorts of questions, it's addictive. Or give your kids a set

Animal Kingdom Projects

- The Cretaceous Trail—a path filled with plants that have survived from the Cretaceous period—is an excellent introduction to botanical evolution.

- Rafiki's Planet Watch is the park's research and education hub, where kids can tour veterinary labs and watch interactive videos about endangered animals.

- It's always fun to do a report on one of the animals you see on Kilimanjaro Safaris or along one of the exploration trails.

amount of mythical money to spend, such as $1,000. Then let them keep track of expenses, deducting purchases from their starting total and making decisions about what they can and cannot afford on their budget.

Other Orlando Educational Programs

Disney World isn't the only place in Orlando that can be educational. Consider one of the following:

SeaWorld

SeaWorld offers daily tours, as well as weeklong classes and cool overnight programs in summer and during holidays. Call 407/ 351–3600 or visit www.seaworld.org for more information. See Chapter 16 for details on touring SeaWorld.

Orlando Science Center

This impressive facility has oodles of hands-on exhibits and programs for kids of all ages. Something is happening all the time—especially in spring and summer when most of the camps are held—and the prices are reasonable.

Admission to the center is $15 for adults, and $10 for kids ages 3 to 11. Classes are individually priced. To see what's happening during your visit call 407/514–2000 or visit www.osc.org.

Kennedy Space Center

Orlando is only about an hour's drive from the Kennedy Space Center so it's an easy day trip. Kids will enjoy seeing the rockets and the IMAX films about space exploration. You can even plan your visit to coincide with a launch.

Crew passes, which include a bus tour of the space center as well as the IMAX film, are $37 for adults and $27 for kids ages 3 to 11. Call 321/867–5000 or visit www.kennedyspacecenter .com for details on launch dates and tours.

Should We Buy a Package?

This is a toughie. There are advantages to package trips, most notably that if you play your cards right, you can indeed save money. It's also helpful to know up front exactly what your vacation will cost. Packages often require hefty prepayments, which are painful at the time, but at least you don't return home with your credit card utterly maxed out.

Package trips can have drawbacks, however. Like buying a fully loaded car off a dealer's lot, you may find yourself paying for options you don't want and don't need. Packages are often padded with perks such as reduced golf fees, which interest only a few families, or free rental cars, which you may not need if you're staying on-site. At the other end of the spectrum are

Money-Saving Tip

Don't automatically assume that a package will save you big bucks. Unless you're sure you need every feature that the package includes, you may end up losing money on the deal.

deeply discounted packages that place you in run-down or out-of-the-way hotels.

Disney Package Vacations

The basic Magic Your Way package includes a hotel room on Disney property and theme park tickets. You can choose any resort from any price range and customize your ticket options in a way that suits your family's needs. Prices for a six-day/seven-night package for a family of four staying at a value resort, such as one of the All-Stars, and choosing the most basic kinds of tickets start at $1,700. The same package with a stay at a moderate resort, such as Port Orleans, will cost you $2,000, and with a stay at a luxury resort, such as the Yacht Club, will cost $2,700.

The rule of thumb is, if your kids are young and this is one of your first trips to Disney World, you'll probably be spending most of your time in the four major theme parks, so choose a basic package. It's a good idea to upgrade to Park Hopper tickets, since they give you the flexibility to move from

Money-Saving Tips

- AAA and travel agents can provide some genuine bargains. Check with an agency for prices and then call Disney directly to compare.
- Look for deals online. Go to Disney's own Web site, www.disneyworld.com, and click on "My Vacation." Or check out www.expedia.com, www.hotels.com, www.vacationoutlet.com, or www.travelocity.com for rooms and packages.
- If you're using Disney's direct line, 407/934–7639 (407/W–DISNEY), to book rooms always ask, "Are there any discounts or special offers available?"

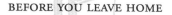
one park to another in the course of the day. How fancy a re-sort you choose and whether or not to include dining is up to you. The more expensive premium options are better for fami-lies who've been to Disney World before and want to do some-thing different, and whose kids are old enough to enjoy the water parks, sporting options, fancier restaurants, tours, and Cirque du Soleil.

Should You Add a Dining Plan?

The Magic Your Way dining plans start at about $40 per day for adults and $12 per day for kids 3–9. The basic plan in-cludes, for each day of your trip, one full-service meal, one counter-service meal, and a snack from a list of the 100+ par-ticipating Disney restaurants.

Is it worth it? If you have big eaters in the party, the plan can save you big money. For families with younger kids or finicky eaters the numbers don't work out quite as well. If 6-year-old Katie eats nothing but cereal and 3-year-old Danny grows so rest-less that sit-down dinners are a nightmare, it's unlikely they'll eat enough food to justify the cost of the dining plan.

One other thing to consider: The plan works on a point system, and certain experiences, like the dinner shows and most of the luxury restaurants, are worth more than your daily full-service meal allowance. For *one* of these exceptional dining ex-periences, you must use the points for *two* of your regular full-service meals. But you can save a bundle on what would otherwise be a very expensive meal. One mother wrote, "By eating at counter-service places for a couple of days beforehand we saved enough points for a full dinner at California Grill and it was superb."

Another mom wrote to us that "the Disney Dining Plan makes a lot of sense if you like character meals. We were able to attend three: at Crystal Palace, Chef Mickey's, and 1900 Park Fare, and we could not have afforded all this without the plan."

On the other hand, a couple from Georgia with three children under age 10 said the meal plans weren't for them: "In our opinion, adding meals to your package only makes sense if you're prepared to eat 6,000 calories a day and spend five hours a day in restaurants.

Airline Packages

If you're flying, check out the airline's own packages, which include airfare, theme park tickets for Disney and other Orlando attractions, and lodging at either on-site or off-site hotels. Again there's a huge range of amenities—you can have valet parking and bottles of champagne if you're willing to pay for them. And again the packages can be fine-tuned to meet your needs.

Insider's Secret

The airlines control a limited number of on-site hotel rooms, so call at least six months in advance if you have your heart set on a particular Disney hotel.

Cruise Packages

Some of the most popular Disney packages are those that combine a cruise on the *Disney Magic* or *Disney Wonder* with a vacation in the parks. Check out www.disneycruise.com, call 800/ 370–0097, or contact your travel agent. See Chapter 13 for more information.

Helpful Hint

Order your tickets online as soon as you know you're going to Disney—it generally takes 2–3 weeks for them to arrive. Or arrange to pick them up at Guest Relations at the theme parks or at any on-site hotel.

What Kind of Tickets Do We Need?

Under Disney's flexible Magic Your Way ticketing system, families can customize their tickets to reflect their priorities and length of stay.

Let's say you have a long weekend to visit and want a three-day ticket. The base price is $181 for ages 10 and up, which comes to $60.33 a day, a slight savings over the one-day ticket price of $63. However, this base price lets you into only one park per day. From there, you can add the Park Hopper option, which allows you to move from park to park within a day. That's $40 more per person. If you want to visit Disney's minor parks and attractions, such as Blizzard Beach, Typhoon Lagoon, DisneyQuest, and Pleasure Island, you can either pay the $21 to $34 one-day price, or for longer stays, add the $50 Water Parks & More option to your package.

Magic Your Way tickets expire 14 days after their first use, so if you're in town for a week and you purchase a four-day ticket, you don't have to go to Disney World four days in a row. You can space out your visits. For $10 to $65 more, depending on the numbers of days in your multiday ticket, you can ensure that any remaining days on your multiday ticket never expire—useful if you plan to return.

So, how do you know what ticketing options to buy? If this is your first trip to Disney World, keep it simple. If you have young kids, you'll likely spend most of your time in the four major parks, so a base ticket is fine. Most families report that the Park Hopper option is worthwhile, especially for longer stays,

Money-Saving Tips

The more days you buy, the less your per-day cost. If you're staying for a week, your ticket price per day drops significantly. An adult buying a seven-day basic ticket ends up paying around $29 per day, a significant savings over the one-day ticket price of $63.

Magic Your Way
Price Chart

TICKET OPTIONS								
TICKET	10-DAY	7-DAY	6-DAY	5-DAY	4-DAY	3-DAY	2-DAY	1-DAY
BASE TICKET Ages 10-up	$210	$204	$202	$199	$195	$181	$125	$63
Ages 3-9	$171	$165	$164	$162	$160	$149	$103	$52

Base Ticket admits guest to one of the four major theme parks per day's use.
Park choices are: Magic Kingdom, Epcot, Disney-MGM Studios, Disney's Animal Kingdom.

ADD: Park Hopper	$40	$40	$40	$40	$40	$40	$40	$40

Park Hopper option entitles guest to visit more than one theme park per day's use. Park choices are any combination of Magic Kingdom, Epcot, Disney-MGM Studios, Disney's Animal Kingdom.

ADD: Water Parks & More	$50 5 visits	$50 5 visits	$50 4 visits	$50 3 visits	$50 3 visits	$50 2 visits	$50 2 visits	$50 2 visits

Water Parks & More option entitles guest to a specified number of visits (between 2 and 5) to a choice of entertainment and recreation venues. Choices are Blizzard Beach, Typhoon Lagoon, DisneyQuest, Pleasure Island, and Wide World of Sports.

ADD: No Expiration	$135	$65	$50	$40	$20	$10	$10	n/a

No expiration means that unused admissions on a ticket may be used any time in the future. Without this option, tickets expire 14 days after first use.

MINOR PARKS AND ATTRACTIONS		
TICKET	AGES 10-UP	AGES 3-9
TYPHOON LAGOON OR BLIZZARD BEACH 1-Day 1-Park	$34	$28
DISNEYQUEST 1-Day	$34	$28
DISNEY'S WIDE WORLD OF SPORTS	$10.05	$7.48
CIRQUE DU SOLEIL'S *LA NOUBA*	$61–$95	$49–$76
PLEASURE ISLAND 1-Night Multi-Club Ticket	$20.95	$20.95

*Admission to *Pleasure Island* clubs is restricted to guests 18 or older unless accompanied by an adult 21 or older. For some clubs all guests must be 21 or older.

*All prices are subject to Florida sales tax.

Helpful Hint

Theme park tickets demagnetize easily, so keep them in a separate pocket away from your credit cards. If your ticket does become demagnetized and won't swipe at the entrance turnstiles, Disney will gladly replace it. But this involves a trip to Guest Relations and it's maddening to have to make this detour when you're itching to get to the rides.

when you might want the flexibility to revisit a park. It's also good for people who've been to Disney World before and know what attractions they want to see. Many of the touring tips in this book assume that you have the ability to move from one park to another in the course of the day. Disney "adjusts"—that is, raises—prices on a regular basis, so you should always confirm prices by calling 407/824–4321 or visiting www.disneyworld .com. Also note that children under age 3 are admitted free.

The Water Parks & More option makes sense if you have older kids who would enjoy the water parks and DisneyQuest, or if you've been to Disney World before and are looking to venture outside the four major parks. On the other hand, if this is your first trip to Disney World you'll have all you can handle just visiting the four major marks. And if your kids are very young, you may find your hotel pool is a far more practical way to cool off than trekking to a water park.

Insider's Secret

If you are or have been a member of the U.S. or foreign military, you're eligible for discount tickets and you can stay at the on-site Shades of Green Resort for a fraction of what it costs to stay at other Disney resorts. For more information call 407/824–1403 or visit www.shadesofgreen.org.

Transportation

If you're flying to Orlando, one of the first major decisions that you should make in advance is whether to rent a car. For families staying on-site and focusing primarily on Disney attractions, the answer is probably no. Quite a few families have reported that they used their rental car less than they anticipated. "We paid $350 for the privilege of driving from the airport to our hotel and back," wrote one father.

But for families staying off-site or anyone planning to visit both Disney and non-Disney attractions, the answer is yes. "We got a great hotel rate but it was about 15 miles from Disney World," one mother reported. "We also spent a day at Universal and a day at SeaWorld, so we would have been sunk if we hadn't had our own transportation."

Insider's Secret

At times it may make more sense to use a taxi than a rental car or Disney's transportation. Consider taking a cab if:

- You'd like quick, direct transportation from the airport to your hotel.
- You'd like quick, direct transportation from one resort to another.
- You're headed to a minor park like Downtown Disney or the water parks and don't want a lengthy shuttle commute.
- You're staying at a Disney hotel but heading to Universal Orlando or SeaWorld for the day.
- Everyone's absolutely exhausted. If you've pushed too far and the kids are in a meltdown, cabs are the fastest way to get back to your room. They're always waiting near the theme park exits and, at times, this is $10 well worth spending.

Transportation with a Rental Car

Some rental car companies, such as Avis, Budget, Dollar, and National, have desks at the Orlando airport, with cars in the adjacent lot. Others, including Hertz and Alamo, are away from the airport and require a separate shuttle ride.

Alamo	800/462–5266	www.alamo.com
Avis	800/331–1212	www.avis.com
Dollar	800/800–4000	www.dollar.com
Hertz	800/654–3131	www.hertz.com
National	800/227–7368	www.nationalcar.com

An average weekly rental fee for a midsize car is around $300. Don't be fooled by the quoted rate of $30 a day; by the time you add on taxes and insurance it's closer to $50.

Transportation Without a Rental Car

If you're staying at a Disney resort, the Magical Express Service makes transport from the airport to hotel room less costly, and if all goes according to plan, more convenient. Here's how it works:

Check your bags at your hometown airport. This is the last time you'll see them until you're in your hotel room in Orlando, so be sure to put anything you may need in the meantime, such as medication or summer-weather clothing into your carry-on. When your plane arrives in Orlando, you don't have to go to baggage claim to pick up your bags—instead, follow a Disney representative, board a motor coach, and head for your resort. Your bags will arrive in your room shortly after you do.

The system saves you the hassle of waiting for your bags to appear on the revolving belt then dragging them through the Orlando airport, and it also saves you money. The Magical Express service is free to all Disney hotel guests. Round-trip shuttle service between the Orlando airport and the Disney resort area runs about $30 a person and a cab ride is about $50 each

Insider's Secret

The Magical Express buses that transport you from the airport usually stop at several different hotels and this can add up to a long commute time. If you're really eager to get your vacation going fast, take a cab. Some families have reported significant wait times before their luggage showed up at their hotel, so pack anything you need for your first day in a carry-on bag and take it with you in the bus.

way, so a family of four is automatically saving $100–$120 on transportation.

If you're not staying at a Disney resort and not renting a car you have two basic options for transport between the airport and your hotel. The fastest and easiest is a cab; prices average about $40 to the Universal-SeaWorld area and $50 to the Disney area, plus tip. The Mears shuttle service is $29 round-trip for adults and $19 for kids, and no tipping is expected. You can reserve your shuttle before leaving home by calling 407/423–5566. If there are two people or more in your party, it'll be as cheap to take a cab as it is to take a shuttle.

Countdown to Disney World

Okay, let's summarize. Here's what needs to be done—and when.

As Soon as Possible

- Choose your resort. To help find the best on-site hotel for you, consult Chapter 2, and once you've narrowed your options, make reservations via www.disneyworld.com or 407/934–7639 (407/W–DISNEY).

Money-Saving Tip

The Orlando Magicard is a great source of savings for families staying at off-site hotels, and another way to slash costs is to buy a discount coupon book for the Entertainment Club in your hometown. The books are best known for their local restaurant coupons, but few people realize that a nationwide directory of hotels offering deep discounts can be found in the back. Several off-site Orlando hotels are listed and a 50% discount can make an upscale resort as inexpensive as an interstate cheapie. But only a few rooms per hotel are earmarked for the discount, so your chances of cashing in improve if you're willing to book early.

- Even if you're staying off-site, booking your room early is smart. A great way to get discounts on off-site lodging is to call the Orlando Visitors Bureau at 800/255–5786 to request a Vacation Planner and Magicard. It takes three to four weeks to get the package, but the card qualifies you for significant discounts at many off-site hotels.

- Want to see a dinner show? Check out Chapter 10 for options. Dinner shows can be booked up to two years in advance by calling 407/939–3463 (407/WDW–DINE).

Six Months in Advance

- Buy your theme park tickets. You can either buy online at www.disneyworld.com, which sometimes offers a slight discount, or call 407/934–7639 (407/W–DISNEY).

- When you purchase your tickets, request maps of the theme parks to aid in your planning. If you need a Guidebook for Disabled Visitors, request that, too.

- Flying? Book now.

- If you need a rental car, reserve it now. There's no need to reserve shuttle service.

Four Months in Advance

- You can arrange for dining reservations 180 days in advance by calling 407/939–3463 (407/WDW–DINE). For a complete explanation of the system, see Chapter 11.

- To book a fireworks cruise call 407/939–7529 (407/WDW–PLAY). See Chapter 10 for more information.

- Interested in golf, parasailing, surfing, or some other sport? Book your time by calling 407/939–7529 (407/WDW–PLAY). See Chapter 10 for details.

Two Months in Advance

- Families who would like to take a behind-the-scenes tour or enroll their kids in one of the Grand Floridian programs, such as the pirate-theme scavenger hunt or tea with Alice and the other *Wonderland* characters, should do that now. Call 407/939–8687 (407/WDW–TOURS) for the tours and 407/939–3463 (407/WDW–DINE) for the Grand Floridian programs.

- Want a spa treatment? Call Saratoga Springs Resort at 407/827–4455 or the Grand Floridian at 407/824–2332 for a reservation.

- For Cirque du Soleil tickets, call 407/939–7600.

Two Weeks in Advance

- You should be good to go. Just check over everything and reconfirm times and reservations, so when you get to Orlando all you'll have to focus on is having fun.

Things to Discuss with Your Kids Before You Leave Home

It's important to include the kids in the vacation planning, so discuss the following topics before you leave home.

The Trip Itself

There are two schools of thought on just how far in advance you should tell the kids you're headed to Disney World. Because many families make reservations as much as a year in advance, it's easy to fall into a "waiting for Christmas" syndrome, with the kids nearly in a lather of anticipation weeks before you leave. To avoid the agony of a long countdown, one couple packed in secret and then woke the kids up at 5 AM one morning and announced, "Get in the car, we're going to Disney World." The best method is probably somewhere between the two extremes. Tell your kids at the time you make the reservations and solicit their opinions about what activities to book in advance, but don't begin poring over the brochures in earnest until about a month before the trip.

The Layout of the Parks

Testimonies from the more than 400 families surveyed or interviewed for this book have shown that the amount of advance research you do directly correlates with how much you enjoy your trip. Don't get me wrong—visitors who show up at Disney World without any preparation can still have fun, but their comment sheets are peppered with "Next time I'll know . . ." and "If only we had . . ."

If you're letting preteens and teens roam around on their own, they should definitely be briefed on the locations of major attractions. But the pleasures of being prepared can extend even to preschoolers. If you purchase a few Disney World coloring books or a kids' touring guide, even the youngest child will arrive able to identify Spaceship Earth and Splash Mountain. A little knowledge before entering the gates is essential to helping you spend your time in the parks wisely.

The Classic Stories of Disney

If your kids are under 8, another good pretrip purchase is a set of Disney books with audiotapes. Even though parental eyes may glaze over when Dumbo rewinds for its 34th straight hearing, these tapes and books help to familiarize kids with the characters and rides they'll be seeing once they arrive.

Some families rent Disney movies before the trip. For example, viewing *Honey, I Shrunk the Kids* before you leave will vastly improve your children's appreciation of Epcot's *Honey, I Shrunk the Audience* as well as the *Honey, I Shrunk the Kids* Movie Set Adventure at MGM.

Special Academic Projects

See the section "Should We Take the Kids Out of School?" earlier in this chapter for ideas. Whatever project you decide upon, it's essential you get the kids on board before you arrive in Orlando. Once there, they'll be too distracted for your lectures on academic responsibility.

Souvenirs and Money

Will you save all souvenir purchases for the last day? Buy one small souvenir every day? Are the children expected to spend their own money or will Mom and Dad spring for the T-shirts? Whatever you decide will depend on your pocketbooks and your particular interpretation of fiscal fairness, but do set the rules before you're in the park. Otherwise the selection of goodies will lure you into spending far more than you anticipated.

One excellent technique for limiting impulse buys is to purchase Disney Dollars the first day you're in WDW. (You can get them at any on-site hotel or at Guest Relations in any park.) Disney Dollars come in denominations of $1, $5, and $10 (with pictures of the characters where presidents would be) and are accepted throughout Disney World. You can give your kids an age-appropriate number of Disney Dollars at the beginning of the trip, explaining that this money alone is for souvenirs.

The Scare Factor

Finally, give some thought to the scare factor. A disappointing meal or boring show can ruin an hour, but if misjudging a ride leaves you with a terrified or nauseated child, that can ruin the whole day.

How frightening a ride is can be tough to gauge because Disney World scariness comes in two forms. First there are atmospheric rides, ranging from the shadows and cardboard witch of Snow White's Scary Adventures to the creepy, cobwebbed old hotel in the Tower of Terror. The other kind of fear factor is motion related: while Space Mountain and other such coasters are obviously risky, some guests can lose their lunch on sweet little charmers like the Mad Tea Party.

Helpful Hint

For many people, the motion-simulation rides are more disturbing than the coasters. In Star Tours at MGM, for example, you barely move, but the visual effects may make you feel like you've been literally spinning through space.

Disney's guidance comes in the form of height requirements, but saying that a 41-inch-tall 5-year-old *can* ride Big Thunder Mountain is no indication that he *should* ride Big Thunder Mountain. As we all know, some 6-year-olds are fearless and some 11-year-olds easily unnerved. Read the ride descriptions and scare-factor ratings in this book to find out what you're dealing with.

Height Requirements

The Magic Kingdom

Barnstormer	35 inches
Big Thunder Mountain	40 inches
Splash Mountain	40 inches
Space Mountain	44 inches
Stitch's Great Escape	40 inches

Epcot

Body Wars	40 inches
Mission: SPACE	44 inches
Soarin'	40 inches
Test Track	40 inches

MGM

Rock 'n' Roller Coaster	48 inches
Star Tours	40 inches
Tower of Terror	40 inches

The Animal Kingdom

DINOSAUR	40 inches
Expedition Everest	44 inches
Kali River Rapids	38 inches
Primeval Whirl	48 inches

If you're still unsure, employ these strategies:

- *Do a Baby Swap.* (No, this does not mean you can trade your shrieking toddler for that angelic napping infant behind you!) If you have doubts about whether a ride is appropriate for your child, inform the attendant that you may need to do a Baby Swap. As you approach the attraction, one parent rides and returns with the verdict. If the first parent thinks the child will do okay, the second parent immediately boards and rides with the child. If the first parent thinks the ride is too wild, the second parent passes the child through to the first parent and then rides him- or herself. It sounds confusing, but the attendants help you and it actually works smoothly.

@ *Slowly increase ride intensity throughout the day.* This advice runs counter to the touring tips you'll find later in this book that recommend you ride the big-deal attractions first thing in the morning, but if you're not sure your 7-year-old is up for a roller coaster, start her off slow. Kids who begin with something relatively mild like Pirates of the Caribbean often build up their nerve throughout the day and close out the night on Space Mountain.

@ *Avoid motion sickness.* Obviously, steer clear of bumpy rides just after eating. If you begin to feel queasy on a motion-simulation ride like Star Tours, stare at something inside the cabin, like the back of the seat in front of you, instead of the screen.

Helpful Hint

One thing you probably don't want to bring with you is the family pet. If you do, board it at the WDW Kennel Club, near the Magic Kingdom. Call 407/824–6568 for reservations; the cost is $9 a night for on-site visitors and $11 for the pets of guests who are staying off-site. Never, repeat, never leave an animal locked in a car, no matter what time of year you're visiting. The Florida heat and humidity are far too dangerous.

Don't Leave Home Without...

✔ *Comfortable shoes.* Forget about wearing sandals or slides in the parks—stick to sneakers. And this is no time to be breaking in new shoes.

✔ *Minimal clothing.* Many hotels have laundry facilities and you can always wash out clothes in the sink. Most families make the mistake of overpacking, not figuring on all the souvenirs they'll be bringing back. Disney T-shirts are not only great for touring but can serve as swimsuit cover-ups and pajamas as well. And unless you're planning a special evening out at Victoria and Albert's, casual clothing is acceptable everywhere.

✔ *Lightweight jackets.* Rain is possible in Orlando year-round, so jackets should be water-resistant.

✔ *Basic necessities.* These include disposable diapers, baby formula, camera, memory cards or film, and blank camcorder tapes. All these are available within Disney World, but at premium prices.

✔ *Sunscreen.* Keep a tube with you, and reapply it often. Sunburn is the number-one complaint at the first-aid clinic in the Magic Kingdom. You need sun protection all through the year in Orlando, not just in summer.

✔ *A waist pouch or fanny pack.* Unlike a purse, a fanny pack frees up your hands for boarding rides, pushing strollers, and holding on to your kids. A backpack is another option and good for carrying snacks and water, which are very expensive in the parks, but even a light one can start to hurt your shoulders after a while. Plus, some rides don't allow backpacks, so you may have to keep putting yours in a locker.

✔ *Ziplock bags.* Disney serves such large dining portions, even on kiddie meals, that some parents report they save some of the fruit or chips for a later snack.

✔ *Sunglasses.* The Florida sun is so blinding that more than once I've reached into my bag for my sunglasses only to realize I already had them on. Kids too young for sun-glasses need wide-billed caps to cut down the glare.

✔ *Strollers.* Most Orlando hotels are huge, so if you have an infant or toddler, you'll need your own stroller just to get around your hotel.

The Frantic Factor

Although I rate rides throughout this book according to their "scare factor," I've often thought that I should include ratings on the "frantic factor" as well, measuring how hysterical the av-erage parent is apt to become in any given situation.

I'm often asked to speak to parent groups on the topic of family travel. Almost inevitably, someone asks me how to make a Disney vacation relaxing. These people are very earnest, but they might as well be asking me to recommend a nice ski lodge for their upcoming trip to Hawaii. The only honest response is, "If you want to relax, you're going to the wrong place." Disney World is a high-stimulation environment, a total assault on all five senses mixed in with a constant and mind-boggling array of choices. This is not the week to take your kids off Ritalin or dis-cuss marital issues with your spouse. This is not the week to relax.

Actually, high stimulation and a lively pace may be the reason most people go to Disney World in the first place. Fam-ilies who slip over the line from happily stimulated to unhap-pily frantic often do so because:

1) they forget to build in adequate rest breaks

2) they've planned their trips for the busiest times of the year

3) they're confused about the logistics of touring

4) they're hell-bent on taking it all in because "We're paying through the nose for this" and "Who knows when we'll get back?"

This book is full of tips to help you avoid the first three mistakes, but your attitude is pretty much up to you. Just remember that doing it all is not synonymous with having the most fun, and if time is tight, limit your touring to those attractions that have the most appeal for your particular group. As for when you'll get back, who knows? But using this as a rationale for pushing everyone in the family past his personal exhaustion limit only guarantees that you'll never want to come back. The way for parents to really relax at Disney (besides spending time in hotel hot tubs with adjacent bars) is to do a little less, and enjoy it a little more.

As one father of three from New Jersey says, "Disney will bring out the best and the worst in you. If your family relationships are strained or your kids are undisciplined, don't expect a Disney vacation to automatically heal everything and make you the all-American family. If you're realistic about it—this is a vacation, not therapy—you can have a great time."

CHAPTER

2

Choosing
a Hotel

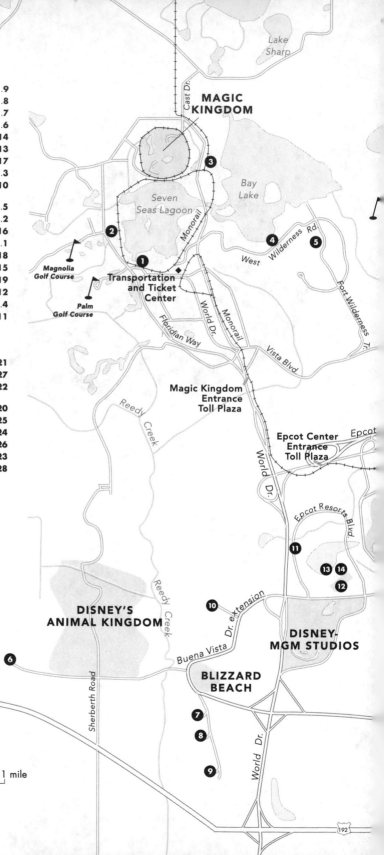

On-Site Hotels

Off-Site Hotel

KEY

1 On-site hotel

10 Off-site hotel

0   1 mile

0   1 km

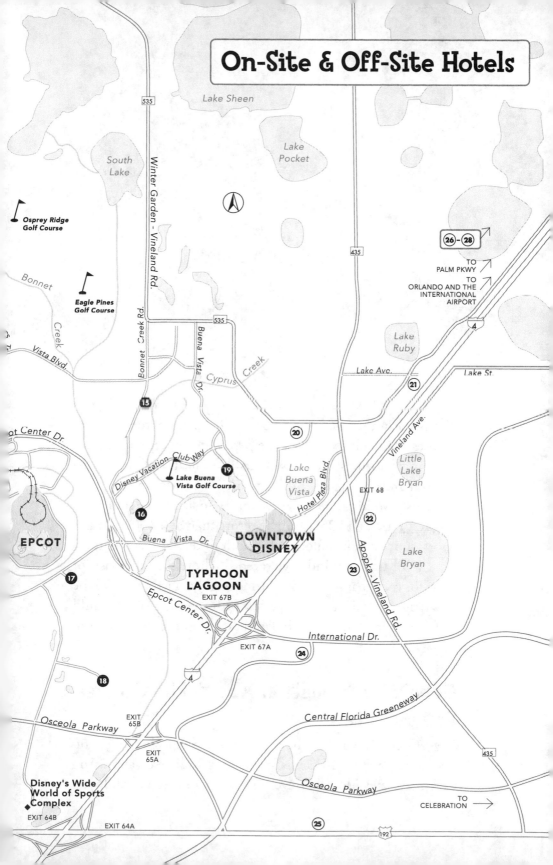

On-Site & Off-Site Hotels

Lake Sheen

535

South Lake

Lake Pocket

Osprey Ridge Golf Course

Eagle Pines Golf Course

Bonnet Creek

Winter Garden - Vineland Rd.

Bonnet Creek Rd.

Vista Blvd.

Buena Vista Dr.

Cyprus Creek

435

26 - 28

TO PALM PKWY

TO ORLANDO AND THE INTERNATIONAL AIRPORT

4

Lake Ruby

Lake Ave.

Lake St.

21

Vineland Ave.

535

15

ot Center Dr

Disney Vacation Club Way

Lake Buena Vista Golf Course

19

20

Lake Buena Vista

Hotel Plaza Blvd

Little Lake Bryan

EXIT 68

22

16

EPCOT

Buena Vista Dr.

DOWNTOWN DISNEY

Apopka - Vineland Rd.

Lake Bryan

17

TYPHOON LAGOON

EXIT 67B

23

Epcot Center Dr.

International Dr.

EXIT 67A

24

18

Central Florida Greeneway

Osceola Parkway

EXIT 65B

4

435

EXIT 65A

Disney's Wide World of Sports Complex

EXIT 64B

Osceola Parkway

TO CELEBRATION

EXIT 64A

25

192

he ratings for the hotels discussed in this chapter are based on three factors: the responses of families surveyed; the percentage of repeat business a resort experiences, which is a reliable indicator of guest satisfaction; and the quality of the resort in relation to the price. Obviously, you'd expect more amenities and a higher employee-to-guest ratio at a $250-a-night resort than at a $100-a-night resort, so it's unfair to hold them both to the same standard.

With that in mind, I've rated the hotels on the basis of value for cost; that is, are you getting what you paid for? Do the advantages of this resort make it worth the price? And would you recommend this resort to families with the same amount of money to spend?

General Information About the On-Site Disney Hotels

@ A deposit equal to the price of one night's lodging is required within 14 days after making your reservation. You may pay with cash, traveler's checks, or credit card. If you cancel at least five days in advance, your deposit will be fully refunded.

@ Disney hotels operate under the family plan, meaning that kids 18 and under stay free with parents.

@ Check-in time is 3 PM at most Disney hotels, but it's 4 PM at the BoardWalk, Wilderness Lodge, Old Key West, and the All-Stars. If you arrive before your room is ready, you can check in, store your bags, pick up your tickets and resort IDs, and go ahead to the parks.

@ Checkout time is 11 AM, but, once again, you need not let this interfere with your touring. Check out early in the morning, store your bags, then go on to enjoy your last day in the parks.

@ When you check in, you'll be issued a resort ID that allows you to charge meals, drinks, tickets, and souvenirs to your room and also gives you access to all Disney World transportation.

Time-Saving Tip

If you pay with a credit card, you can arrange for automatic checkout—a definite time-saver. An itemized statement is hung on your doorknob early on the morning of your departure. If it's correct, you can keep it as your receipt and leave immediately.

Is It Worth the Expense to Stay On-Site?

Staying at one of the Disney-owned hotels is very convenient, and with rates as low as $77 a night at the All-Star resorts and Pop Century Resort, it's more affordable than you might think.

Off-site hotels fight back with special promotions and perks of their own, arguing that the Disney hotels still cost more and bring you only slightly closer to the action. On-site or off-site? Ask yourself the following questions to help you decide:

What time of year are you going?

If you're visiting Disney World in summer or during a major holiday, you'll need every extra minute, so it's worth the cost to stay on-site.

How old are your kids?

In the Florida heat and humidity it's nearly a medical necessity to keep young kids out of the sun in the middle of the afternoon, and an on-site hotel room makes it easier to return for a nap. If your kids are preteens or teens who can handle a whole day in the parks, commute time is less of a factor.

Are you flying or driving?

If you're flying and doing only Disney World, it may make more economic sense to stay on-site and use Disney World's transportation system in lieu of a rental car. But if you're driving to Orlando, it's just as easy to stay off-site. You'll be able to drive into the parks at hours that suit you without having to rely on shuttles.

What's your budget?

If money isn't a major issue, stay on-site. If money is a primary consideration, you'll find your best deals at the budget hotels along Interstate 4. Exits 62 and 68 are chock-full of chain hotels and restaurants.

How much do your kids eat?

Food is expensive at Disney World, both in the parks and the on-site hotels. If you're staying off-site, you can always eat in the numerous fast-food and family-style restaurants along Interstate 4, Route 192, and International Drive. Many off-site hotels have complimentary

Money-Saving Tip
Disney isn't exactly known for deep discounts, but when times are slow they're as eager to fill their rooms as any other hotel chain. The trouble is, they don't always announce these discounts to people who seem ready and willing to pay the full price. When you call in to make your resort reservations always ask, "Are there any special offers available during the times I'll be visiting?"

breakfast buffets, while the all-suites properties often have in-room kitchens where you can fix your own meals.

@ *Do you plan to visit other attractions?*

If you'll be spending half your time at SeaWorld, Universal Orlando, or the other non–Disney World attractions, stay off-site—at least during those days. There's no need to pay top dollar for proximity to Disney if you're headed for Islands of Adventure.

@ *Will your party be splitting up at times?*

Does Dad want to golf one afternoon? Do you have teenagers who can spend a day at Blizzard Beach on their own? Will there be times when it would make sense for Dad to take the younger kids back to the hotel while Mom stays in the park with the older ones? Is your 5-year-old raring to go at dawn, whereas your 15-year-old sleeps until noon? If so stay on-site, where the use of the Disney World transportation system makes it easy for all of you to go your own way.

@ *What's your tolerance level for hassles?*

If you don't want to deal with interstate traffic, big parking lots, toting luggage, and carrying cash, stay on-site.

The Advantages of Staying On-Site

Extra Magic Hours

Extra Magic Hour works like this. Each day year-round, one of the four major theme parks opens for Disney resort guests an hour early or stays open an extra hour or two after the regular closing time. This gives resort guests the chance to ride some featured attractions and greet the characters in a relatively uncrowded park. (Note the word "relatively." There are so many Disney resort guests that there are still plenty of people around, just not as many as you can find when the parks reach peak capacity later in the day.) When you check into your hotel, you'll receive a leaflet printed with the Extra Magic Hours schedule for the week. If you need this information in advance to help you create your touring plan, call Guest Services at the resort where you'll be staying.

Generally only a few attractions per park are open for the Extra Magic Hour, but this is your chance to ride them easily with little wait. Just as important—in the morning you'll be deep inside the theme park when it officially opens so you can dash to other big-deal attractions before the rest of the crowd gets there.

For evening Extra Magic Hours, get a special bracelet from marked booths before the regular park closing time. You'll need to show your resort ID/room key card, so be sure to keep it handy.

Magical Express Service

Disney's latest perk for on-site guests allows you to check your bags at your hometown airport and not see them again until you walk into your hotel room in Walt Disney World. You also get free shuttle service from the Orlando airport to your resort.

When it's time to go home, the system works in reverse. You check your bags and receive your boarding passes before departing your Disney resort. Take another complimentary shuttle back to the airport and go directly to your flight. Your luggage will be waiting for you at baggage claim in your hometown. This also saves you the inconvenience of having to store your bags on the last day of your trip.

Transportation

On-site guests have unlimited use of the monorails, buses, and boats of the WDW transportation system.

Insider's Secret
The system is supposed to save you time and money, but in reality it doesn't always work seamlessly. Quite a few of our readers have complained of long delays. Comments range from "We stopped at three hotels, and it took over an hour to get to ours from the airport" to "You have to tip somebody every two minutes" to "Thanks to this so-called benefit we began the whole trip with confusion and irritation." The general consensus seems to be that the system works well at times when it's not too crowded, but during peak travel times slow service is common. If you're traveling at such a time, consider handling your own bags and arranging for your own transportation between the airport and your hotel.

Helpful Hint
If you're using the Magical Express system be sure to allow plenty, and I do mean plenty, of extra time to get to the airport. Otherwise, you may make so many stops at various Disney hotels that you come close to missing your flight.

Use of Other On-Site Hotel Facilities

If you want to use the child-care or sports facilities of other Disney hotels or dine at their restaurants, you can receive preferential treatment over off-site visitors. (Each hotel, reasonably enough, allows its own guests first shot at its services.) This means that even if you're staying at the midprice Port Orleans, you can use the kids' club at the Polynesian or take a tennis lesson at the Contemporary.

Free Parking at the Theme Parks

If you opt to drive your car to the theme parks, you don't have to pay to park. The attendant will wave you through when she sees your resort parking ID.

Package Delivery

Don't lug your souvenirs around while touring. When you make a purchase, you can fill out a form and Disney will deliver the package to your hotel gift shop for free. It's generally the next day before your purchases show up, so don't use the package delivery service on the last day of your visit.

Charging Privileges

If you're staying on-site, everyone in your party will be issued a resort ID the day you arrive. The ID allows adults to charge tickets, food, and souvenirs back to the hotel room. (Vendors selling small things like ice cream or bottled water still require cash.) It's certainly easier not to have to carry huge amounts of cash around, especially at the pool, water parks, and marinas.

It's up to you whether older kids have charging privileges.

Giving them this privilege makes it easier to send Johnny to the snack bar for a round of Cokes, but be sure to impress upon kids that these IDs work like credit cards. They're not an open invitation to order pizza for all the kids at the arcade, purchase all seven dwarfs from the hotel gift shop, or, heaven forbid, obtain cash advances.

Family Atmosphere

All of the on-site hotels are designed with families in mind. The ambience is casual, security is tight, and there are always other children around to play with. The on site ho tels have laundry facilities, generally located near the pools, and arcades so that you can run a quick load while the youngsters play; there's late-night pizza delivery to your room; and if there's not a child-care facility at your particular hotel, Guest Services can help you arrange for an in-room sitter. The emphasis at the Disney hotels is on making life more convenient for parents.

Helpful Hint

If an ID with charging privileges is lost, it should be reported to the front desk immediately to avoid unauthorized charges.

Cool Themes

All the on-site hotels have themes that are carried out in megadetail. At the Polynesian, the staff greets you with "Aloha"; at the Port Orleans, jazz music plays all day; and at the All-Star Sports, the dressers in the rooms look like gym lockers. This makes

Insider's Secret

The on-site resorts, especially the luxury ones, often have fun little activities for kids such as scavenger hunts, pool races, or unbirthday parties. Activity schedules are usually posted around the pool areas or child-care centers.

staying at an on-site hotel almost as exciting for kids as being inside the parks.

In fact, because the on-site hotels are all so different from each other and so cool, it's fun to visit other hotels. Many families surveyed told us they enjoyed eating dinner at a different resort from their own.

Helpful Hint

Disneyworld.com is a great planning tool, allowing you to compare the prices of different on-site hotels during the week you'll be visiting. You can comparison shop at leisure without a travel agent or phone reservation agent nudging you into a quick decision.

Rating the On-Site Disney Hotels

Orlando has more than 120,000 hotel rooms and a fair percentage of these rooms are Disney owned.

For decades, cost was the primary reason families opted to stay off-site. But with the opening of the All-Star resorts and the gargantuan new Pop Century Resort, there are suddenly many more on-site budget rooms up for grabs.

All this expansion means that even if a family has decided to stay on-site it still faces a bewildering number of choices. Does the convenience of being on the monorail line justify the increase in price? Do you want to stay amid Victorian splendor, or is a fort more your style? At which park do you plan to spend most of your time? As with all of WDW, making the best choice hinges on your awareness of what your family really needs.

On-Site Luxury Hotels

Luxury hotels are full-scale resorts with fine dining, health clubs and spas, valet parking, on-site child-care facilities, full room service, and lots of sporting options. There's a price attached—the Disney luxury hotels cost, on average, twice as much a night as the mid-price hotels. Luxury hotels include the BoardWalk, Yacht and Beach Clubs, Contemporary, Grand Floridian, Polynesian, Swan, Dolphin, Wilderness Lodge, and Animal Kingdom Lodge. (Note: The Wilderness Lodge and Animal Kingdom Lodge are at the lowest price point in this category.)

On-Site Mid-Price Hotels

"Mid-price" is something of a misnomer because both the price and the quality are higher than what you'd find in an off-site chain hotel in Orlando. You may pay a little more but the hotels are beautifully maintained and landscaped, with their themes carried out to the nth degree. Resorts that fall into this category include the Caribbean Beach, Port Orleans, and Coronado Springs.

On-Site Budget Hotels

The on-site budget hotels include the All-Star Music, All-Star Movies, All-Star Sports, and Pop Century resorts.

Again, the resorts are well maintained and have eye-popping catchy graphics that dazzle the kids. You can find a food court but no sit-down dining; a swimming pool but no other sporting options; a lengthier check-in line and smaller staff but rates that more than compensate for the minor inconveniences. The most important on-site benefits—transportation to the parks, help with tickets and priority-seating reservations, Extra Magic Hour, and charging privileges—are just as available to those paying $77 a night at All-Star Sports as to those paying $377 a night at the BoardWalk. And, hey, the housekeepers still leave your kids' stuffed animals in the window to greet them in the evening, so who can complain?

Quick Guide to

Hotel	Description
All-Star Resorts	Very popular, great price
Animal Kingdom Lodge	An exotic African theme
Beach Club Resort	Homey, lovely, and not one bit fancy
Beach Club Villas	Big suites in a great location
BoardWalk Inn	Rooms are spacious, modern, and attractive
BoardWalk Villas	Great location for both Epcot and MGM
Caribbean Beach Resort	The price is right
Contemporary Resort	Convenient and lively
Coronado Springs Resort	Elaborate pool with pyramid slide
Dolphin Resort	Geared toward convention trade
Fort Wilderness Campground	Great for families who like to camp
Grand Floridian	Expensive, but luxurious
Old Key West Resort	Lots of room, quiet
Polynesian Resort	Relaxed and casual with a loyal, repeat clientele
Pop Century Resort	5,760 more budget rooms
Port Orleans Resort	With French Quarter or Riverside options
Saratoga Springs Resort	Amazing grotto pool
Swan Resort	Adult-oriented and expensive
Wilderness Lodge	Rustic looking, with an intimate feel
Wilderness Lodge Villas	Great setting, a bit more space
Yacht Club Resort	On the door of the World Showcase

NOTE: *The central reservations number for on-site hotels is 407-W-DISNEY.*

On-Site Hotels

Location	Rating	Price Range
Animal Kingdom	★★	$79–$137
Animal Kingdom	★★★	$205–$625
Epcot	★★★	$305–$695
Epcot	★★★	$305–$1070
Epcot	★★★	$305–$710
Epcot	★★★	$305–$2020
Epcot	★	$139–$215
Magic Kingdom	★★	$249–$725
Animal Kingdom	★★	$139–$215
Epcot	★	$259–$525
Magic Kingdom	★★	$39–$349
Magic Kingdom	★★	$359–$890
Downtown Disney	★★	$269–$1545
Magic Kingdom	★★★	$315–$780
Animal Kingdom	★★	$79–$137
Downtown Disney	★★★	$139–$215
Downtown Disney	★★	$269–$1545
Epcot	★	$259–$525
Magic Kingdom	★★★	$205–$500
Magic Kingdom	★★★	$295–$1040
Epcot	★★★	$305–$695

Villa-Style Accommodations

Larger families or those who like to prepare their own meals may want to rent a villa. Resorts included in this category are the Wilderness Lodge Villas, Saratoga Springs Resort, BoardWalk Villas, Yacht and Beach Club Villas, and Old Key West Resort.

On-Site Camping

The Fort Wilderness Campground is a great choice for families who love to camp and is by far the cheapest way to stay on-site and get on-site privileges.

Definition of Star Ratings for Hotels

★★★ This resort was a favorite among families surveyed and offers solid value for the money.

★★ Surveyed families were satisfied with this resort and felt they got what they paid for.

★ This resort is either more adult oriented, with fewer amenities designed to appeal to families, or is more expensive than you'd expect considering the location or level of service.

Magic Kingdom Resorts

If you'll be spending most of your time at the Magic Kingdom—and you're willing to spend the bucks—consider one of these resorts.

The Polynesian Resort   ★★★ 407/824–2000

Designed to emulate an island village, the Polynesian is relaxed and casual. Activities take place at the Great Ceremonial House, where all the shops and restaurants encircle a beautiful garden with orchids, parrots, and fountains. Guests stay in one of the sprawling "long houses" along the lagoon.

Best On-Site Choices at a Glance

BEST MAGIC KINGDOM RESORT: WILDERNESS LODGE

The Wilderness Lodge gets a lot of repeat business; once families stay here, they report having little interest in going anywhere else.

BEST EPCOT RESORT: THE YACHT AND BEACH CLUBS

You like Epcot and MGM? They're both easy to get to from this prime location— and the pool is to die for.

BEST MID-PRICED RESORT: PORT ORLEANS

Relaxed and homey, the Port Orleans resorts have the charm of the luxury resorts at a reduced cost. The French Quarter is smaller and quieter than its sister, Riverside, so it gets our nod as being easier for families with young kids.

BEST BUDGET RESORT: THE ALL-STAR RESORTS

Kids love the wacky themes at these simple but totally adequate hotels.

BEST VILLAS: VILLAS AT WILDERNESS LODGE

Families stay loyal to the Wilderness Lodge in any form. The BoardWalk Villas also gets many votes.

Proximity to the Magic Kingdom:	Excellent, via direct monorail, boat launch, or ferry
Proximity to Epcot:	Good, via monorail with one change at the Transportation and Ticket Center (TTC)
Proximity to MGM:	Fair, via bus
Proximity to the Animal Kingdom:	Fair, via bus

Pluses

+ The Polynesian offers the most options for transport to the Magic Kingdom. You have monorail, ferry, and launch service.
+ There's a private beach with an attractive pool, plus numerous boating options. Canvas shells shade napping babies and toddlers digging in the sand.
+ The Kona Café is one of the best places for desserts in all of Disney World.
+ Excellent on-site child-care center.

Minuses

— Without a discount, expect to pay $315 a night and up.
— Like the Contemporary, the Polynesian is an older resort. The color scheme screams 1970s.

Overall grade: ★★★ The Polynesian enjoys a loyal repeat clientele, and that says it all.

Wilderness Lodge and Villas	★★★ 407/824–3200

Starting at $205 a night, the rustic-looking, Western-spirited Wilderness Lodge is aimed at filling the gap between the mid-price and luxury resorts.

The theme of the Wilderness Lodge extends into every aspect of the hotel's design. The pool begins indoors as a hot spring and then flows through the lobby into a waterfall that tumbles over rocky caverns and culminates in the outdoor pool. The awe-inspiring lobby, which looks like a Lincoln Log project run amok, centers on an 82-foot fireplace that blazes all year round. The Native American–theme wallpaper, the staff dressed like park rangers, and even the stick ponies children ride to their tables in the Whispering Canyon Café all combine to evoke the feel of a National Park Service lodge built in the early 1900s.

Proximity to the Magic Kingdom:	Good, via launch
Proximity to Epcot:	Fair, via bus
Proximity to MGM:	Fair, via bus
Proximity to the Animal Kingdom:	Fair, via bus

Pluses

+ The lodge is heavily themed and the pool area, with its erupting geyser and stone hot tubs, is especially dramatic.
+ On-site child-care facilities.
+ Tons of happy quasi campers here. Families return to the Wilderness Lodge again and again.

Minuses

- Although it's one of the least expensive luxury options, at $205 a night and up, it still isn't cheap.
- This is the only Magic Kingdom resort without monorail service. The boat takes slightly longer than the bus.
- The rooms sleep only four people; the other luxury resorts sleep five.

Overall Grade: ★★★ A great family-pleasing setting and a favorite with many of our readers.

Contemporary Resort ★★
407/824–1000

You'll either love or hate Disney's original resort, which has 1,050 rooms surrounding a mammoth, high-tech lobby full of shops and restaurants. This place is always hopping.

Proximity to the Magic Kingdom:	Excellent, via monorail
Proximity to Epcot:	Good, via monorail with a change at the TTC
Proximity to MGM:	Fair, via bus
Proximity to the Animal Kingdom:	Fair, via bus

Pluses

+ On the monorail line.

+ The easiest Magic Kingdom resort to book; discounts are sometimes available.

+ Exceptional sporting options, including WDW's largest tennis center and a full marina, with parasailing and waterskiing options.

+ Outstanding dining choices, including the California Grill, Disney's premiere restaurant, and Chef Mickey's, a great place to meet the characters for breakfast and dinner.

Minuses

— It's loud with a big-city feel, which is exactly what some families come to Florida to escape. "Like sleeping in the middle of Space Mountain," wrote one mother. Note that the Garden Wings are quieter, cheaper, and more spacious than those in the main building.

— Like all the other hotels on the monorail line, the Contemporary is expensive, with prices starting at $249 a night.

Overall Grade: ★★ Convenient and lively. Perhaps a little too lively.

The Grand Floridian

★★
407/824–3000

Modeled after the famed Florida beach resorts of the 1800s, the Grand Floridian is possibly the prettiest of all Disney hotels, with 900 rooms ensconced among its gabled roofs, soaring ceilings, and broad white verandas. This elegant and stately lady is also the hub of many activities, including a variety of programs for children.

Proximity to the Magic Kingdom:	Excellent, via monorail or launch
Proximity to Epcot:	Good, via monorail with a change at the TTC

Proximity to MGM: Fair, via bus
Proximity to Animal Kingdom: Fair, via bus

Pluses

+ Convenient location on monorail line.
+ A private beach and marina on the Seven Seas Lagoon and numerous boating options.
+ On-site child-care center.
+ Three programs for children: Grand Adventures in Cooking, Disney's Pirate Adventure, and Wonderland Tea Party.
+ On-site health club and full-service spa.
+ Exceptional dining. Citricos and Victoria and Albert's are among the finest restaurants in all of WDW. If you have the kids along, check out 1900 Park Fare, which hosts breakfast and dinner character buffets.
+ Lots of special little touches, such as afternoon tea and live music in the lobby each night.

Minuses

− The most expensive rooms on Disney property.
− The elegance puts off some families who feel funny trooping past a grand piano with squalling babies in their arms.

Overall Grade: ★★ Expensive but luxurious.

Fort Wilderness Campground
★★
407/824–2900

Fort Wilderness has campsites for tents and RVs as well as air-conditioned cabins. The cabins, which sleep six, rent for approximately the same nightly rate as a luxury hotel. The wide-open spaces of the campground are perfect for volleyball, biking, and exploring, making the resort perfect for families with kids old enough to enjoy all the outdoor options.

Proximity to the Magic Kingdom: Good, via bus or launch
Proximity to Epcot: Fair, via bus

Helpful Hint

Fort Wilderness Campground is so sprawling that many families rent a golf cart to make it easier to get around.

Proximity to MGM: Fair, via bus
Proximity to the Animal Kingdom: Fair, via bus

Pluses

+ Fort Wilderness offers a huge variety of activities for kids, such as hayrides, horseback and pony riding, and a petting zoo.

+ Hookups and tent sites are by far your cheapest lodging options at WDW.

+ Groceries are available at the on-site trading post.

Minuses

— Camping may not seem like a vacation to you.

— A large number of people are sharing relatively few facilities; the pools and the beach can get very crowded.

— This place is so spread out that it requires its own in-resort bus system to get guests from one area to another. You can rent golf carts or bikes, but make no mistake: Fort Wilderness is huge and hard to navigate.

Overall Grade: ★★ If you like to camp and are willing to put up with a little inconvenience for great savings, this is a good option.

Epcot Hotels

The Epcot resorts share their own "back-door" entrance into Epcot's World Showcase, accessed by water taxis and walkways. Unfortunately—and somewhat ironically considering these properties are marketed as "Epcot resorts"—it can be tricky to get to Epcot's front gates. The Future World section of Epcot usually opens at 9 AM but Epcot resort guests enter through the World Showcase, where the rides, shops, and restaurants don't open until 11 AM. That means Epcot hotel guests have to walk through the World Showcase and enter Future World at a special rope-drop area. (Many people assume the Epcot hotels offer bus service to the main entrance of Epcot. They don't.) The bad news is that this stroll through the World Showcase adds 10 minutes to your commute. The good news is that there are fewer people at this entrance point so you can still get a jump on the crowds, a key factor if you're heading to a popular attraction like Soarin'.

In contrast, getting to MGM is a breeze. Water taxis leaving from the Epcot resort marinas will have you at the MGM gates within minutes.

The BoardWalk Inn and Villas ★★★
407/939–5100

The BoardWalk Inn and Villas form the hub of a large complex with convention space, several restaurants and shops, the ESPN sports club, and a dance club and piano bar. The mood is turn-of-the-20th-century Atlantic City. Bright, attractive rooms are clustered above an old-fashion boardwalk and the action on the waterfront goes on until late at night.

"Once you stay at the Boardwalk, nothing else is good enough," wrote one enthusiastic grandmother of two in Ohio. "The location is perfect for both Epcot and MGM, and there's always free entertainment, like jugglers or comedians, to keep the kids happy."

Proximity to the Magic Kingdom:	Fair, via bus
Proximity to Epcot:	Excellent, via a short stroll or water taxi
Proximity to MGM:	Excellent, via water taxi
Proximity to the Animal Kingdom:	Fair, via bus

Pluses

+ Lots of entertainment: surrey bikes for rent, midway games, and a wider variety of restaurants and bars than you'd find at most resorts.
+ On-site health club.
+ On-site child-care facilities.
+ Great location for both Epcot and MGM.

Minuses

− Expensive, at $305 and up per night.
− Maybe too lively and hopping for families with very young kids. The boardwalk can get loud at night, and you can hear the revelers from some rooms.

Overall grade: ★★★ You'll feel like you're right in the middle of the action—because you are.

The Yacht and Beach Clubs

★★★
407/934–7000

Designed to resemble a turn-of-the-20th-century Nantucket seaside resort, the Yacht and Beach Clubs have sunny, airy rooms overlooking a 25-acre freshwater lake. Both hotels are charming yet casual (think Polo Ralph Lauren), with a wide variety of restaurants and sporting options close at hand.

Proximity to the Magic Kingdom:	Fair, via bus
Proximity to Epcot:	Excellent, via a short stroll or water taxi
Proximity to MGM:	Excellent, via water taxi
Proximity to the Animal Kingdom:	Fair, via bus

Pluses

+ Stormalong Bay, the water recreation area shared by the two resorts, is like a private water park. The sand-bottom "bay" contains pools of varying depths, whirlpools, waterslides, and a wrecked ship for atmosphere. This is by far the best resort pool in all of WDW.

+ The Yacht and Beach Clubs are perfectly situated for easy travel to both Epcot and MGM.
+ On-site child-care facilities.
+ Disney characters are on hand for breakfast at the Cape May Café in the Beach Club.
+ The two resorts share an on-site health club.

Minuses

— Price is the only real drawback. Rates begin at $305.

Overall Grade: ★★★ These hotels enjoy a lot of repeat business from satisfied families.

Caribbean Beach Resort

★

407/934–3400

This family-priced, 2,112-room resort is on 200 acres with a private lake surrounded by beaches. Each section of this mammoth hotel is painted a different tropical color and named for a different Caribbean island and each "island" has its own shuttle bus stop, beach, and pool with water slide. The rooms, although small, are attractively decorated.

Proximity to the Magic Kingdom:	Fair, via bus
Proximity to Epcot:	Fair, via bus
Proximity to MGM:	Fair, via bus
Proximity to the Animal Kingdom:	Fair, via bus

Pluses

+ The price is right, at $139 to $215 a night.
+ Caribbean Cay, an artificial island with a playground, climbing fort, and small aviary is fun for young kids.
+ A marina with watercraft is available.

Minuses

— Although the buses are regular, they must stop at all of the resort's many "islands." Expect a longer commute time to the parks.

— The place is huge. It may be a major hike from your hotel room to the food plaza or marina. If you have young kids, bring your own stroller.

— Caribbean Beach is the oldest of the mid-price hotels and some of the rooms show their age. The resort is in a constant state of refurbishment; there are always some rooms that look newly remodeled and others that look old and tired. Ask for a recently refurbished room when you book.

Overall Grade: ★ Solid value for the money, but try the newer mid-price resorts first.

Swan and Dolphin
★
407/934–3000

This convention–resort complex made up of two side-by-side hotels is connected to Epcot and MGM by water taxi and bridges. The Swan and Dolphin are the only hotels not owned by Disney that are on Disney property and whose guests qualify for on-site perks. Sometimes called "sister" hotels (like the nearby Yacht and Beach Clubs), the Swan and Dolphin have separate check-ins but are alike in architecture and mood. Despite the hotels' sophisticated, adult-oriented feel, both have made strides in the past few years to become more family oriented.

Proximity to the Magic Kingdom:	Fair, via bus
Proximity to Epcot:	Excellent, via a moderate walk or water taxi
Proximity to MGM:	Excellent, via water taxi
Proximity to the Animal Kingdom:	Fair, via bus

Pluses

+ On-site child-care facilities.

+ The beach area has a playground, kiddie pools, water slides, and a small marina with swan-shape paddleboats.

+ Bike rentals, tennis courts, and a health club.

Minuses
- Expensive, with rates beginning at $259.
- Although they're on Disney property, these hotels are not owned by Disney and have less of a family feel. What you find instead are many conventioneers, and although the restaurants and amenities are top-notch, they are more oriented to adults than families with young kids.
- Since these resorts are not owned by Disney, they do not qualify for the Magical Express Service, and they don't have their own airport shuttles, so you'll have to arrange for transportation.

Overall grade: ★ A great place to go if the company is picking up the tab. Otherwise, try the Yacht and Beach Clubs first.

Downtown Disney Hotels

Port Orleans	★★★
	407/934–5000

The mid-price resort called Port Orleans has two sections. The French Quarter has manicured gardens, wrought-iron railings, and streets with cute names like Rue d'Baga. The Mardi Gras mood extends to the pool area, where alligators play jazz while King Triton sits atop a funky-looking waterslide, regally surveying his domain.

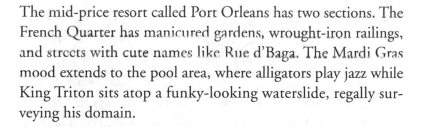

Insider's Secret

If you can't decide which section of Port Orleans is best for your family, keep in mind that the French Quarter is smaller and quieter. There's more activity at Riverside. A mom from Illinois wrote to us that "the Port Orleans French Quarter is amazing, especially the pool. We stay there every time and request building two or five so we'll be close to the action."

The Riverside section is a bit more down-home, with a steamboat-shape lobby, general stores run by gingham-clad girls, and a swimming area themed on *Song of the South*. Schizophrenic in architecture, with white-column buildings encircling fishing holes and cotton mills, Riverside manages to mix in a variety of Southern clichés without losing its ditzy charm. If Huck Finn ever married Scarlett O'Hara, this is where they'd come on their honeymoon.

Since the French Quarter is only half the size of Riverside, the odds are that you'll be close to the lobby, pool, food court, and shuttle bus station; at Riverside, getting around is a bit more of a headache. Both resorts have a fast-food court and a bar that offers live entertainment.

Proximity to the Magic Kingdom: Fair, via bus
Proximity to Epcot: Fair, via bus
Proximity to MGM: Fair, via bus
Proximity to the Animal Kingdom: Fair, via bus

Pluses

+ Great pool areas (especially at the French Quarter), which can easily keep the kids entertained for an afternoon. Riverside also offers on-site fishing.

+ So well designed and maintained that you won't believe you're staying on-site for half the price of the other resorts.

+ Both hotels have marinas with a selection of watercraft as well as bike rentals.

+ Horse-and-carriage tours are available around the resort, and are especially romantic at night.

+ The Sassagoula Steamboat offers easy water transport from both resorts to Downtown Disney.

Minuses

– The two resorts share a bus to all major theme parks, which means a slightly longer commuting time.

Overall Grade: ★★★ You get a good deal here in more ways than one.

Disney's Old Key West

★★
407/827–7700

Although part of the Disney Vacation Club, the villas of Old Key West are available for nightly rentals. You'll get all the standard amenities of a Disney resort, plus a lot more room. The setting is pleasant, casual, and very Floridian in spirit. "We love the quieter atmosphere of Old Key West," wrote a mother of three from Maryland. "Our kids are young (ages 2, 5, 7), so even with naps they're often too exhausted at night for us to take them to a restaurant and expect them to behave. We like being able to go 'home' to a villa and order pizza or make sandwiches. We like the fact the villas are more like an apartment than a hotel room."

Proximity to the Magic Kingdom:	Fair, via bus
Proximity to Epcot:	Fair, via bus
Proximity to MGM:	Fair, via bus
Proximity to the Animal Kingdom:	Fair, via bus

Pluses

+ If you have more than two children and need to spread out or you'd like a kitchen to prepare your own meals, Old Key West is a good on-site option.

+ A water taxi provides swift transit to Downtown Disney.

+ Tennis courts, pools, bike rentals, shuffleboard, basketball, a marina, a sand play area, an arcade, and a fitness room are all on-site.

+ Prices run from $269 for a studio with kitchenette to $1,545 for a Grand Villa that can accommodate up to 12 people. If you're willing to swap proximity to the parks for more space, Old Key West may be just what you need.

Minuses

− Still pricier than off-site villas such as the Embassy Suites on Hotel Plaza Boulevard.

− Quieter, with less going on than at other resorts.

— No on-site child-care facilities, which is unusual in a resort at this price point.

Overall Grade: ★★ Very homey, with nice touches. One of the best options for families seeking peace and quiet at the end of the day.

Saratoga Springs Resort and Spa	★★ 407/827–1100

Saratoga Springs is the latest addition to the Disney Vacation Club family. The mood recalls the posh upstate–New York retreats of the 1890s, complete with a horse-racing theme. As with the other Vacation Club villa properties, units are available for rent by the general public.

Proximity to the Magic Kingdom:	Fair, via bus
Proximity to Epcot:	Fair, via bus
Proximity to MGM:	Fair, via bus
Proximity to the Animal Kingdom:	Fair, via bus

Pluses

+ The resort opened in 2004, and the units are still fresh and cheery.

+ Proximity to the restaurants and entertainment of Downtown Disney via water taxi.

+ Access to the biggest and best health club in WDW and a full-service spa.

+ The location is great for golfers—Saratoga Springs is adjacent to the Lake Buena Vista course.

+ A good choice for family reunion groups seeking larger accommodations and a relaxed atmosphere with plenty of space for the kids to play.

+ The grotto pool, complete with man-made hot springs, is one of the most dramatic hotel pools in WDW.

Minuses
  — More expensive than off-site villa accommodations.
  — Saratoga Springs is often used by corporations for retreats and conferences so you may find yourself in the middle of a group of businesspeople.
  — Limited dining options on-site, although you do have the option to cook your own meals or head over to the restaurants of Downtown Disney.
  — Since you're pretty far out of the Disney loop, expect a longer commute time via bus to any of the major parks.
  — At 65 acres, Saratoga Springs is so spread out that you might find yourself in a room far from the food court and large themed pool. Request to be as close as possible to the main building when you make your reservation.

Animal Kingdom Hotels

Animal Kingdom Lodge ★★★
407/938–4760

Step inside the massive lobby of the Animal Kingdom Lodge and you'll be transported . . . outdoors. From the thatch roof to the enormous mud fireplace, and from the rope bridges to the tribal art to the lighting that is designed to simulate sunrise to sunset, the resort creates the feel of a game lodge in the middle of a wildlife preserve.

The Animal Kingdom Lodge is in the middle of a 33-acre savanna where more than 200 animals freely roam. Thirty-six species of mammals, including giraffes, zebras, and gazelles, and 26 species of birds, such as the sacred ibis and African spoonbill, live within the working wildlife preserve. The kopje, a series of rock outcroppings, serves as a natural barrier but is also an elevated walkway that offers panoramic views of the landscape and the chance for guests to come within 15 feet of the animals. If you'd rather engage in animal viewing from the comfort of your own balcony, most of the guest rooms have a view of the savanna.

Proximity to the Magic Kingdom:	Fair, via bus
Proximity to Epcot:	Fair, via bus
Proximity to MGM:	Fair, via bus
Proximity to the Animal Kingdom:	Excellent, via a short bus ride

Pluses

+ A dramatic and exotic setting.
+ The Animal Kingdom Lodge has truly fantastic restaurants, including Boma, a buffet restaurant with especially good breakfasts, and Jiko, which serves excellent and authentic African food and an exclusively South African wine list.
+ Lots of extras for the kids, including tours that tell about the animals and games held in the lobby.
+ On-site child-care facilities, spa, and health club.
+ Proximity to the Animal Kingdom and Blizzard Beach.

Minuses

— Although not as expensive as many of the other luxury hotels, the Lodge can be pricey, with rates beginning at $205 a night.
— The out-of-the-way location means a longer-than-average bus ride to the Magic Kingdom, Epcot, and MGM.
— Rooms are small and basic despite the African theme, and if the animals aren't right outside, the views are pretty dull.

Overall Grade: ★★★ The most unique resort on Disney property.

★★

All-Star Sports, All-Star Music, 407/939–5000,
and All-Star Movies Resorts 407/939–6000,
and 407/939–7000

The All-Star resorts have rapidly built such a loyal following that, despite having nearly 6,000 rooms, they fill up quickly.

There are three reasons for the resorts' success—price, price, and price. The All-Star resorts make staying on-site possible for families who previously could only dream of such a splurge.

All-Star Sports has five sections, each decorated with a tennis, football, surfing, basketball, or baseball theme. At the Music Resort, you can choose between jazz, rock and roll, country, calypso, and Broadway tunes. All-Star Movies offers *The Love Bug, Toy Story, Fantasia, 101 Dalmatians,* and *The Mighty Ducks.*

The in-your-face graphics of the brightly colored buildings and the resort's general zaniness appeal to kids. There are giant tennis-ball cans and cowboy boots, a walk-through jukebox, and footballs the size of houses. At the diamond-shape baseball pool at the All-Star Sports, you'll find Goofy as pitcher; Mickey conducts sprays of water in the Fantasia pool of All-Star Movies; and show tunes play all day under the marquee in the Broadway district of All-Star Music. It may be budget, but it ain't boring.

Proximity to the Magic Kingdom:	Fair, via bus
Proximity to Epcot:	Fair, via bus
Proximity to MGM:	Fair, via bus
Proximity to the Animal Kingdom:	Good, via a short bus ride

Pluses
+ In a word, cost. Rooms start at $79.
+ All-Star Resorts offer an affordable option for families with a disabled member. For $94 a night, you can have a slightly larger ground floor suite with roll-in showers.

Insider's Secret
If your child adores *101 Dalmatians* or is a big football buff, you can indeed ask to be lodged in that section of the hotel when you make your reservation. Disney won't guarantee you'll get your request, but they'll try.

Time-Saving Tip

The All-Star resorts are enormous and check-in time (4 PM) is a madhouse. If you arrive before then, go ahead and try to check in early. If your room isn't available, you can store your bags and return later, when you'll only have to wait in the shorter, swifter-moving "key pickup" line.

+ The free shuttle buses are a good transportation option, considering the price. When you get into this price range at off-site hotels, you often have to pay for a shuttle.
+ Proximity to Blizzard Beach and the Animal Kingdom.

Minuses
- Food options are limited to fast-food courts and pool bars only, with no restaurants or indoor bars.
- Sports options are limited; swimming is it.
- The rooms are very small. They sleep four, but you'll be bunched.
- Long check-in lines.
- By breaking each resort into five separate sections, Disney is striving to eliminate that sleeping-in-the-middle-of-Penn-Station feel. But the bottom line is, it takes more effort to get around a huge hotel than a small one.

Overall Grade: ★★ Lots of bang for the buck here.

Helpful Hint

If you don't care what All-Star section you're in, request a room near the lobby when you make your reservation. This can save you lots of walking each time you leave your room to catch a bus or eat a meal.

Coronado Springs Resort

★★
407/939–1000

Disney's first moderately priced convention hotel has a Mexican theme with Spanish-tile roofs, adobe walls, and a pool area that is dominated by an imposing Mayan temple. The rooms are scattered around a 15-acre lake.

Proximity to the Magic Kingdom: Fair, via bus
Proximity to Epcot: Fair, via bus
Proximity to MGM: Fair, via bus
Proximity to the Animal Kingdom: Good, via a short bus ride

Pluses

+ Dramatic pool area with water slide, arcade, bar, fast-food stand, and themed playground.
+ Marina with standard boat and bike rentals.
+ On-site health club—a rarity in this price range.
+ Proximity to the Animal Kingdom and Blizzard Beach.

Minuses

− Coronado Springs is a convention hotel, meaning it has more businesspeople and fewer families than is typical for a Disney resort.
− The fast-food court is too small to accommodate 2,000 rooms and can get very crowded, especially in the morning.
− The resort is quite spread out, even by Disney standards. If you're in one of the more far-flung rooms, you face a 15-minute walk to the food court and shuttle bus stop.

Overall Grade: ★★ Because of the convention trade, Coronado Springs has more amenities than are typical in this price range.

Pop Century Resort

★★
407/938–3000

Disney's newest resort is also in the budget category, bringing 5,760 more affordable rooms into the mix. At Pop Century, each pair of buildings is themed to a different decade, from the 1900s to the 1990s. Expect the same larger-than-life icons that earmark the All-Stars. Cultural touchstones from each decade, including giant yo-yos, Big Wheel bikes, and Rubik's Cubes, mark the entrances and the roofs are lined with catchphrases from each area.

Proximity to the Magic Kingdom: Fair, via bus
Proximity to Epcot: Fair, via bus
Proximity to MGM: Fair, via bus
Proximity to the Animal Kingdom: Fair, via bus

Pluses
+ The price is affordable, starting at $79 a night.
+ Free transportation, a rarity in this price range.
+ Everything is brand new, and looks it.

Minuses
− Food options are limited to a fast-food court.
− The retro music is relentless and sometimes overwhelming. Do-wop and disco aren't dead at Pop Century.
− Sporting options are limited to swimming.

Insider's Secret
Request placement in the '60s section when you make your reservation. It's a bit louder, but you're close to the bus stops, food court, and the fun Hippie Dippy pool. The '80s and '90s sections are a long walk from most of the hotel services and some of the buildings also overlook a construction site.

— The rooms are small; they sleep four but you'll be crowded.
— Longer check-in than is typical for Disney resorts.
— The out-of-the-way location means a slightly longer commute by bus to all of the theme parks.

Off-Site Hotels: Which Location Is Best?

Here's the scoop on the three main off-site areas that tourists frequent: Exits 62 and 68 off Interstate 4, and International Drive.

Exits 62 and 68 are within a 10-minute drive of the theme parks. Exit 68 (U.S. 535) has a vast number of chain hotels and eateries, and the area underwent some major development and expansion in the last few years, so many of the hotels are relatively new. It's your best bet if you want to get close to Disney without paying Disney prices.

Helpful Hint
One of the best sites for Disney World bargain hunters is the appropriately named www.mousesavers.com. It's a great source for family-friendly off-site hotels.

Exit 62, which leads to U.S. 192, has similar hotel chains represented but the rates are about $20 less per night. Why? The hotels are, in general, older and a bit farther off I–4 than the hotels of Exit 68. The whole area is a little less spiffy, but still safe and still close to Disney property.

International Drive is farther out, about 20 minutes from the Disney theme parks, but it's modern and well kept. This area has representatives from every chain restaurant and hotel you've ever heard of, as well as entertainment options like malls, ice-skating, and miniature golf. International Drive is the conduit that runs between SeaWorld and Universal Orlando, so it's a smart central location if you're planning to visit those parks as well as Disney.

Time-Saving Tip

Many off-site hotels claim to run shuttles to the theme parks, but beware. Relying on off-site transportation can sometimes make for a long commute. The worst situations are when two or three hotels share a shuttle and you have to make stops at all of them. Even if a resort has its own shuttle, it may make stops at all of the major parks on each run, meaning commutes of up to an hour just to get from your hotel to the theme park of your choice. A lengthy bus ride is maddening in the morning when the kids are eager to get to the rides, and at night, when you're all exhausted, it can be disastrous.

To make matters worse, some off-site hotels charge you for shuttle rides. They may tell you that by buying shuttle tickets you'll save the "horrendous" cost of Disney parking, but the truth is Disney parking is $9 for the whole car and the shuttle bus tickets can be from $5 to $10 per person. And it still may take you an hour to get there!

This is why I suggest that families staying off-site either drive to Orlando or get a rental car. If you do decide to use an off-site resort shuttle be sure to ask if it's a private shuttle and if service to theme parks is direct. If you don't like what you hear, rent a car or call a cab.

How to Get the Best Deals on Off-Site Hotels

Orlando has more hotel rooms than any other U.S. city besides Vegas, so there are plenty of beds out there for the taking. Here are a few tips to make sure you're getting the most for your money.

The Orlando Magicard is free and offers 20% to 30% discounts on area hotels, as well as restaurants and non-Disney attractions. Delivery takes four weeks, so order well in advance of your trip by calling 800/255–5786 or visiting www .go2orlando.com.

Money-Saving Tip
Try calling both the hotel chain's 800 number and the direct line to the particular hotel. You may be quoted different rates.

Buying an Entertainment Book is another source of major discounts; dozens of hotels in the greater Orlando area offer price breaks of up to 50% to cardholders. For more information, visit www.entertainment.com.

If you especially like a particular hotel chain, you can simply call their 800 number and ask for the hotel nearest Disney World. This eliminates the element of surprise, because one Hampton Inn looks pretty much like another. Big chains have multiple Orlando locations, so stress that

Money-Saving Tip
Always ask for a discount. If none is available, ask for an upgrade on your room.

you'd like to be as close as possible to the Disney gates, preferably near Exit 62 or 68. Proximity to Disney raises the rate about 20%, but location is important; if you end up in a hotel near the airport or downtown, that means a major daily commute, and Orlando traffic can be brutal.

Some visitors swear that condos or all-suites hotels are the way to go. Condolink (800/733–4445) handles many different properties in the area.

Finally, six magic words can save you major bucks. When

Helpful Hint

One note of caution: An extremely cheap hotel rate, say $55 or less, generally means that the hotel is in a less desirable part of town than those I've listed, both in terms of theme park proximity and general security.

talking to a reservation clerk always ask, "Do you have any discounts available?" Remember that the reservation clerk works for the hotel, so if he can sell you a room at $95 a night there's no incentive for him to tell you how you can drop the rate to $79. But if you specifically inquire about discounts, he has to tell you.

Things to Ask When Booking a Room at an Off-Site Hotel

There's a wide range of amenities and perks among the hundreds of hotels in the Orlando area. To make sure you're getting top value for your dollar, take nothing for granted. Some $250-a-night hotels charge you for shuttle service to the parks; some $75 ones do not. Some hotels count 12-year-olds as adults, others consider 19-year-olds to be children. Some relatively inexpensive hotels have kids' clubs; some larger and more costly ones are geared to convention and business travelers and don't even have an arcade. The moral is, always ask.

Money-Saving Tip

If you're staying off-site and thus will be eating at least some of your meals outside of Disney property, pick up a few of those free tourist magazines that are available in the airport and all around Orlando. They're full of dining discount coupons, some of them for family-oriented restaurants near the theme parks.

The following questions should help you ferret out the best deal.

- Does the hotel provide in-room babysitters? Is there an on-site child-care center or kids' club? What's the cost? How far in advance do you have to make reservations?
- Does the hotel provide direct shuttle service to the theme parks? How often do the buses run? How early do they begin and how late do they run? How many stops do they make? Is there a fee?
- Do kids stay free? Up to what age?
- Do you have any suites with kitchens? If not, can we rent refrigerators or microwaves?
- Does the hotel provide a free buffet breakfast?
- What fast-food or family-style restaurants are nearby?
- Are laundry facilities on the premises?
- Can I buy tickets to area attractions through the hotels? Are the tickets discounted? (Note: Disney tickets are rarely discounted but sometimes off-site hotels offer discounts to Universal Orlando, SeaWorld, and area dinner shows.)

Great Off-Site Hotels for Families

Orlando has plenty of hotel rooms, so how is a family to choose? The ten properties listed below are tried-and-true family favorites based on proximity to Disney World, amenities, and value. For descriptions of the Universal Orlando resorts, see Chapter 14.

Two notes: Since the hotels listed below are all recommended as good family choices we did not provide star ratings. And since Walt Disney World is so huge and spread out, our "proximity to Disney" rating is based on the distance between the hotel and Disney's main entrance gate.

Quick Guide to

Hotels	Description
Embassy Suites Lake Buena Vista	Good location, solid value
Enclave Suites	Upscale amenities, easy access to parks
Holiday Inn SunSpree	Child-oriented activities all day long
Hyatt Regency Grand Cypress	Luxury hotel with lots of activities for adults and kids
Magic Memories Villas	Private homes and condos for rent
Nickelodeon Holiday Inn	Nonstop Nick-theme action for the kids
Residence Inn SeaWorld	Quiet and homelike suites
Royal Pacific Resort	Elegant, upscale resort on Universal grounds
Sheraton Vistana	A favorite with our readers
Studios Plus Deluxe Studios	Especially well supplied for longer stays

Off-Site Hotels

Phone #	Nearest Theme Park	Price Range
407/239–1144	Walt Disney World	Moderate: $139 and up
407/351–1155	Universal Studios and SeaWorld	Budget: $89 and up
407/239–4500	Walt Disney World	Budget: $79 and up
407/239–1234	Walt Disney World	Luxury: $269 and up
407/390–8200	Depends on location	Moderate: $114 and up
407/387–5437	Walt Disney World	Moderate: $124 and up
407/313–3611	SeaWorld	Luxury: $154 and up
407/503–3000	Universal Studios	Luxury: $199 and up
407/238–5000	Equidistant from all	Moderate: $124 and up
407/370–4428	Universal Studios	Budget: $69 and up

Off-Site Luxury Hotels

Hyatt Regency Grand Cypress	407/239–1234 www.hyattgrandcypress.com

This beautiful hotel—so close to Disney that it's almost on-site—has expansive grounds, lush landscaping, an elegant lobby, and numerous sporting options. It's a serene oasis and a great choice for families who want the option to escape from Disney in the evenings and yet remain conveniently close to the parks. Prices begin at $269 for a standard room.

Proximity to Disney World: Excellent, via a 5-minute drive

Proximity to Universal: Good, via a 15-minute drive

Proximity to SeaWorld: Good, via a 15-minute drive

Pluses

+ The pool area is gorgeous, with 12 waterfalls and several very secluded whirlpools.

+ You can golf, play tennis, and ride horses at the equestrian center. Pleasant trails wind through the grounds for walkers and runners.

+ Camp Hyatt has great activities for kids, such as pool games, nature walks, poolside movies, canoeing, tennis lessons, and pitch-and-putt golf.

+ Sophisticated dining options include Hemingway's, dramatically perched atop one of the pool waterfalls.

+ The Hyatt basically backs up to Disney World grounds and offers an easy commute to any Disney theme park.

Minuses

– Price: both the rooms and restaurants are very expensive. The standard-room rates here can get you a suite with a kitchen at a midrange or budget property.

– The Hyatt sometimes hosts conventions and attracts a more adult crowd than other area hotels.

Residence Inn SeaWorld International Center

407/313–3611
www.residenceinn.com

The suites at the Residence Inn are especially homelike and you can choose among one- to three-room units, all with separate areas for eating and relaxing. Plus the hotel is practically at the backdoor of SeaWorld and Discovery Cove. Disney World and Universal Studios are each about 5 miles away. Prices begin at $154 for a two-room suite with sofa bed and $269 for a three-room (two bedrooms and a living room with sofa bed) suite. "My husband hates crowds and noise and was very skeptical about taking a vacation in Orlando," a woman wrote to us. "But even he had to admit that the Residence Inn was very relaxing and that SeaWorld was a wonderful theme park."

Proximity to Disney World:	Good, via a 10-minute drive
Proximity to Universal:	Good, via a 10-minute drive
Proximity to SeaWorld:	Excellent via a 5-minute drive or shuttle ride

Pluses

- ✦ Suites are spacious and the kitchens are well equipped.
- ✦ Complimentary hot breakfast buffet is included.
- ✦ The hotel is relatively new so everything looks crisp and well-maintained.
- ✦ Packages including SeaWorld tickets are available.

Minuses

- — All those big suites aren't cheap.
- — The hotel is a bit off the main drag of International Drive. For families seeking peace and privacy, that actually may be a plus, but you'll have to drive for every meal unless you're eating in your own kitchen.

Off-Site Mid-Price Hotels

Nickelodeon Holiday Inn   407/387–5437
Family Suites   www.nickhotel.com

Okay, you say you're totally doing this trip for the kids? You'll never find a hotel any more kid oriented than this one. First of all, you're not going to miss it while driving in from the airport—the lime green and hot orange façade of the building looks like it's been slimed. Once there, you'll find a never-ending array of Nick-theme activities, including a character breakfast with SpongeBob SquarePants, nightly live stage shows, and poolside games. There are two separate water park–style pools. One is oriented toward older kids with big-deal slides and a 400-gallon "dump tank" that periodically, without warning, splashes gigantic waves of water down the slides and flumes. The other pool is geared to younger kids, with preschooler-size slides, climbing areas, and games. Other types of recreation include basketball, miniature golf, and one of the largest arcades in Orlando. There's even a kids' spa offering manicures, pedicures, hair braiding and wraps, and air-brush tattoos. Whew! While several hotels in Orlando offer a limited number of so-called kidsuites (multi-room suites in which one of the rooms is decorated to please children, with amenities like video-game consoles and bunk beds), the Nickelodeon Holiday Inn is all about kidsuites. Rates begin as low as $124 in the off-season.

Proximity to Disney World: Good, via a 10-minute drive
Proximity to Universal: Fair, via a 20-minute drive
Proximity to SeaWorld: Good, via a 15-minute drive

Pluses
+ Entertainment options for kids are practically unlimited.
+ This is the ultimate family-focused hotel; you'll find virtually nothing but parents with kids here.
+ If your kids are into Nick characters like SpongeBob, this place will be heaven to them.

+ Some effort is made—such as having two separate pool areas—to keep the hyperexcited older kids from trampling the overwhelmed younger kids.
+ The kidsuites are numerous and well priced.

Minuses

— No question: this has to be the loudest, most garish hotel in the world.
— The nonstop stimulation may make it hard to persuade your kids to nap in the afternoon, or even go to sleep at night.
— Dining options consist of fast food and buffets, which appeal to kids and are fairly priced, but don't offer much variety or nutrition.

Embassy Suites Lake Buena Vista	407/239-1144 www.embassysuites.com

The Embassy Suites chain is very popular with our readers, especially this location. The suites include kitchenettes, the hotels are generally exceptionally well maintained, and a bountiful breakfast is included in the price. There are four Embassy Suites in Orlando; rates at the Lake Buena Vista location, which is the closest to Disney World, begin at $139 during the off-season. The two International Drive locations—Embassy Suites International Drive South and Embassy Suites International Drive Jamaican Court—are also convenient to area theme parks, being closest to SeaWorld.

Proximity to Disney World:	Good, via a 10-minute drive
Proximity to Universal:	Fair, via a 20-minute drive
Proximity to SeaWorld:	Good, via a 15-minute drive

Pluses

+ There are many all-suite hotels in Orlando but this is one of the closest to Disney. You can access Disney property through the Downtown Disney gate without the hassle of getting on I-4.

+ Complimentary breakfast buffet with made-to-order pancakes and eggs.
+ Kitchenettes make it easy to keep snacks and sandwich supplies on hand.
+ A shopping center with a grocery and fast-food restaurants is nearby.
+ Lots of sports options: an indoor–outdoor pool, a gym, tennis courts, basketball, shuffleboard, and volleyball.

Minuses
– Proximity to I-4 means a consistently high noise level.
– This Embassy Suites is on Palm Parkway surrounded by many other hotels, which means you may hit traffic getting to the parks—another reason to start early.

Magical Memories Villas	407/390–8200 www.magicalmemories.com

One can only imagine how thrilled Disney is that this independent rental agency has adopted the word "magical"—perhaps the most frequently employed word in Disney promotional materials. But Magical Memories, while having no affiliation with Disney, can offer good deals for families. The company handles both condo and house rentals in nine different neighborhoods throughout Orlando. If you want to pay for a home with a private pool in a gated community, that's certainly available, but the majority of the rentals are simply furnished, clean, safe apartments in condo complexes. Rates start surprisingly low, at $114 for a two-bedroom condo and at $169 for a five-bedroom house. Be sure to browse the Web site to see all your options. There's a substantial range of amenities and prices.

Proximity to Disney:	minimum 5 miles, maximum 8 miles
Proximity to Universal:	maximum 16 miles
Proximity to SeaWorld:	maximum 13 miles

Pluses

+ Good choice for large families and groups, since you can get a multibedroom house or condo with a well-equipped kitchen and all the conveniences of a hotel.

+ Daily cleaning service during your stay isn't automatically included, which helps keeps the rates low, but it can be added for an extra fee.

Minuses

− This isn't like a familiar hotel chain where you know what to expect. There's a range in the quality of accommodations.

− For condo rentals of two nights or less and home rentals of four nights or less you'll be charged a cleaning fee based on the size of your unit. The cleaning fee is waived for longer rentals.

− A stay of three nights (or possibly five in the on-season) is required.

− There's a very strict reservations and payment policy. You have to pay a $100 deposit when you reserve. If you don't cancel your reservation within 24 hours, you are charged $50. You must pay for your entire stay at least 15 days in advance and you get no refund if you cancel after that date.

Sheraton Vistana	407/238–5000
	www.starwood.com

The Sheraton Vistana has been a perpetual favorite with our readers since we first began doing resort surveys. One mom wrote, mirroring many other letters, "We found the resort to be very pretty, very quiet, and very clean. And it took us only 15 minutes to drive to Disney World."

Unusually well decorated and maintained, these villas supply almost anything a family could require, and the location is nearly equidistant between the major Orlando theme parks.

One-bedroom villas begin at $124 in low season and $154 in high season; two-bedroom villas begin at $214 in low season and $268 in high season.

Proximity to Disney World:	Good, via a 15-minute drive
Proximity to Universal:	Good, via a 15-minute drive
Proximity to SeaWorld:	Good, via a 15-minute drive

Pluses

+ Children's programs and in-room babysitting allow parents to have some quiet time.

+ A central location between International Drive and I-4, makes it easy to get to all the theme parks and to family-friendly restaurants and minor attractions along International Drive.

+ The villas are larger and more comfortable than those in most other all-suites hotels.

Minuses

− The resort is expanding and renovating until early 2007. Unless you specify otherwise while booking, you may find yourself in a room near the construction zone.

Budget Off-Site Hotels

Holiday Inn SunSpree	**407/239–4500**
Lake Buena Vista	**www.kidsuites.com**

While not quite as wild and woolly as its sister, the Nickelodeon Holiday Inn, the SunSpree offers lots of ways to keep kids entertained, as well as a smaller price tag and a location that's actually closer to Disney. Kidsuites, rooms with one king bed and two bunk beds in a cheerfully-decorated cubicle, begin as low as $99 and standard rooms begin at $79. In-room microwaves and refrigerators allow families to fix snacks and simple meals and an on-site grocery store makes it easy to get supplies.

A mom from North Carolina expressed her appreciation:

"We were at the Holiday Inn SunSpree in the summer when they offer a kiddie program called Camp Holiday Inn. They had games and movies to entertain children in a nice child-care center. Parents can drop off their children, rent a pager so they can be contacted in case of an emergency, and then go out to dinner. It's a marvelous benefit."

Proximity to Disney World:	Good, via a 10-minute drive
Proximity to Universal:	Fair, via 20-minute drive
Proximity to SeaWorld:	Good, via a 15-minute drive

Pluses

+ Kids will feel special here: there's a separate kid registration desk, an arcade, a sports deck, a playroom, and two pools.
+ Kids eat free at the buffet restaurant.
+ Free shuttle service to Disney.
+ Unusually good prices considering the proximity to Disney.
+ On-site child care in the on-season.
+ A good choice for families who don't need suites with full kitchens, but who would still like some of the amenities, such as a fridge and microwave, that a suite would offer.

Minuses

— The resort is fairly old and while some rooms were renovated in 2005, others are in need of a little sprucing up. Request a recently refurbished room when you book.

— Like most of the kid-oriented hotels in Orlando, this place is always loud. The noise volume in the main hallway is enough to make your eyes cross.

— As you might anticipate from the lower price, the kid-suites here are not large and don't have separate bedrooms for parents and kids. What you do get is one big room and a room-within-a-room, really a cubicle, that has bunk beds for kids.

Studios Plus Deluxe Studios— Orlando/Universal Studios   407/370–4428   www.studioplus.com

Besides being possibly the only hotel in the world to have the word "studios" in its name three times, the Studios Plus has much to recommend it. The hotel was created for business travelers on extended trips and thus has all the amenities you have at home, including full kitchens and a laundry room. More to the point, Studios Plus offers maximum space for minimal price. Prices begin as low as $69 a night for a studio with a queen bed and sofa sleeper.

Proximity to Disney World:	Fair, via a 20-minute drive
Proximity to Universal:	Excellent, via a 5-minute drive
Proximity to SeaWorld:	Good, via a 10-minute drive

Pluses
+ Well-supplied suites that appeal to families and those who will be in town more than a few days.
+ Pricewise, this is about as low as a suite in this area gets.

Minuses
− Virtually no entertainment options and a simply functional design. What you see here is what you get.

Enclave Suites of Orlando   407/351–1155   www.enclavesuites.com

Just off International Drive, the Enclave Suites offers easy access to all the major theme parks and an endless number of family-oriented restaurants. A studio with a queen bed and sofa bed begins at $89 during the off-season. Some suites feature KidsQuarters, cubicles with bunk beds and murals depicting SeaWorld or Universal Studios themes. Of this hotel, one Texas mom wrote, "After paying $200 a night to be crammed into a single hotel room on our last visit to Orlando, we found the Enclave Suites to be a great bargain. Our two-bedroom suite was very spacious and we still paid only about $140 a night."

Proximity to Disney World: Fair, via a 15-minute drive
Proximity to Universal: Good, via a 10-minute drive
Proximity to SeaWorld: Good, via a 10-minute drive

Pluses

+ Fully-equipped kitchens in the standard suites.
+ Rooms have either a balcony or patio.
+ Complimentary hot breakfast buffet.
+ Because the hotel is as popular with business travelers as with tourists, the list of amenities is longer than you might expect at this price point. There's an indoor pool and hot tub, a 24-hour fitness center, tennis courts, and complimentary newspaper delivery.

Minuses

- The KidsQuarters are basically just kiddie-theme corners of the parents room. Don't expect much privacy.
- Lots of business travelers make the mood here a little less family oriented than at many other Orlando hotels.
- The International Drive location, while offering plenty of dining and entertainment options, also increases the traffic and noise level.

CHAPTER

3

Once You
Get There

Bare Necessities: Strollers, Babies, and First Aid

Whether you're pregnant, traveling with a baby, or nursing a sore ankle, Disney World is prepared to accommodate your needs.

Strollers

Single and double strollers are available for rent at each theme park for $10 and $18, respectively. Wheelchairs rent for $10, and self-powered electric vehicles are available for $35, with $5 of that refundable upon the return of the vehicle. At these rates, if you need a stroller every day it's obviously most cost-effective to bring one from home. But if you have an older child who will only need a stroller at Epcot, a rental isn't a bad option.

- All kids 3 and under need a stroller, for napping as well as riding and resting.

- For kids 4 to 6, the general rule is this: Strollers are a must at Epcot, nice in the Magic Kingdom, and less needed at the Animal Kingdom or MGM, where the walkable area of the parks is smaller and you spend a lot of time sitting in shows.

@ Tie something like a bandanna or a balloon to your stroller to mark it; otherwise, when you emerge from a ride it may be impossible to find your stroller in a sea of look-alikes. Also,

Money-Saving Tip

If you plan to park-hop in a single day, you don't have to pay for a stroller twice: Keep your receipt and show it for a new stroller when you arrive at the next park.

people sometimes just grab the nearest stroller without checking the name tag, but most people stop short of taking a personal belonging.

Helpful Hint

Just because your stroller isn't where you left it doesn't mean it's been taken—it may simply have been moved aside. Families often stop in midstride when they see an appealing attraction and abandon their stroller in the middle of the sidewalk. There are Disney cast members whose sole duty it is to collect and rearrange these strollers, lining them up outside rides and packing them as close together as possible. Keep looking—you'll likely find your stroller a few yards away from where you left it.

@ Still can't find your stroller? In the Animal Kingdom and MGM, you'll have to go back to the entrance for a replacement. In the Magic Kingdom, check in at Tinkerbell's Treasures in Fantasyland. At Epcot you can get a new stroller at the World Traveler shop between France and the United Kingdom. As long as you've kept your receipt there's no additional charge for a new stroller.

@ If at 8 AM your 5-year-old swears she doesn't need a stroller but at noon she collapses in a heap halfway around Epcot's World Showcase, head for the World Traveler shop. The World Traveler is also the place to rent a stroller if you're coming from the Yacht and Beach Clubs, Board-Walk, Swan, and Dolphin and thus using the "back-door" entrance.

@ If you're renting a stroller for more than one day, you don't have to get in line every morning. On your first park visit, tell them you want, for example, a four-day stroller rental and they will give you coupons for four days. After that you can skip the rental line and go directly to the stroller pick-up booth.

@ Families staying at one of the more sprawling resorts, such as Pop Century, Caribbean Beach, Coronado Springs, Port Orleans, Fort Wilderness, or the All-Star resorts, should bring a stroller from home for any child under 4. You'll need it just to get from your room to the food court or shuttle bus stop.

Baby Services

Each park has a Baby Services Center where rockers, bottle warmers, high chairs, and changing tables are available; diapers, formula, and jars of baby food are also for sale.

In the Magic Kingdom, Baby Services is beside the Crystal Palace Restaurant. In Epcot, it's on the bridge that connects Future World to the World Showcase. At MGM, it's in the Guest Services building; and in the Animal Kingdom, it's behind the Creature Comforts gift shop.

Disposable diapers are available in the larger shops, but they're kept behind the counter, so you'll have to ask for them. Changing tables are provided in most women's rest rooms and some men's as well. If fathers have trouble locating a changing table in a men's room, they can always make a stop in Baby Services.

Nursing Moms

Disney World is so casual and family-oriented that you shouldn't feel self-conscious about using a towel or blanket and discreetly nursing anywhere that's comfortable. If you're too modest for these methods or your baby is easily distracted, try the rockers in the Baby Services Center.

First Aid

First Aid Clinics are beside the Baby Services Center in each park. Although the clinics mostly treat patients with minor problems such as sunburn, motion sickness, and boo-boos, they're equipped for major emergencies and, when necessary, can provide ambulance service to an area hospital.

If you do suffer a medical emergency, take comfort in the fact that hundreds of families that I've interviewed have given ringing endorsements to Disney cast members in times of crisis. I've gotten dozens of e-mails and letters from people who have broken their arms, fainted from heat, gone into premature labor, come down with the chicken pox, and everything else you can imagine—and each person has lauded the Disney cast members for their quick medical response and emotional support. One mother of two from Maryland wrote, "We visited Walt Disney World with our son, who has cystic fibrosis, and found everyone there to be extremely helpful and aware of what our needs might be. In fact, they often anticipated our needs before we did."

> **Helpful Hint**
> Seek medical advice the moment you suspect there may be a problem. Waiting it out only makes the solution more painful and more expensive.

Insider's Secret

If anyone in your family is prone to a recurring medical condition—your son frequently gets ear infections, for example—bring a prescription from your doctor at home in case you need medication while in Orlando.

General First Aid Tips

@ If someone begins to feel ill or suffers an injury while in the parks, head for the nearest first aid clinic. If the nurses there can't fix the problem, they'll find someone who can.

@ All on-site hotels and many off-site hotels have physicians on call 24 hours a day. Contact either the Guest Services desk at your own hotel or Doctors on Call at 407/399–3627.

@ Centra Care Walk-In Medical Care, as the name implies, accepts walk-in patients and has in-house pharmacies. There are two locations near Disney World. For directions and more information, call 407/238–2000. Most area hotels provide courtesy transport to area medical clinics and pharmacies for guests in need.

@ Of course, no matter where you're staying, in a true emergency call 911.

More Things You Don't Want to Think About

A Rainy Day

Unless there's a full-out hurricane headed inland, the parks operate as usual. If there's an electrical storm, outdoor rides and shows are suspended until the weather clears and water parks may close down for the day.

But if you just run into one of those afternoon cloudbursts so common to Florida, soldier on. Rain slickers are available throughout the parks for $5 and they're much more practical than umbrellas because your hands are free to hang on to your kids. The only problem is that on a rainy day half the people in the park are wearing the slickers and thus everyone looks alike. It makes it easier to lose your kids in the crowd, so stay especially alert.

Here are some tips to make sure that a rainy day doesn't turn into a total washout.

@ MGM is a good choice when the weather is iffy because most of the rides and shows are indoors. The Animal Kingdom has mostly outdoor attractions, but it can also be a good rainy day choice because the animals are more active. The Magic Kingdom, where many rides are outside, and Epcot, which requires a lot of walking, are a bit tougher to navigate.

@ There's always plenty to do at Downtown Disney: shopping, movies, Cirque du Soleil, and DisneyQuest. But be forewarned—DisneyQuest is especially swamped when the weather turns bad.

@ Remember, a rainy morning doesn't necessarily mean a rainy day. Weather conditions can change rapidly in Orlando, and if it clears up later in the day the parks will be less crowded than usual. If you see a storm approaching, duck into a show or indoor attraction and give it some time. You may walk out to find sunny skies.

"My advice is 'Pray for rain,'" wrote a father of two from Pennsylvania. "We were standing in a long line for Dumbo and it began to shower. Everyone left, but we just went into a nearby

Insider's Secret

Everyone designates Cinderella Castle or Spaceship Earth as a meeting spot, which is one of the reasons these places are always mobbed. Plan to catch up with your crowd in a more out-of-the-way locale.

shop and it stopped raining after just a couple of minutes. When we emerged, Fantasyland was practically empty and we got on Dumbo with no wait at all."

Lost Kids

Obviously, your best bet is not to get separated in the first place. Savvy families set up prearranged meeting places.

If you do get separated and your kids are too young to understand the idea of a meeting place, act fast. Disney employees are well briefed about what to do if they encounter a lost child, so the odds are good that if your preschooler has been wandering around on his own for more than a couple of minutes, he's been intercepted by a Disney staff member and is on

Helpful Hint

The one glitch in the system is that lost kids are sometimes so interested in what's going on around them that they aren't crying and they don't look lost, and thus no Disney employee intercepts them. Explain to your kids that if they get separated from you to approach the nearest person wearing a Disney name tag. That person can call in the child's name to Baby Services and, assuming you've also called in to report the child as missing, the attendant can tell you where your child is.

his way to Baby Services. Flag down the nearest person you see wearing a Disney name tag and ask to call Baby Services and see if the child has been reported found.

> **Insider's Secret**
> Where and when are kids most apt to get lost? During character signings, in play areas, and just after parades.

In real emergencies— when the child is very young or disabled, or when you're afraid she's been nabbed—bulletins are put out among employees. So if you lose a child, don't spend a half hour frantically searching on your own. Contact the nearest Disney employee and let the system take it from there.

Closed Attractions

Because Disney World is open 365 days a year, there's no downtime for repainting and repairing rides. Thus, on any given day, two or three attractions throughout Disney World may be closed for refurbishment, although this is more likely in low season. You can check to see which attractions are scheduled to be closed for maintenance during the time you'll be in Orlando by visiting www.disneyworld.com or calling 407/824–4321. That way, if the Rock 'n' Roller Coaster is shut down for the week at least you'll know before you hit the gates.

There's still a slight chance that a ride will be malfunctioning and thus temporarily closed when you visit, but this is relatively rare and the rides usually come back on line quickly. The one exception to this is Test Track, which is closed for servicing more than any other Disney attraction.

Auto Breakdowns

If you return to the parking lot at the end of the day to find your battery dead or your tire flat, walk back to the nearest tram stop. The parking lots are patrolled continuously by security staff and they're happy to help. Twelve thousand visitors locked their keys in their cars last year at Disney World, so the staff is used to these fun moments.

A full-service gas station and branch of AAA are near the toll plaza at the Magic Kingdom entrance. The station provides towing and minor repairs.

Helpful Hint

By far the most common problem is forgetting where you parked. Be sure to write down your row number as you leave your car in the morning. Pluto 36 seems easy to remember at first, but you may not be able to retrieve that information 14 brain-numbing hours later.

Running Out of Money

ATMs are located throughout Disney property. For more complex transactions—foreign-currency exchange, lost traveler's checks, taking out a second mortgage on your house—visit the Sun Bank across the street from Downtown Disney.

Crime

Use common sense, especially in trying to avoid the most common crime: theft. Make use of lockers so that you don't have to carry valuables or new purchases around the parks and take cameras and camcorders on rides with you when possible. Be especially cautious at water parks, where you may be tempted to leave your belongings heaped in a lounge chair while you swim. Either rent a locker or use a waterproof money pouch. In case you forget to bring one from home, these are for sale in gift shops throughout the parks.

Don't let paranoia ruin your trip—statistically, Orlando is a pretty safe town—but do keep your wits about you, making sure you bolt the hotel door, lock the rental car, and stick to major roads while exploring.

Saving Money

Saving money at Disney World is somewhat of an oxymoron, but there are ways to contain the damage.

- Be aware that once you cross the Florida state line, there's an inverse relationship between time and money. You have to be willing to spend one in order to save the other. It's worth taking a few minutes to really analyze if cost-cutting measures are worth it; given the high cost of tickets, it doesn't make sense to spend hours trying to save a few bucks.

- How should you spend your arrival day at Disney World? It's tempting to rush straight to the parks but that's rarely the best use of your money. Since it will probably be at least afternoon before you arrive and settle into your hotel, you'll be using a full day of your expensive ticket for only a few hours in the park. Instead, relax around your resort pool or spend the evening at Downtown Disney, which doesn't require a ticket. Then you can start your first full day rested and raring to go.

- Staying hydrated is essential—and expensive. Even bottled water is ungodly costly inside the parks so bring your own bottles and keep refilling them at fountains. Also, on-site hotels offer a deal where you can buy a souvenir beverage mug the first day of your trip and get free refills at the resort for the remainder of your stay. Because soft drinks and coffee are so costly, families who plan to eat a lot of meals at their hotel can save as much as $20 per person with the souvenir mugs.

@ Eat at least some of your meals outside the parks. If you get a suite, it's easy to keep at least breakfast food and snacks in your room. Many off-site Orlando hotels offer free breakfast buffets to their guests and there are numerous fast-food and family-friendly chain restaurants along the I–4 exits that flank Walt Disney World.

@ Dining in Epcot's World Showcase can be very special, but book them for lunch, when prices are considerably lower than at dinner. And remember that portions are huge, even for kiddie meals. Consider splitting a meal with a family member. Or toss a few Ziplock bags in your tote and save some of those french fries or grapes for a later snack.

@ Keep an eye out for full-service restaurants with early-bird value meals. Signs are prominently displayed announcing the restaurants that offer this perk.

@ The dinner shows are expensive, costing a family of four about $130, and even a character breakfast can set you back $60 or more. If the budget is tight, skip those extras and concentrate on ways to meet the characters inside the parks.

@ Except for maybe an autograph book and a T-shirt, hold off on souvenir purchases until the last day. By then the kids will really know what they want and you won't waste money on impulse buys.

@ Buy film, blank videotapes, diapers, and sunscreen at home before you leave. These things are all for sale in the parks but you'll pay dearly for the convenience.

@ If you move from park to park in the course of a day, save your parking receipt so you'll only have to pay the fee once. Also, remember that parking is free for on-site guests.

@ Buy your tickets when you make your hotel reservations, so you'll have them before Disney decides it's time for another price increase.

Meeting the Disney Characters

Meeting the characters is a major objective for some families and a nice diversion for all. If your children are young, prepare them for the fact that the characters are big and thus often overwhelming in person. I once visited Disney World with a 2-year-old whose happy babble of "my Mickey, my Mickey" turned into a wary "no Mickey, no Mickey" the minute she entered the Magic Kingdom gates and saw that everyone's favorite mouse was much, much larger than he appears on TV.

That reaction is not unusual. Many kids panic when they first see the characters and pushing them forward only makes matters worse. The characters are trained to be sensitive and sensible (in some cases more so than the parents) and will always wait for the child to approach them. It's a good idea to schedule a character breakfast near the end of the trip; by then the kids have had plenty of time to observe the characters around the park and even cautious youngsters have usually warmed up.

On the other hand, some kids fall in love with the characters from the start. A father from Ohio said, "We were really surprised at how fast our 3½-year-old daughter became a character groupie. Even when in her stroller she could spot them from a mile away, and she loved getting autographs. This took a lot of time but was worth it just to see the excitement on her face."

Many children, even older ones, enjoy getting character autographs and an autograph book can become a cherished souvenir. Before lining up, prepare the kids for the fact that the characters don't talk with the exception of face characters, those without masks, like Aladdin or Cinderella. As many as 30 young people in Mickey suits (mostly women, because the suits are pretty small) might be dispersed around Disney World on a busy day and they can't all be gifted with that familiar squeaky voice. So the characters communicate through body language.

Helpful Hint

The characters are usually available in greeting locations for about 20 minutes, before they are suddenly whisked away to another location. There is always a character escort close at hand, and if the line to meet a certain character is long, check with the escort before you line up. He or she can tell you approximately how much longer the character will be there and save you from waiting patiently only to have the heartbreaking experience of having the character leave just as your child makes it to the front of the line.

Also be aware that because of the construction of their costumes, the characters can't always see what's happening beneath them too clearly. Donald and Daisy, for example, have a hard time looking over their bills, and thus small children standing at their feet might be ignored. If this appears to be happening, lift your child to the character's eye level.

Times and places for meeting the characters are listed on theme park maps, tip boards, and entertainment schedules.

Pal Mickey

While this guide encourages you to get as much information as possible before you leave home, there's a cool new way to get information once you're inside the parks, and it's called Pal Mickey.

Pal Mickey may look like a cuddly plush toy, but he can turn even the youngest child in the family into a knowledgeable theme park guide. Mickey giggles and vibrates whenever he has something to say and you hold him to your ear and squeeze his hand to get the message. But this isn't just random chatter—oh no, Mickey is one savvy mouse. As you walk through the parks, Mickey knows where he is and different messages are triggered by location. For example, he can tell you where the characters are by saying "Hey, Goofy is on Main Street—let's drop by and say hi."

Via sensors inside the toy that are tripped by sensors around WDW property, Mickey knows about the attractions you're approaching and can make recommendations, such as telling you about height restrictions, warning you about the witch in Snow White's Adventures, or predicting that he might get wet on Kali River Rapids. Via timed signals, Mickey also prompts you when it's time to find a seat for the parade or an upcoming show and gives tips like "Italy is a great place to watch *IllumiNations*."

Helpful Hint

Since Pal Mickey knows what's going on in "real time" he can update you on current conditions in the park, like when lines are unusually short for certain attractions.

Most of Mickey's messages are about the parks, but he also tells jokes and fun facts. And when a child is waiting in line for a ride or restaurant service is slow, he steps in to entertain. Squeeze both hands and he plays three child-oriented games.

With messages coming approximately every two minutes, parents may fear Pal Mickey overload, but if you don't want to hear the message, you can ignore the giggle. If Mickey is in a backpack or bag (and thus can't "see"), he won't send messages at all. Also, if you walk past a location twice, he remembers that he's been there so he doesn't tell you the same thing over and over. Pal Mickey was once available for rent but is now only available for sale, at a price of $60. Once you get him home, he no longer picks up message signals, but he can still play games.

CHAPTER

4

Touring Tips and Plans

General Disney World Touring Tips

The size of Disney World is often a shock to first-time visitors, many of whom arrive with vague notions that they can walk from Epcot to the Magic Kingdom or even that they are separate sections of the same theme park. There can also be confusion over the names: Some people use "Walt Disney World" and "Magic Kingdom" synonymously, whereas in reality the Magic Kingdom is a relatively small part of the much larger Disney World complex. There's more to this place than Cinderella Castle and Space Mountain. Thus it's vital that you have at least a basic understanding of the Disney World layout and transportation system before you leave home.

The tips in this chapter encourage you to visit more than one park a day—to follow a morning hitting the water slides at Blizzard Beach, for example, with an afternoon taking in the shows at MGM. The best way to avoid overstimulation and burnout is to work a variety of experiences—some active, some passive, some educational, some silly—into each day.

When it comes to touring, families tend to fall into three

groups. The first group sleeps in, has a full-service meal at their hotel, and lollygags over to the parks around 11 AM They wander around aimlessly, finding the lines for major rides to be so long that their only choices are either to wait 90 minutes for Splash Mountain or to spend the whole afternoon riding minor attractions. By the time they begin to get in a groove (i.e., they figure out time-saving systems like Fastpass), it's 5 PM and they're exhausted. They retreat back to their hotel room frustrated at how little they've seen, irritated by how much they've spent, and carping at each other. This is a vacation?

The second group is what I call Disney World Commandos. These hyperorganized types have elaborate tour plans and march determinedly from ride to ride, checking off their "to do" list as they go. Amanda wants to ride Dumbo twice in a row? No way! It'll throw them off their schedule. Jeffrey wants to hang out at Innoventions? Sorry, it's not on the list. If anything unforeseen happens—Space Mountain opens late or there's a glitch in the bus system—the whole group goes into a psychological meltdown. This is a vacation?

Disney-savvy families find the sweet spot between the two extremes. They have an overall plan but make sure to leave empty spaces in the day to allow for spontaneity. They get an early start each morning, but factor in plenty of downtime to rest, particularly in the afternoon. Most important, they're familiar enough with each park and its attractions that they arrive with a clear idea of what they want to see, but they don't feel compelled to do it all. One father of four from Washington State wrote, "People need some kind of plan before they go. Disney World is so big and so overwhelming that the first time we went down we spent hours just aimlessly drifting around."

The following tips should help you make the most of your time without pushing anyone, parents or kids, past their endurance level.

@ For families with kids, it's especially important to avoid the exhaustion that comes with just trying to get there. If you're staying off-site, it can easily take two hours from the time you leave your hotel until you board your first ride, which is enough to shatter the equanimity of even the most well-behaved kid. Your children have been waiting for this vacation a long time, and now they've been flying and driving for a long time. You owe it to them to get into the parks quickly.

Insider's Secret

Come early! If you follow only one tip in the whole book, make it this one. Although in recent years the mornings have become more crowded than they used to be, you'll still find far shorter waits for big-deal rides than you do in the afternoon.

@ Every Disney World guidebook on the market tells people to come early and in the 17 years since I've written my first edition, the mornings have become more crowded. But the majority of people visiting Disney World still arrive between 10 and 11 AM, many of them proudly announcing that this is their vacation and they'll sleep in if they want. (These same people seem to take a strange inverse pride in bragging about how long they stood in line and how little they saw.) Arriving early is like exercising regularly; everyone knows you should do it, but most people don't. So an early start is still the best way to ride major attractions with little or no wait time.

@ On the evening you arrive, check with your hotel to see what time the park you'll be visiting the next day opens. (All on-site and most off-site hotels display this information prominently.) If you learn, for example, that the Magic Kingdom is scheduled to open at 9 AM, be at the gate by 8:30. At least part of the park is usually open early and you can be at the end of Main Street awaiting the rope drop while the other 50,000 poor saps are still crawling along I–4.

If you're indeed allowed to enter the first section of the park early, use your time wisely. Take care of any business— get maps and entertainment schedules, rent strollers, make dining reservations, take a potty break—before the main park opens. If you haven't had breakfast, there's always a kiosk where you can grab juice and muffins. The characters are usually on hand to greet kids, which is a fun way to start the day. But be sure to be at the ropes about 10 minutes before the stated opening times.

> **Insider's Secret**
> What if everyone comes early? They won't.

Because people were practically stampeding each other after the rope drop, Disney is now controlling how fast you can enter the main body of the park. Once the whole park opens, proceed quickly but calmly (they'll nab you if you run) to the first ride you'd like to board. Sometimes the

Time-Saving Tip
To maximize your time in the parks, either eat breakfast back at your hotel or buy fast food while you're waiting for the rope drop. There's always at least one sit-down place to get breakfast in each park, but you don't want to waste the relatively uncrowded morning hours in a restaurant.

Fastpass system doesn't start working until 20 or 30 minutes after park opening, so it's definitely better to ride your top-priority attraction first and get your Fastpass second.

@ Eat at "off" times. Some families eat lightly at breakfast, have an early lunch around 11 AM and supper at 5 PM. Others eat a huge breakfast and then a late lunch around 3 PM and have a final meal back at their hotels after the parks close. If you tour late and you're really bushed, all on-site hotels and many off-site hotels have in-room pizza delivery service.

Helpful Hint

Plan to see the most popular attractions either early in the day, late at night, or during a time when a big event siphons off other potential riders (such as the afternoon parade in the Magic Kingdom).

@ Kids usually want to revisit their favorite attractions and parents who overschedule to the point where there's no time to revisit risk a mutiny. One way to handle this is to save the entire last day of your trip as a "greatest hits" day and go back to all your favorites one more time, even if this means maximum park-hopping. If you feel like lugging the camcorder around only once, make this the day.

@ Use the touring plan to cut down on arguments and debates. It's a hapless parent indeed who sits down at breakfast and asks, "What do you want to do today?" Three different kids will have three different answers.

@ When making plans, keep the size of the parks in mind. MGM is small and can be easily crisscrossed to take in various shows. Likewise, the Animal Kingdom can be toured in four or five hours. The Magic Kingdom has more attractions and more crowd density, slowing you down; although some cutting back and forth is possible, you'll probably want to tour one land fairly thoroughly before heading to another. Epcot is so enormous that you're almost forced to visit attractions in geographic sequence or you'll spend all your time and energy in transit.

℮ Try park-hopping. Families with a multiday pass might figure: We'll spend Monday at the Magic Kingdom, Tuesday at MGM, Wednesday at Blizzard Beach, Thursday at Epcot, and Friday at the Animal Kingdom. Sounds logical, but a day at the Magic Kingdom is too much riding, 14 hours at Epcot is too much walking, the Animal Kingdom simply doesn't require that much time, a whole day at MGM is too many shows, and anyone who stays at Blizzard Beach from dawn to dusk will wind up waterlogged. Mix it up a bit.

℮ If you're trying to predict how crowded a ride or show will be, four factors come into effect:

The newness of the attraction. In general, the newer it is, the hotter it is, especially if it's an attraction that's gotten a lot of media attention like *Mickey's PhilharMagic* or Mission: SPACE.

The quality of the attraction. Space Mountain, *Fantasmic!,* and other Disney classics will still be mobbed years from now.

Speed of loading. Continuous-loading attractions such as Pirates of the Caribbean, Spaceship Earth, and It's a Small World can move thousands of people through in an hour. The lines at start-and-stop rides such as Dumbo, Triceratops Spin, and the Mad Tea Party move much more slowly.

Capacity. Shows like Muppet*Vision 3-D, Universe of Energy, and *Mickey's PhilharMagic* have theaters that can accommodate large crowds at once. Lines form and disappear quickly as hundreds of people enter the theater for a show. For this reason, theater-style attractions are good choices in the afternoon, when the park is at its most crowded and you need a rest.

@ Take some time to familiarize yourself with the sprawling WDW transportation system. If you're staying on-site you'll be given a transportation map at check-in, and Guest Relations can help you decide the best route to take to out-of-the-way locations.

@ For families with young children, seeing the characters is a major part of what makes Disney World special, so don't overplan to the point where you don't have time to hang with Mickey and the gang. Your theme park map indicates when and where they'll appear, but the one place you probably won't see them is just walking down the street. At Disney, the characters are the equivalent of rock stars and security around them is tight. If you want that photo, autograph, or hug, you'll need to either line up or schedule a character breakfast.

@ In the off-season, the Magic Kingdom, MGM, and the Animal Kingdom sometimes close at 5 or 6 PM, but Epcot always stays open later, even during the least crowded days of the year. Ergo, spend your days at one of the parks that close early, and evenings at Epcot. This buys you more hours in the parks for your money and besides, many of the best places for dinner are at Epcot.

@ If you'll be at Disney World for more than four days, consider planning a "day off" in the middle of your vacation. A day in the middle of the trip devoted to sleeping in, hanging around the hotel pool, shopping at Downtown Disney, and maybe taking in a character breakfast at an on-site hotel, can make all the difference. Not only will you save a day on your multiday ticket, but also you'll start the next morning refreshed and energized.

@ You need a strategy for closing time. Except for the Animal Kingdom, the major parks all have nighttime extravaganzas that result in huge logjams as nearly every guest in the park convenes for the show and then mobs the exits en masse when it's over. See the "Tips for Leaving" sections in each park for specific information on how to best exit each park.

Touring Tips for Visitors Staying On-Site

@ By far the greatest advantage of staying on-site is the shortened commute to the theme parks, making for an easy return to your hotel for a mid-afternoon nap or swim. You can reenter the parks in the early evening. Remember the mantra: Come early, stay late, and take a break in the middle of the day.

@ Take advantage of the Extra Magic Hour program. You're given a brochure at check-in telling you which park is featured on which day of your visit. If you want to use this information in your pretrip planning, you can call 407/824–4321 or Guest Relations at the resort where you'll be staying to verify which park will have extended hours on which day.

Touring Tips for Visitors Staying Off-Site

@ Time your commute. If you can make it from your hotel to the theme park gates within 30 minutes, it may still be worth your while to return to your hotel for a midday break. If your hotel is farther out and your commute is longer, it's doubtful you'll want to make the drive four times a day.

@ If it isn't feasible to return to your hotel, find afternoon resting places within the parks. (See the sections headed "Afternoon Resting Places" in each theme park chapter.) Sometimes kids aren't so much tired as full of pent-up energy. If that's the case, take them to the play areas in each park (Tom Sawyer Island and Toontown in the Magic Kingdom; the play fountains in Epcot; the *Honey, I Shrunk the Kids* Adventure Zone at MGM; and the Boneyard at the Animal Kingdom) and let them run around for a bit.

@ The hotel restaurants in the Magic Kingdom are rarely crowded at lunch, and dining there is much more relaxed and leisurely than eating lunch in the parks. An early dinner can also effectively break up a summer day, when you'll be staying at the park until late. If you do take the monorail to a Magic Kingdom resort, be sure to line up for the train marked "Monorail to the MK Resorts." Most of the monorails run express back to the Transportation and Ticket Center (TTC).

@ Off-site visitors tend to tour all day, so get strollers for preschoolers. Few 4-year-olds can walk through a 14-hour day.

@ If you have a multiday ticket, you're entitled to use Disney transportation to move from park to park. Spend the morning in a park where you'll be active (like the Animal Kingdom or Magic Kingdom) and in the afternoon transfer to a park (such as Epcot or MGM) that has more shows and thus more places to sit and rest.

Tips to Save Your Sanity

Use Your Time Wisely

This boils down to one thing: Avoid the lines. Big-deal attractions draw long lines early and stay crowded all day.

Head for the most crowded, slow-loading attractions first. In the Magic Kingdom that's Splash Mountain, Space Mountain, and Big Thunder Mountain—although some Fantasyland attractions, such as Dumbo, Peter Pan, and the Many Adventures of Winnie the Pooh, can also draw long lines. In Epcot, it's Test Track and Mission: SPACE. At MGM it's Rock 'n' Roller Coaster, the Tower of Terror, and *Voyage of the Little Mermaid*. At Animal Kingdom, it's Kilimanjaro Safaris and *Festival of the Lion King.*

Ride as many of the big-deal rides as you can in the morning, when waits are shorter. In general, except for those noted, save theater-style attractions for the afternoon. And if you can't get to all the big-deal rides during the first couple of hours the park is open, try again during the parades, or during the last hour before closing.

Be Willing to Split Up

By this point in the planning process, it's probably beginning to dawn on you that every single member of the family expects something different from this vacation.

Discuss which attractions you'll enjoy as a family; some rides, shows, restaurants, and parades will be a blast for everyone. But there are also bound to be some attractions that won't have such universal appeal, and this is especially true if there's a significant gap in the ages of your children.

If an attraction holds appeal for only one or two family members, there's no need to drag the whole crew along. A 13-year-old boy on It's a Small World is not a pretty sight.

Teenagers, in fact, often like to split off from the family for an hour or two and simply shop, hang out in arcades, or ride a favorite over and over. Security in Disney parks is tight, so this is an option worth considering. Just make sure to have a clearly designated meeting time and place. About splitting up, one mother of three from Ohio wrote, "Playhouse Disney is a wonderful attraction for young children, but my preteen son wasn't that thrilled with the idea of standing in line for an hour to see Bear. We let him shop and walk around on his own for an hour while we took the younger kids to Playhouse Disney. Normally, I would worry about letting him on his own but at Walt Disney World we feel pretty safe about it. And he was in a much better mood after a break from his little sisters."

Master Fastpass

Disney World's Fastpass system is designed to reduce the time you spend waiting in line. Attractions offering Fastpass are listed in each theme park chapter.

Here's how it works: Let's say you enter the Animal Kingdom at 10 AM and find that a long line has already formed for Kilimanjaro Safaris. Rather than standing in line for an hour, go to the Fastpass kiosk and insert your theme park ticket. You'll get the theme park ticket back, along with a small paper Fastpass that looks like a movie admission stub. The Fastpass

Helpful Hint

Only a limited number of Fastpasses are available for each attraction. At the most popular rides on crowded days, Fastpasses can run out by mid-afternoon. So if you want to guarantee you'll get a Fastpass for Splash Mountain or Test Track, visit the kiosk as soon as possible after you enter the park.

Must-See List for WDW

At the Magic Kingdom
Big Thunder Mountain
Buzz Lightyear's Space Ranger Spin
Dumbo
Evening parade and fireworks
Mickey's PhilharMagic
Space Mountain
Splash Mountain

At Epcot
Honey, I Shrunk the Audience
IllumiNations
Mission: SPACE
Soarin'
Test Track
World Showcase Entertainment

At MGM
Fantasmic!
Lights, Motors, Action! Extreme Stunt Show
The Magic of Disney Animation
Rock 'n' Roller Coaster
Star Tours
Twilight Zone Tower of Terror
Voyage of the Little Mermaid

At Animal Kingdom
Expedition Everest
Festival of the Lion King
It's Tough to Be a Bug!
Kali River Rapids
Kilimanjaro Safaris

(along with a digital clock at the kiosk) will tell you when to return. There's usually an hour-long window of opportunity, which in this case might be between 11:30 AM and 12:30 PM.

Go on to tour the rest of the Animal Kingdom and return to Kilimanjaro Safaris sometime within that one-hour period. Show your Fastpass to the attendant and you'll be allowed to enter a much shorter line and proceed directly to the boarding area. The waits with Fastpass average 10 to 15 minutes, a vast improvement over the 90-minute waits that big attractions can post on crowded days.

Insider's Secret

To keep the line short, a finite number of Fastpasses are issued for each five-minute interval. If a lot of park guests use the Fastpass system for a popular ride, the time frame between when the Fastpass is issued and when you return keeps getting longer. For example, if you get a Fastpass for Tower of Terror on a relatively uncrowded day, you may be able to return in an hour. On a more crowded day, when many people have gotten Fastpasses before you, you might visit the kiosk at noon and get a Fastpass that tells you to return at 6 PM. And if you wait until afternoon, you may not be able to get a Fastpass at all.

To let as many guests as possible take advantage of the Fastpass system, you can only get one Fastpass at a time. Once you've either used it or it has expired, you can get another. (The exact time at which you can get another Fastpass is printed on your current Fastpass ticket.) Periodically, there's buzz that Disney may change the system and let people get multiple Fastpasses, but at present, it's still one to a customer.

Helpful Hint

Four family members will need four Fastpasses, but that doesn't mean you all have to line up at the kiosk. Let one family member be in charge of holding on to all the tickets and all the Fastpasses. That way you won't find that Tyler has somehow managed to lose his Fastpass just as you're set to board Test Track.

Also, as an Ohio mom says, "Be careful when you're getting your Fastpass to make sure you retrieve your park ticket. We left our multiday tickets in a Fastpass machine in Epcot and didn't realize it for hours. Disney eventually got it straightened out, but it took a while and it was very stressful."

Fastpass is so popular that Disney is always looking for ways to expand the system, and you never know when they'll be offering some new perk. Check the information flyers you get with your park maps for any new information about the Fastpass program. Disney has already experimented with giving out bonus Fastpasses, wherein a second Fastpass for a different attraction is automatically distributed when you get your first Fastpass of the day. There's also talk that Disney hotel guests may be able to order Fastpasses before they even get to the park through an in-room ordering system.

When You Don't Need Fastpass

As great as Fastpasses are, you don't always need one. Don't use the Fastpass system if 1) the wait time in the general-admittance line is 25 minutes or less, 2) the attraction in question is a theater-style show that admits hundreds of people at once, or 3) you plan to later ride an even more popular attraction. Essentially, you want to use your Fastpass privilege where it's most effective, for big-deal rides that get the most crowds.

Tips for Big Families

Disney has instituted a new program called Magical Gatherings specifically to help make it easier for groups, such as family reunions, to vacation in Disney World. Specialists can help you arrange rooms, tickets, and dining for the whole party, and they help handle details such as individual payment. Plus, Magical Gathering groups get some great little perks not available to the general public, such as private character breakfasts or fireworks cruises on the Seven Seas Lagoon. Even if you'd rather not hire a specialist, there are lots of great tips and planning tools that you can read and use for free in the Magical Gatherings section of www.disneyworld.com. The following tips may also make things a little less hectic.

@ Consider renting a villa or condo. Many have kitchens so you can save on eating out. On-site resorts with villa-style lodging include Old Key West, Saratoga Springs, BoardWalk Villas, the Beach Club Villas, and the Villas at Wilderness Lodge. Good sources for information about off-site condo and villa properties include Condolink (800/733–4445) and www.travelocity.com.

Helpful Hint
A gratuity of 18% is added for parties of eight or more—even at buffet restaurants.

@ If you'd like a little less togetherness, book as many rooms as you need at a resort, but ask for adjoining rooms.

@ Transportation can be an issue, especially if there's a wide variation in the ages, stamina, and risk tolerance of the family members. Older kids will probably want to stay at the park all day, while the toddlers and grandparents might be burned out and ready to rest by noon. Either way, stay on-site so you can use the Disney transportation system at your leisure, or, if you're driving, bring more than one vehicle to the parks so that family members have the option to leave early.

@ Bring cell phones or rent pagers at Guest Relations in each theme park. Large groups tend to scatter and you don't want to spend half your time trying to get the group re-assembled.

@ Have everyone wear the same color T-shirt or hat each day. A tour operator passed along this tip, which makes it easier to spot "your people" in a sea of faces.

Money-Saving Tip

If the adults plan to head out for a night, an in-room sitter is generally less expensive than drop-off child care when three or more children are involved.

@ Orlando can be the ultimate multigenerational destination for grandparents traveling with their grandchildren, but if possible avoid summers, since the Florida heat and humidity can be very taxing on older adults, and make sure you build in adequate rest stops. There's also no shame in wheelchair rental (see below) even if the older members of the party are mobile. The average amount one walks in a Disney day is 6.5 miles, and that's a lot for anyone.

Tips for Guests with Disabilities

@ Request a copy of the "Guidebook for Guests with Disabilities" when you buy your ticket or pick one up when you rent your wheelchair. It offers information on how to approach each attraction.

@ Wheelchairs can be rented at any stroller rental booth ($10 standard, $35 if motorized) and many attractions are accessible by wheelchair. Attendants are on hand to help guests with special needs board through their own gates, so parties traveling with a disabled guest can often avoid waiting in line altogether. (This has prompted some young and able-bodied people to rent wheelchairs solely to avoid the lines, an obviously unethical little scam that Disney is trying to eliminate.)

@ People with disabilities give the Disney resorts high marks for convenience at reasonable prices. The All-Star resorts, for example, have several wheelchair-accessible rooms that begin as low as $84 a night. The monorail, buses, boats, and other forms of transportation are all wheelchair accessible and (if you request it in advance) you can have a complimentary wheelchair waiting for you upon check-in. Most of the on-site resorts offer rooms with specially equipped bathrooms and extra-large doors; life jackets are available at resort pools and the water parks.

@ For more detailed information on hotel options for people with disabilities, call Central Reservations at 407/934–7639 (407/W–DISNEY) and ask for the Special Reservations Department.

@ Guests with visual disabilities should be aware that guide dogs are welcome at all parks and many area hotels. Guests can also rent a tape recorder and cassette describing the attractions at each park and a Braille guidebook with a $25 refundable deposit. Just visit Guest Relations.

@ Guests with hearing disabilities can rent listening devices that amplify attraction music and words through Guest Relations with a $25 refundable deposit. TTYs are available throughout Disney World and guests can also contact Disney Reservations via TTY at 407/939–7670.

@ All on-site hotels and most off-site hotels are equipped to refrigerate insulin and other medications.

Finally, not a tip, but a word of reassurance. If you're traveling with someone who has a chronic health problem or disability, rest assured that the Disney World cast members will help you in any way they can. Because Disney World is frequently visited by children sponsored by the Make-A-Wish Foundation and other programs like it, the Disney staff is accustomed to dealing with a wide range of situations, even cases in which visitors are seriously ill. The key is to make sure that Disney employees both at your hotel and within the parks are aware of your presence and that you may need assistance. With a few preliminary phone calls, you'll find that Disney World is one of the best possible travel destinations for families who have a child with special needs. A mom from Connecticut writes, "We informed our hotel (the Contemporary) in advance of our daughter's health problems and when we checked in we were delighted to learn that our family had been invited to ride in the first car of the afternoon parade at the Magic Kingdom. The cast member told us that there is no way to guarantee such an invitation, but that if they know a special needs child is visiting, they try to offer some special treats. Riding in the convertible and waving to the crowd was the highlight of our daughter's week."

Tips for Pregnant Guests

I've personally toured Disney World twice while pregnant and not only lived to tell the tale but honestly enjoyed both trips. However, a few precautions are in order.

- Make regular meal stops. Instead of buying a sandwich from a vendor, get out of the sun and off your feet at a sit-down restaurant.

- If you aren't accustomed to walking as much as 7 miles a day, begin getting in shape a couple of months before the trip by taking 30- to 40-minute walks at home.

- Dehydration is a real danger. Keep water in your tote bag and sip frequently. You can refill your bottle at water fountains throughout the parks.

Helpful Hint
Most important of all, check out rest room locations in advance.

- Consider staying on-site so that you can return to your room in the afternoon to rest.

- Mothers-to-be are welcome to rest in the rocking chairs inside Baby Services.

- Standing stock-still can be more tiring than walking when you're pregnant, so let your husband stand in line for rides. You and the kids can join him as he's about to enter the final turn of the line.

Birthdays and Special Occasions

While Disney has no set protocol for birthdays, anniversaries, and other special occasions, the general rule is "Ask and you shall (probably) receive." If you're staying at a Disney resort, inform Guest Relations or the concierge in advance if you'd like flowers, balloons, or a gift delivered on a special day. It's also a good idea to make reservations at your restaurant of choice weeks in advance and let the manager know if you have any preferences. Most are happy to oblige.

One mother wrote that her son celebrated his birthday at a character breakfast featuring Pooh and friends. The cake was delivered to the table by Tigger, the child's favorite character, who then led the birthday guests in an impromptu parade around the restaurant. Or consider the young man who proposed to his girlfriend at the Coral Reef in the Living Seas pavilion at Epcot. The couple was having dinner next to the mammoth glass aquarium when, at the key moment, one of the divers swam by the table carrying a sign that read, "Will you marry me?" When the girl turned to look at her boyfriend, he was on one knee with the ring—and the whole restaurant stood up and cheered when she said yes.

What do these stories have in common? They were arranged in advance. So if you'd like to add some treats and surprises to a special occasion, contact the management at the hotel or restaurant. With their help, you should have no trouble finding a way to make the day memorable.

Helpful Hint

Even if you decide not to arrange a special dinner, you can drop by any Guest Relations desk to pick up an identifying pin for the birthday boy or girl. It's free and it guarantees the child will receive lots of special treatment throughout the day from cast members. One mother reported that when the characters in the afternoon parade saw her daughter's birthday pin, they made a special point to come over and high-five her or shake her hand.

How to Customize a Touring Plan

Get Some General Information

Request maps and transportation information at the time you make your hotel reservations. Disney's Web site, www .disneyworld.com, is also a good source of preliminary information, including theme park hours during the time that you'll be visiting.

Ask Yourself Some Basic Questions

Consider how long you'll want to stay at each park. If your kids are under 10, you'll probably want to spend more time in the Magic Kingdom. Older kids? Plan to divide your time fairly equally among the major parks, and save some time for the water parks and Downtown Disney.

The time of year you'll be visiting is a major factor, too; although you may be able to tour MGM thoroughly in a single day in October, it will take you twice as long to see the same number of attractions in July. In summer the combination of the crowds, the heat, and extended park hours mean you'll need to build in more downtime.

Plan at least one evening in Magic Kingdom, MGM, and Epcot so that you can see all the closing shows.

Set Your Priorities

Next, poll your family on what attractions they most want to see and build these priorities into the plan. I'd let each family member choose three must-sees per park. For example, at MGM, 10-year-old Jeremy wants to ride Star Tours, the Tower of Terror, and Rock 'n' Roller Coaster. His 6-year-old sister Elyce chooses Muppet*Vision 3-D, *Beauty and the Beast,* and *Voyage of the Little Mermaid.* Mom thinks the Prime Time Café sounds like a hoot, and wants to ride the Great Movie Ride and

Star Tours. Dad is all over the Tower of Terror thing, wants to play the Millionaire game, and thinks the *Lights, Motors, Action!* stunt show sounds interesting.

Okay, because of some overlap you have 10 items on this family's personal must-see list. They should make sure that they experience these attractions even if they don't do anything else. With any luck, they'll have some extra time and may be able to work in a few other things as well, but the key is to make sure you honor everyone's top three choices.

Cut Some Deals

Building each family member's must-sees into the touring plan has many advantages. You're seeing the best of the best, you've broken out of that "gotta do it all" compulsion, and the kids feel that they're giving input and are full partners in the vacation planning.

There's another huge advantage: A customized touring plan minimizes whining and fights. Your 12-year-old is more apt to bear a character breakfast with good grace if she knows that you'll be spending the afternoon at Blizzard Beach, one of her top choices. Kids understand fair. They might fidget a bit in Chefs de France, but if you've already covered Test Track and Mission: SPACE, you're perfectly justified in saying, "This is Mom's first choice in Epcot, so be quiet and eat your croquette de boeuf."

Break Up the Days

Divide each day of your visit into three components: morning, afternoon, and evening. It isn't necessary to plan where you'll be every hour on the hour—that's way too confining—but you need some sense of how you'll break up the day.

Pencil in things that have to be done at a certain time. You have a character breakfast for Wednesday morning, for example, or you must be in the Magic Kingdom on Friday night because that's the only time the evening parade is scheduled during your visit.

The final product may look something like this:

Monday
Morning: Magic Kingdom
Afternoon: Rest by hotel pool
Evening: Epcot

Tuesday
Morning and afternoon: Animal Kingdom
Evening: MGM

Wednesday (rest day)
Morning: Character breakfast
Afternoon: Downtown Disney then early to bed

Thursday
Morning and afternoon: Blizzard Beach
Evening: Epcot

Friday
Morning: MGM
Afternoon: Rest by pool
Evening: Magic Kingdom

Note: This plan assumes you have the Park Hopper option on your tickets.

Favorite Attractions for Preschoolers

IN THE MAGIC KINGDOM
Aladdin's Magic Carpet
Country Bear Jamboree
Dumbo
It's a Small World
Jungle Cruise
Mad Tea Party
The Many Adventures of Winnie the Pooh
Mickey's PhilharMagic
The parades
Peter Pan's Flight
Pooh's Playful Spot
Toontown

IN THE ANIMAL KINGDOM
The Boneyard
Festival of the Lion King
It's Tough to Be a Bug!
Kilimanjaro Safaris
Triceratop Spin

AT EPCOT
Family Fun Kidcot Stops
Innoventions
Journey into Imagination
The Living Seas

AT MGM
Beauty and the Beast
Honey, I Shrunk the Kids Movie Set Adventure
Muppet*Vision 3-D
Playhouse Disney
Voyage of the Little Mermaid

Favorite Attractions for Kids 5-8

IN THE MAGIC KINGDOM
Aladdin's Magic Carpet
Buzz Lightyear's Space Ranger Spin
Country Bear Jamboree
Dumbo
It's a Small World
Jungle Cruise
Mad Tea Party
The Many Adventures of Winnie the Pooh
Mickey's PhilharMagic
The parades
Peter Pan's Flight
Pirates of the Caribbean
Toontown

IN THE ANIMAL KINGDOM
The Boneyard
Festival of the Lion King
It's Tough to Be a Bug!
Kali River Rapids
Kilimanjaro Safaris
Triceratop Spin

AT EPCOT
Honey, I Shrunk the Audience
Innoventions
Journey into Imagination
The Seas with Nemo and Friends
Soarin'

AT MGM
Beauty and the Beast
Honey, I Shrunk the Kids Movie Set Adventure
Muppet*Vision 3-D
Playhouse Disney
Voyage of the Little Mermaid

Whatever you do, save plenty of time to meet the
characters. It's a major thrill for kids this age.

Favorite Attractions for Kids 9-12

IN THE MAGIC KINGDOM
Big Thunder Mountain Railroad
Buzz Lightyear's Space Ranger Spin
Haunted Mansion
Mickey's PhilharMagic
Pirates of the Caribbean
Space Mountain
Splash Mountain

IN THE ANIMAL KINGDOM
Dinosaur
Expedition Everest
The exploration trails, including Gorilla Falls and Maharajah
Festival of the Lion King
It's Tough to Be a Bug!
Jungle Trek
Kali River Rapids
Kilimanjaro Safaris
Primeval Whirl

AT EPCOT
Body Wars
Cranium Command
Honey, I Shrunk the Audience
IllumiNations
Live entertainment around the World Showcase
Mission: SPACE
The Seas with Nemo and Friends
Soarin'
Spaceship Earth
Test Track

AT MGM
Beauty and the Beast
Fantasmic!
Great Movie Ride
Indiana Jones Epic Stunt Spectacular
Lights, Motors, Action! Extreme Stunt Show
Muppet*Vision 3-D
Rock 'n' Roller Coaster
Star Tours
Twilight Zone Tower of Terror
Voyage of the Little Mermaid

IN THE REST OF DISNEY WORLD
Blizzard Beach
Cirque du Soleil
DisneyQuest
Typhoon Lagoon
Water Sprite boats

Favorite Attractions for Teens

IN THE MAGIC KINGDOM
Big Thunder Mountain Railroad
Buzz Lightyear's Space Ranger Spin
Haunted Mansion
Mickey's PhilharMagic
Pirates of the Caribbean
Space Mountain
Splash Mountain

IN THE ANIMAL KINGDOM
Dinosaur
Expedition Everest
The exploration trails
It's Tough to Be a Bug!
Kali River Rapids
Kilimanjaro Safaris

AT EPCOT
Body Wars
Cranium Command
Honey, I Shrunk the Audience
IllumiNations
Live entertainment around the World Showcase
Mission: SPACE
Soarin'
Test Track

AT MGM
Fantasmic!
Great Movie Ride
Indiana Jones Epic Stunt Spectacular
Lights, Motors, Action! Extreme Stunt Show
Rock 'n' Roller Coaster
Star Tours
Twilight Zone Tower of Terror
Who Wants to Be a Millionaire—Play It!

IN THE REST OF DISNEY WORLD
Blizzard Beach
Cirque du Soleil
DisneyQuest
Downtown Disney
Surfing Lessons at Typhoon Lagoon
Typhoon Lagoon
Water Sprite boats

CHAPTER

5

The Magic Kingdom

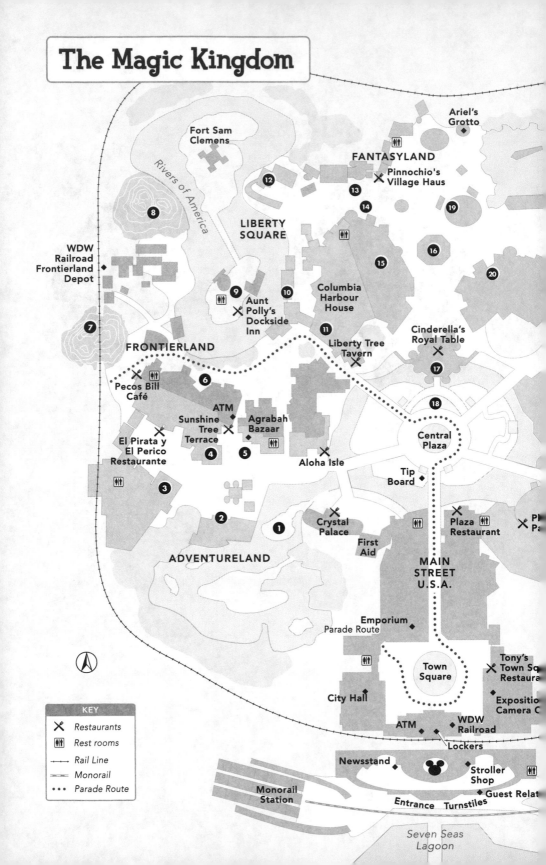

The Magic Kingdom

Fort Sam Clemens

Rivers of America

FANTASYLAND

Ariel's Grotto

Pinnochio's Village Haus

LIBERTY SQUARE

WDW Railroad Frontierland Depot

Aunt Polly's Dockside Inn

Columbia Harbour House

Liberty Tree Tavern

Cinderella's Royal Table

FRONTIERLAND

Pecos Bill Café

ATM

Sunshine Tree Terrace

Agrabah Bazaar

El Pirata y El Perico Restaurante

Aloha Isle

Central Plaza

Tip Board

Crystal Palace

First Aid

Plaza Restaurant

ADVENTURELAND

MAIN STREET U.S.A.

Emporium
Parade Route

Town Square

Tony's Town Sq Restaura

Expositio Camera C

City Hall

ATM

WDW Railroad

Lockers

KEY

✕   Restaurants

🚻   Rest rooms

—|—   Rail Line

⊶   Monorail

••••   Parade Route

Newsstand

Stroller Shop

Guest Relat

Monorail Station

Entrance   Turnstiles

Seven Seas Lagoon

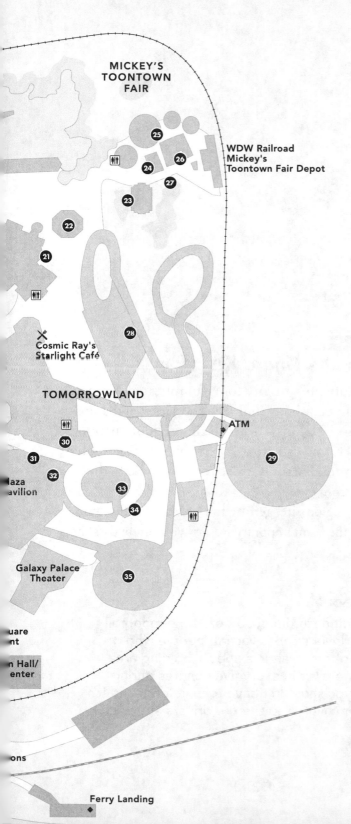

MICKEY'S
TOONTOWN
FAIR

WDW Railroad
Mickey's
Toontown Fair Depot

Cosmic Ray's
Starlight Café

TOMORROWLAND

ATM

Plaza
Pavilion

Galaxy Palace
Theater

Square
nt

Hall/
enter

ons

Ferry Landing

Getting to the Magic Kingdom

If you're staying off-site, prepare for a complicated journey. Either drive or take your hotel shuttle to the Ticket and Transportation Center (TTC) inside the Magic Kingdom parking lot. From the TTC you can cross the Seven Seas Lagoon by either ferryboat or monorail. Both deliver you directly to the Magic Kingdom front gates.

If you're staying on-site, getting to the Magic Kingdom is a lot easier. From the Contemporary Resort, you can bypass the

Insider's Secret

Make it a habit each time you board the monorail to ask if the driver's cab is vacant; people who'd like to ride up front wait in a special holding area. Because monorails run every five minutes during peak times, you shouldn't have to wait long, and it's a real kick for children to see the drivers at work.

TTC and take the monorail to the Magic Kingdom or walk to the park. From the Grand Floridian, you can either take the monorail or the ferry. From Fort Wilderness Campground or Wilderness Lodge, take the ferry. Polynesian guests have all the options: the monorail, a water taxi, or the ferry.

Guests at Disney hotels that are not Magic Kingdom resorts will take shuttle buses that deliver them directly to the Magic Kingdom gates, bypassing the TTC. Sometimes families who stay on-site but have a car prefer to drive to the parks, which can save you time at every park *except* the Magic Kingdom. If you're headed for the Magic Kingdom, take Disney transportation even if you have your own car just so you can avoid the TTC.

Helpful Hint

Driving? The Magic Kingdom parking lot is the most confusing of the four parks. Even if you come early enough to park near the gate, still take the tram just to make sure you wind up at the right place.

Through the Turnstiles

Each of your park tickets will be a different color and have a different Disney character on the front. When you get your tickets, assign each one to a different family member and have everyone write their name on the back of their ticket. You can designate one person (i.e., Mom) to hold on to all the tickets, but when you get to the turnstiles, everyone will need to hold their own ticket. Disney's security system, called Ticket Tag, requires each ticket holder to place their second and third fingers into an electronic reader as they slide their ticket through a machine at the turnstiles. Disney makes a quick electronic measurement of your fingertips, allowing the system to link your park ticket to you and you alone. Ticket Tag makes it easier to get new tickets if your originals are lost or stolen, but it does require that each family member hold his or her own ticket at the entrance. So if Brendan uses the purple Mickey ticket for entrance to the Magic Kingdom in the morning, he'll need to use the same purple Mickey ticket when he enters MGM that evening.

Getting Around the Magic Kingdom

The Disney World Railroad leaves from Main Street with stops near Splash Mountain in Frontierland and Toontown. A lap around the park takes 20 minutes; trains depart from Main Street every four minutes during busy times and every 10 minutes during slower times. Even so, this is not your fastest way to get around the park. In the morning, when crowds are heaviest, you may have to wait for a second or even third train; by that time, you could have walked.

Walking, in fact, is the fastest means of transport in the Magic Kingdom. The train, vintage cars, and horse-drawn carriages are fun, but think of them as rides, not as a serious means of getting around the park.

Helpful Hint

Be prepared to make frequent rest stops while touring the Magic Kingdom. You won't walk as much as you do in Epcot, but you're likely to spend more time standing in line. Standing still is ultimately harder on the feet—and the nerves—than walking.

Tips for Your First Hour in the Magic Kingdom

- Be through the gates 30 minutes earlier than the stated opening time. Get strollers and pick up a map and entertainment schedule as you enter. The entertainment schedule is crucial because it gives you showtimes and character meeting times for that day.

- On Extra Magic Hour mornings, Fantasyland and Tomorrowland open first. Older kids should head straight for Space Mountain and Buzz Lightyear while younger kids should start with Dumbo, Peter Pan's Flight, and the Many Adventures of Winnie the Pooh.

Helpful Hint

On days that are anticipated to draw large crowds, guests are allowed to travel the length of Main Street before the park officially opens. On less crowded days, people are usually held in the town square just in front of the railroad. Either way, several characters will be on hand to give the kids something to do while you're waiting for the ropes to drop.

- On regular mornings all sections of the park open at once. If your kids are up for it, head for Splash Mountain when the ropes drop, then on to Big Thunder Mountain Railroad. Both may have long lines even by 9:15—if you arrive to find a 30-minute wait, get a Fastpass.

- If there's a gap in the ages of your children and the 9-year-old is ready for a coaster but the 5-year-old isn't, consider splitting up during this crucial first hour of the day when

Quick Guide to Magic

Attraction	Location	Height Requirement
Astro Orbiter	Tomorrowland	None
Big Thunder Mountain Railroad	Frontierland	40 inches
Buzz Lightyear's Space Ranger Spin	Tomorrowland	None
Carousel of Progress	Tomorrowland	None
Cinderella's Golden Carousel	Fantasyland	None
Country Bear Jamboree	Frontierland	None
Dumbo	Fantasyland	None
Enchanted Tiki Birds	Adventureland	None
Goofy's Barnstormer	Toontown	35 inches
Hall of Presidents	Liberty Square	None
Haunted Mansion	Liberty Square	None
It's a Small World	Fantasyland	None
Jungle Cruise	Adventureland	None
Liberty Square Riverboat	Liberty Square	None
Mad Tea Party	Fantasyland	None
Magic Carpets of Aladdin	Adventureland	None

Scare Factor
0 = Unlikely to scare any child of any age.
! = Has dark or loud elements; might rattle some toddlers.
!! = A couple of gotcha! moments; should be fine for school-age kids.
!!! = You need to be pretty big and pretty brave to handle this ride.

Kingdom Attractions

Speed of Line	Duration of Ride/Show	Scare Factor	Age Range
Slow	2 min.	!	5 and up
Moderate	3 min.	!!	5 and up
Fast	6 min.	0	3 and up
Fast	22 min.	0	10 and up
Slow	2 min.	0	All
Moderate	15 min.	0	All
Slow	1 min	0	All
Fast	20 min.	0	All
Moderate	1 min.	!!	5 and up
Fast	20 min.	0	10 and up
Slow	9 min.	!!	7 and up
Fast	11 min.	0	All
Slow	10 min.	0	All
Fast	15 min.	0	All
Slow	2 min.	0	4 and up
Slow	1 min.	0	All

(continued)

Quick Guide to Magic

Attraction	Location	Height Requirement
The Many Adventures of Winnie the Pooh	Fantasyland	None
Mickey's PhilharMagic	Fantasyland	None
Peter Pan's Flight	Fantasyland	None
Pirates of the Caribbean	Adventureland	None
Snow White's Scary Adventures	Fantasyland	None
Space Mountain	Tomorrowland	44 inches
Splash Mountain	Frontierland	40 inches
Stitch's Great Escape	Tomorrowland	40 inches
Swiss Family Robinson Treehouse	Adventureland	None
Timekeeper	Tomorrowland	None
Tomorrowland Indy Speedway	Tomorrowland	None
Tomorrowland Transit Authority	Tomorrowland	None
Tom Sawyer Island	Frontierland	None

Scare Factor

0 = Unlikely to scare any child of any age.
! = Has dark or loud elements; might rattle some toddlers.
!! = A couple of gotcha! moments; should be fine for school-age kids.
!!! = You need to be pretty big and pretty brave to handle this ride.

Kingdom Attractions

Speed of Line	Duration of Ride/Show	Scare Factor	Age Range
Moderate	5 min.	0	All
Moderate	20 min.	0	All
Moderate	3 min.	0	All
Fast	8 min.	!!	6 and up
Slow	3 min.	!!	5 and up
Moderate	3 min.	!!!	7 and up
Moderate	10 min.	!!	5 and up
Moderate	15 min.	!!!	7 and up
Slow	n/a	0	4 and up
Fast	20 min.	0	3 and up
Slow	5 min.	0	2 and up
Fast	10 min.	0	All
Slow	n/a	0	4 and up

you can ride popular attractions with relatively short waits. Mom can take one child, Dad the other, and you can meet back up in an hour.

@ Want to ride lots of big-deal rides? Get your first Fastpass early in the day, but after you take advantage of the usually uncrowded first hour to ride your first-choice attraction.

Attractions in the Magic Kingdom Offering Fastpasses

Space Mountain

Splash Mountain

Big Thunder Mountain Railroad

Jungle Cruise

Buzz Lightyear's Space Ranger Spin

Haunted Mansion

Mickey's PhilharMagic

Peter Pan's Flight

The Many Adventures of Winnie the Pooh

Stitch's Great Escape

Main Street

Main Street is where the stage is set. With its pristine sidewalks, Victorian shops, flower stalls, and antique cars, strolling down Main Street is like walking through an idealized circa-1890 American town. It also provides a transition from the unglamorous parking lots and buses to the charms of the park and people visibly relax as they move closer toward Cinderella Castle. Usually by the time they arrive, they're thoroughly Disney-fied.

The Magic Kingdom Don't-Miss List

IF YOUR KIDS ARE 8 OR OLDER

Any Fantasyland rides that catch their fancy

Big Thunder Mountain Railroad

Buzz Lightyear's Space Ranger Spin

Haunted Mansion

Mickey's PhilharMagic

The parades

Pirates of the Caribbean

Space Mountain

Splash Mountain

IF YOUR KIDS ARE UNDER 8

Buzz Lightyear's Space Ranger Spin

Country Bear Jamboree

Dumbo

It's a Small World

Mad Tea Party

The Magic Carpets of Aladdin

The Many Adventures of Winnie the Pooh

Mickey's PhilharMagic

The parades

Peter Pan's Flight

Pirates of the Caribbean

Splash Mountain and Big Thunder Mountain,
if they're bold enough and if they pass
the height requirement.

Toontown

Main Street Touring Tips

@ Although you might spend a few minutes mingling with the characters as you enter, don't take too much time checking out the shops and minor attractions of Main Street. One mom who made the mistake of shopping too early said, "We bought souvenirs on the way into the park and I spent the whole day dragging things around. I looked like a Disney bag lady!" Instead, focus on getting to the major rides.

@ A blackboard posted at the end of Main Street provides up-to-date information about the approximate wait times of major Magic Kingdom attractions, as well as showtimes and information on where to meet the characters. Consult it whenever you're unsure about what to do next.

@ Return to Main Street to shop mid-afternoon. Main Street is also a good place for lunch.

@ If you're touring the Magic Kingdom late and your party splits up, choose a spot on Main Street as your meeting place. Disney cast members clear people out of other sections of the park promptly at closing time, but Main Street stays open at least an hour after the rides shut down. It's the best place to reassemble the family before heading home.

Insider's Secret

After shopping, either stow your purchases in the lockers beneath the Railroad Station or, if you're a guest at a Disney resort, you can have them returned directly there for free. Not planning to see the parade? Be off Main Street by 2:30 PM After that, it's a mob scene.

Fantasyland

Fantasyland, located directly behind Cinderella Castle, is home to many of the Magic Kingdom's classic kiddie rides. It's also the most congested section of the park.

Fantasyland Touring Tips

- Visit Fantasyland either before 11 AM, after 7 PM, or during the parades.

- Wait times for Dumbo, Peter Pan's Flight, and the Many Adventures of Winnie the Pooh are always longer than for other Fantasyland rides. Visit these first or use Fastpass.

- Don't eat or shop in Fantasyland. Similar foods and souvenirs are available elsewhere in less crowded areas of the Magic Kingdom.

- Park your strollers in one spot and walk from ride to ride. Fantasyland is geographically small, so this is easier than constantly unloading and reloading the kids, only to push them a few steps.

Fantasyland Attractions

Cinderellabration

A musical show starring the Disney princesses is held several times each day in front of Cinderella Castle. Little girls go wild as each princess in turn— Cinderella, Snow White, Belle, Aurora, Jasmine, and Ariel—appears on stage, escorted by her prince. There's no seating, however, and the whole area is exposed to the sun, meaning it's possible to wait 30 minutes

Helpful Hint

Stay alert. Because the kiddie rides tempt them to wander off, this is the most likely spot in all of Disney World to lose your children.

in crowded and uncomfortable conditions even before the 18-minute show even starts. Consult your entertainment schedule for showtimes and try to time your visit for the end of the day or when there's cloud cover.

Mickey's PhilharMagic

A 3-D show projected onto a mammoth screen, *Mickey's Phil-harMagic* is Fantasyland's newest attraction and one of the best in Walt Disney World.

The Scare Factor

Although the theater is dark and some of the special effects are startling—Donald leaps right out the screen at you more than once—the presence of beloved Disney characters usually calms the kids down. Unless you have a baby or toddler who is afraid of loud noises, children of any age will love the show.

The story begins when maestro Mickey is called away from the stage and Donald steps in as conductor. He promptly loses control of the orchestra and is whisked away on a magical, musical, madcap journey. A slew of other Disney characters get into the act—you see Donald falling in love with Ariel and sailing through the skies with Aladdin. You'll smell pastries during "Be Our Guest" and flowers during romantic scenes. The show is funny, the animation is breathtaking, and the music is stirring; in short, it's a great introduction to the 3-D experience for kids. "It was our 4-year-old's favorite attraction at the Magic Kingdom," concurs one dad from Ohio. "We were surprised at how much she enjoyed all the shows (even more than the rides), but this was the best."

Insider's Secret

Mickey's PhilharMagic offers Fastpass, but you'll only need it during the on-season. The theater seats many people at once, so during the off-season, you'll probably be able to get in with a minimal wait. Save your Fastpass for rides that always have lines, like Peter Pan and Pooh.

It's a Small World

Completely renovated in 2004, the sets and audio-animatronics of It's a Small World shine brighter than ever. During this 11-minute boat ride, dolls representing children of all ages greet you with a song so infectious that you'll still be humming it at bedtime. The line moves steadily, even during the most crowded parts of the afternoon. Babies, toddlers, and preschoolers seem to be especially enchanted.

Helpful Hint

Although beloved by preschoolers, It's a Small World can be torture for older siblings. One 10-year-old wrote that Disney should offer an "I Survived It's a Small World" T-shirt similar to those they sell outside of Splash Mountain or the *Twilight Zone* Tower of Terror. In other words, if older kids opt to skip the ride, don't press the point.

Peter Pan's Flight

Tinker Bell flutters overhead as you board miniature pirate ships and sail above Nana's doghouse, the night streets of London, the Indian camp, and Captain Hook's cove. Of all the Fantasyland attractions, this one is most true to the movie that inspired it and the level of detail is so captivating that even

Helpful Hint

Upon entering Fantasyland, immediately get a Fastpass for either The Many Adventures of Winnie the Pooh or Peter Pan's Flight. Both attractions draw longer-than-average lines.

older kids tend to enjoy the ride. It only lasts three minutes, though, so if the wait's longer than 30 minutes, use Fastpass or come back during the parade.

The Many Adventures of Winnie the Pooh

This upbeat attraction follows Pooh and friends through a "blustery" day, so be prepared for your honey pot–shape car to swirl and sway along the way. Designed especially for younger kids, the ride is gentle and fine for any age. Pooh's Thotful Spot, at the exit, has great souvenirs for Pooh fans.

Insider's Secret

Many Disney purists mourned the passing of Mr. Toad's Wild Ride, an original Fantasyland attraction that was torn down to make way for Pooh. In a nod to the dear departed amphibian, there's a painting inside the ride that shows Mr. Toad passing along a deed to Owl.

Pooh's Playful Spot

This whimsical play area just across from the Many Adventures of Winnie the Pooh has spurting fountains of water, crawl-through logs and honey pots, a slide, and a tree house for climbing. Everything is pint-size and geared toward the pre-school set (and there are benches for parents to rest while the kids play). The Playful Spot is a great place for the youngest members of the family to romp around while older siblings ride some of the more intense attractions in Fantasyland.

Cinderella's Golden Carousel

Seventy-two white horses prance while a pipe organ toots out "Chim-Chim-Cheree" and other classic Disney songs. The carousel is especially gorgeous at night.

Snow White's Scary Adventures

The main focus of this ride is on the part of the movie when Snow White flees the evil witch. You ride mining cars through the dark, and the witch, with her toothless grin and gleaming red apple, appears several times quite suddenly.

The Scare Factor

It's hard to decide exactly whom this ride was designed for. It's boring for older kids and too scary for preschoolers. The music, the witch, and the mood of the ride are foreboding enough to give toddlers the willies.

Dumbo

There's something very special about Dumbo. Although the lines move slowly—you could stand in line an hour for the 90-second ride—most kids seem willing to wait for a chance to ride in one of Disney's most enduring icons: a flying elephant. If you visit first thing in the morning, you can cut the wait time way down.

The Scare Factor

You control the height of your flight via a joystick, so the ride is appropriate for any age. All the elephants do rise for a couple of high-flying laps at the end, but by then kids are generally used to the sensation.

Mad Tea Party

Spinning pastel cups, propelled by their riders, swirl around the Soused Mouse, who periodically pops out of his teapot. Because you largely control how fast your teacup spins, this ride can be enjoyed by all ages. Just don't go right after lunch.

Time-Saving Tip

Rider volume ebbs and flows at the Mad Tea Party. If the line looks daunting, grab a drink or make a bathroom stop. By the time you return, the crowd may have dispersed.

Ariel's Grotto

A small play area with squirting fountains, the grotto is a good place for kids to cool off on a hot afternoon. Go inside the cave to meet Ariel and get her autograph only if the line is short. This is the only place in the Magic Kingdom where Ariel appears on a regular basis.

Mickey's Toontown Fair

Mickey's Toontown Fair (most often referred to as just "Toontown") makes you feel as if you're immersed in a giant cartoon. The land is really just one giant play area designed to appeal to the 2- to 8-year-old set.

Begin by walking through Minnie's pastel house where the oven bakes a cake before your eyes. Mickey's house is right down the block, and Donald's boat is a great play area with squirting fountains.

Toontown is the best place in the park to meet the characters. After you tour Mickey's house, signs lead you to a backyard tent where the Main Mouse is holding court. You enter in relatively small groups and have plenty of time for pictures, autographs, and hugs. In the Toontown Hall of Fame you'll find three separate lines leading you to three rooms where you can meet more characters for pictures and autographs. Signs that say "Princesses," "Villains," or "The Hundred Acre Wood" tell you who's inside. After you've visited one group, you can always rejoin the line and visit another.

Toontown Touring Tips

- Like Fantasyland, Toontown can become unbearably crowded in mid-afternoon. By early evening, however, the crowds thin out.

- The Donald's Boat water-play area is a great place to cool off. Many parents let their children wear bathing suits under their clothes, then have them strip down to the suits when they want to get wet. They'll get semidry pretty quickly in the hot weather, at which point you can dress them again. Babies can play in waterproof diapers. There's a changing table in the Toontown rest rooms.

- The very best time to visit Mickey and the other Toontown characters is Sunday morning, when the crowds are light.

- When you're lining up to meet the characters in the Toontown Hall of Fame, be aware that any queue featuring "face characters," such as Cinderella, Snow White, or Peter Pan, will move slowly. The reason is that face characters, unlike Mickey and his gang, can talk and interact with the children. This can slow the line to a crawl, but once you do make it to the front, your kids are in for a real treat.

Toontown Attractions

Goofy's Barnstormer
The centerpiece of Toontown is a zippy little roller coaster called Goofy's Barnstormer, which takes you on a wild trip

The Scare Factor

Goofy's Barnstormer is a good first test to see how kids will handle the bigger coasters like Splash Mountain. The drops are steep and the thrills are definitely there, but the ride is so short that you barely have time to get out one good scream before it's over. Watch it go around once or twice before you decide to ride. "Goofy's Barnstormer is much faster than you think it would be, considering it's in Toontown," wrote a mom from New York. "My 6-year-old was terrified." The height requirement is 35 inches.

through Wise Acre Farm with the Goofman himself as the pilot. The ride only lasts 60 seconds, but it's more intense than it looks.

Tomorrowland

Tomorrowland has a 1930s sci-fi look that reflects "the future that never was." We're talking metal and chrome with a few robots and plenty of neon thrown in for effect.

Tomorrowland Touring Tips

- If you plan to ride Space Mountain, go early—by 9:15 it has substantial lines. If you arrive to find a 30-minute wait, get a Fastpass.

- The arcade across from Space Mountain is a good place for the less adventurous members of your party to wait while the coaster warriors tackle Space Mountain.

- Looking for fast food during peak dining hours? Tomorrowland food stands are rarely as busy as those in other lands. Cosmic Ray's Starlight Café, the largest fast-food place in the Magic Kingdom, moves you in and out fast.

Tomorrowland Attractions

Space Mountain

This three-minute roller-coaster ride through inky blackness is one of the few scream-rippers in the Magic Kingdom. The cars move at a mere 32 mph, a fairly tame pace compared to the monster coasters at some theme parks, but since the entire ride takes place in the dark, it's almost impossible to anticipate the turns and dips.

The Scare Factor

This is the most intense ride in the Magic Kingdom, with a 44-inch height requirement. Most kids in the 3 to 8 age range find Space Mountain too scary, but the 9 to 11 age group gives it a solid thumbs-up. It's the highest-rated attraction in the park among teens.

Time-Saving Tip

Kids often like to ride Space Mountain more than once. If so, ride in the morning and then immediately get a Fastpass. That way you can return later in the day and avoid the inevitable crowd.

Buzz Lightyear's Space Ranger Spin

This attraction is an "interactive fantasy in which riders help Buzz save the world's supply of batteries." More specifically, the ride transports guests into the heart of a video game where they pass through various scenes, spinning their cars and shooting at targets. Your car tallies your score and at the end you learn whether you're a Space Ace or a lowly Trainee. Buzz is addictive, but the lines do move swiftly and Fastpass is available. "Buzz Lightyear is great for all ages," wrote a mother from Texas. "Our

Insider's Secret

Attention Space Ace wannabes: The tougher the target, the higher the points, so don't waste all your time taking cheap shots. There are 100,000-point targets on the palm of the orange robot's left hand in the Robot Attack scene and another on the bottom Z of the spaceship in Zurg's Secret Weapon.

family members ranged from 2 to 83 and this was one ride everybody got into. Of course, we all got a little too competitive . . . "

Astro Orbiter

A circular thrill ride similar to Dumbo, Astro Orbiter is a bit too much for preschoolers and a bit too little for teens. If you ride at night, the astro-ambience is more convincing.

The Scare Factor

Astro Orbiter is a good choice for children ages 5 to 10 who might not be quite up to Space Mountain. But it's not for anyone prone to motion sickness.

Tomorrowland Speedway

Tiny sports cars circle a nifty-looking racetrack and although the ride itself isn't anything unusual, kids under 11 rate it highly, perhaps because young drivers can steer the cars themselves. (Kids 52 inches and taller can drive solo; others must be accompanied by an adult.)

Helpful Hint

Try to persuade your child not to rush through Tomorrowland Speedway; loading and reloading the race cars takes time and you may as well drive slowly rather than sit for five minutes in the pit waiting to be unloaded.

Tomorrowland Transit Authority

This little tram circles Tomorrowland and provides fun views, including a glimpse inside Space Mountain and the Buzz Lightyear attraction. The trip lasts 10 minutes and the ride is never crowded, so the attendant will usually let you stay on for more than one cycle. The rocking of the train has lulled more than one cranky toddler into a nap and, in fact, cast members report that the ride is often full of parents holding sleeping youngsters.

Timekeeper

In this Circle-Vision 360 film, Jules Verne and H.G. Wells take the audience from 19th-century Paris into the future. The voices of Robin Williams and Rhea Perlman, your time-travel pilot and ship, add to the fun. Unfortunately, you stand during the presentation, making this a hard attraction to view with young kids. A clock outside the attraction lets you know how long until showtime; don't amble in until the wait is five minutes or less.

Carousel of Progress

This is another fairly long show (22 minutes), another high-capacity attraction, and thus another good choice for the crowded times of the af-

Helpful Hint
Carousel of Progress and *Timekeeper* are both closed in the off-season.

ternoon. Kids might be bored by this salute to modern inventions, especially once they've seen the more high-tech presentations of Epcot. That said, the show does have a nostalgic appeal for parents; Carousel of Progress was one of Walt's contributions to the 1964 World's Fair.

Stitch's Great Escape

The Great Escape tells the story of what Stitch was like before he came to Earth in the hit movie *Lilo & Stitch*. Stitch is captured by the Galactic Federation and taken to a prisoner processing facility. Since Stitch's reputation as a troublemaker precedes him, visitors to the attraction are recruited to provide additional security. But you can't keep a good alien down, and Stitch eludes security, causing mayhem everywhere he goes. The show features Disney's most sophisticated audio-animatronics to date, including the remarkable, three-dimensional Stitch figure. It's also loud, dark, and far more forbidding than the advertisements indicate.

We receive a lot of mail about Stitch's Great Escape, the majority of it negative. It seems Disney missed the boat here in much the same way they did years ago with Snow White's Scary Adventures. They named an attraction after a familiar movie character beloved by young children, and then they created an experience so intense that it scares the daylights out of the very age group it was designed to attract. While Disney is constantly tinkering with the Stitch attraction, like raising the light level during the most intense scenes, it remains, as one seven-year-old put it "scary scary, not fun scary."

A mom from Delaware echoed the sentiment. "The worst thing about shows like Stitch (and *It's Tough to be a Bug* in the Animal Kingdom) is that they take beloved Disney characters and make children afraid of them. My seven-year-old son wanted to ride Stitch but now he's telling everyone at home that he would never go on it again."

The Scare Factor

The height requirement to see Stitch is only 40 inches, but the darkness and volume are still too scary for many preschoolers. There's often at least one terrified child screaming through the show. Plus, lines can be pretty long for a fairly short show. Unless you have brave kids and you love Stitch, you can skip this attraction.

Adventureland

Thematically the most bizarre of all the lands—sort of a Bourbon Street meets Trinidad by way of Congo—Adventureland definitely conveys an exotic mood.

Adventureland, Frontierland, and Liberty Square Touring Tips

- If you have two days to spend touring the Magic Kingdom, begin your second day in Frontierland, at Splash Mountain. Move on to Big Thunder Mountain, then the Haunted Mansion in Liberty Square. All three attractions are relatively easy to board before 10 AM.

- These lands stay crowded between noon and 4 PM, when the crowds lined up to watch the afternoon parade finally disperse. If you miss Splash Mountain, Big Thunder Mountain Railroad, or the Haunted Mansion early in the morning, wait until early evening to revisit them.

- Should you find yourself stuck in these lands in the afternoon, you'll find a bit of breathing space on Tom Sawyer Island, with the Enchanted Tiki Birds, or in the Hall of Presidents. Surprisingly, Pirates of the Caribbean can be a smart choice even when the park is crowded. At least you wait inside, and this is one of the fastest-loading attractions in Disney World.

> **Time-Saving Tip**
>
> If you hustle to Frontierland only to find that Splash is posting a 30-minute wait, get a Fastpass and ride Big Thunder Mountain Railroad first.

Insider's Secret

Guests who have visited the Magic Kingdom before and want to try something a little different should consider the Family Magic Tour. This adventure is designed for kids 4 to 10 and their families. You follow clues throughout the park, and end by solving the mystery and finding a character. See Chapter 10 for details.

Adventureland Attractions

Jungle Cruise

You'll meet up with headhunters, hyenas, water-spewing elephants, and other varieties of frankly fake wildlife on this 10-minute boat ride. It's dated looking in comparison to the attractions in the Animal Kingdom, but still fun, thanks largely to the amusing patter of the tour guides. These young guides in pith helmets somehow manage to tell jokes and puns that are so corny you're groaning and laughing in the same breath.

The cruise is not at all scary and fine for any age, but the lines move with agonizing slowness and most of the queue area is exposed to the sun. If you decide to take the cruise, go in the morning or during the afternoon parade when the lines abate somewhat.

The Magic Carpets of Aladdin

This colorful, appealing, and relatively new attraction is a circular aerial ride similar to the Dumbo ride. The added twist is

The Scare Factor

Because the carpets pitch around a bit, the Aladdin ride is slightly more intense than Dumbo, but most kids love it.

that riders can make their carpets tilt, rise, or drop on command, and these evasive maneuvers may be necessary if you wish to avoid the spitting camels that guard the ride.

The Enchanted Tiki Birds

These singing and talking birds represent Disney's first attempt at the audio-animatronics that are now such an integral part of theme-park magic. The addition of Iago from *Aladdin* and Zazu from *The Lion King* as the new co-owners is good news for kids, and although this is hardly the most exciting show in the Magic Kingdom, the theater is a good place to get off your feet and out of the heat. Be sure to stick around for Iago's stream of insults as you exit the theater; it's the funniest part of the show.

The Scare Factor

The revamped show is louder than the original version. When the Tiki gods are angered, the theater darkens and lightning and thunder begin. The noise level alone is enough to frighten some toddlers.

Pirates of the Caribbean

This attraction inspires great loyalty and since the success of the movie series by the same name the Pirates are hotter than ever, especially Captain Jack Sparrow (Johnny Depp's character) and his nemesis Barbossa. The pair joined the audio-animatronic cast of the attraction in 2006. If you've been on the ride before, you'll notice a new twist to the story line as Sparrow and Barbossa race to a cache of plundered treasure. It's a kick to see the new figures interacting with some of the older animatronic buccaneers. All the audio-animatronics figures are remarkably life-like, right down to the hair on their legs, and the theme song is

The Scare Factor

The queue winds through a dark, drafty dungeon, so many kids are nervous before they even board. After that, the scariest elements of the ride occur in the first three minutes—there are skeletons, cannons, and periods of shadowy darkness. By the time you get to the mangy-looking and politically incorrect buccaneers themselves, however, the mood is up-tempo, as evidenced by the cheerful theme song. This ride is fine for most kids over 6, unless they're afraid of the dark.

positively addictive. Even though the story is dark, violent, and brutal, in the hands of Disney it all somehow manages to come off as a lighthearted, happy adventure.

Swiss Family Robinson Treehouse

There's a real split of opinion here—some visitors revel in the details and love climbing through this replica of the ultimate tree house, while others rate it as dull. Kids who have seen the movie tend to like it a lot more.

Frontierland

Kids love the rough-and-tumble Wild West feel of Frontierland, which is home to several of the Magic Kingdom's most popular attractions.

Frontierland Attractions

Big Thunder Mountain Railroad

A roller coaster designed as a runaway mine train, Big Thunder Mountain is one of the most popular rides in the park with all age groups. The glory of the ride is in the setting. You zoom through a deserted mining town and although the details are best observed by day, the lighting effects make this an especially atmospheric ride after dark. Be warned that the ride is very bouncy and jerky, but the effects are more apt to make you laugh than to make you scream.

The Scare Factor

When it comes to coasters, Big Thunder Mountain is more in the rattle-back-and-forth style than the lose-your-stomach-as-you-plunge style. Most children over 7 should be able to handle the dips and twists and many preschoolers adore the ride as well. The height requirement is 40 inches. If you're debating which of the three mountains— Space, Splash, or Big Thunder—is most suitable for a child who has never ridden a coaster, Big Thunder is your best bet.

Splash Mountain

Based on "Song of the South" and inhabited by Brer Rabbit, Brer Fox, and Brer Bear, Splash Mountain takes riders on a winding, watery journey through swamps and bayous.

Because it's the first thing you see as you approach, most of the attention is given to that 40-mph drop over a five-story waterfall, but there's a great story to the ride as well. You get into a log boat and follow Brer Rabbit's adventures throughout the attraction, and each time he gets into trouble, you get into trouble, too. In other words, each dangerous moment is followed by an escape through a water drop and the ultimate danger culminates in the ultimate water drop. The interior scenes are delightful and "Zip-a-Dee-Doo-Dah," perhaps the most hummable of all Disney theme songs, fills the air.

The Scare Factor

The intensity of that last drop, which gives you the feeling that you're coming right out of your seat, along with the 40-inch height requirement, eliminates some preschoolers. Watch a few cars make the final drop before you decide. Our mail indicates that most kids over 5 love the ride.

Splash Mountain can get very crowded; ride early in the morning or in the last hour before closing. You can get soaked, really soaked, especially if you're in the front row of the log, and especially if you're sitting on the right. This can be great fun at noon in June, less of a thrill at 9 AM in January. Some people bring ponchos or big black garbage bags for protection and then discard them after the ride.

Hidden Mickey

When you and the kids are keeping an eye out for Mickey Mouse, you may not realize that you're walking right past him. No, we're not talking about the life-size Mickeys, we're talking about those silhouettes and abstract images that are cleverly tucked throughout Walt Disney World.

These "Hidden Mickeys" began as an inside joke among the Imagineers and artists who design theme park attractions. Spotting a Hidden Mickey is a real treat. In the final scene of Splash Mountain, as you pass the *Zip-A-Dee-Lady* paddleboat, look for a pink cloud floating high in the sky. It's a silhouette of Mickey lying on his back.

Helpful Hint

Just because your toddler can't ride Splash Mountain doesn't mean she can't get a thrill. There's a certain place you can stand to watch the log boats on their final drop. The shrieks combined with the sprays of water will delight any child. A father of three from Florida agreed. "Our two-year-old's favorite ride was Splash Mountain. She couldn't ride it, of course, but she stayed outside with Dad while Mom and her brothers rode, and she loved watching the boats splash down. Water shoots up after the boats, and she squealed every time."

Country Bear Jamboree

Kids love the furry, funny, audio-animatronics critters featured in this 15-minute show. From the coy Trixie, who enters via a ceiling swing, to the wincingly off-key Big Al, each face is distinctive and lovable.

The Jamboree seats large numbers of guests for each show, and it's a good choice for the afternoon, when you'll welcome the chance to sit and rest. Kids 10 and up often think the bears are hokey, so parents can take younger kids to the Jamboree while their older siblings visit Splash Mountain and Big Thunder Mountain Railroad.

Time-Saving Tip

A clock outside the Country Bear Jamboree tells you how long you have until the next show. Don't enter the waiting area until the countdown is 10 minutes or less.

Tom Sawyer Island

A getaway playground full of caves, bridges, forts, and wind-mills, Tom Sawyer Island is the perfect destination for kids full of pent-up energy who just need to run wild for a while. Adults can sip lemonade at Aunt Polly's while the kids play, but you'll want to accompany them through the Mystery Cave and Injun Joe's Cave, both of which can be dark, confusing, and a little scary. Across the bouncy suspension bridge is Fort San Clemens, the perfect spot to play cowboy.

The big drawback is that the island is accessible only by raft, which often means you have to wait to get there and wait to get back. If your kids are under 5, don't bother making the trip. The terrain is too wild and widespread for preschoolers to play without careful supervision; young kids can better blow off steam in the padded playgrounds of Toontown. Likewise, there's little on the island for teenagers and adults to do. But for kids 5 to 12, a trip to Tom Sawyer Island is the ideal afternoon break. "Tom Sawyer Island was my 6-year-old's favorite place in the Magic Kingdom," wrote a mom from Texas. "It's so detailed with a lot for a boy his age to do. We definitely thought it was worth the wait to catch the raft."

Liberty Square

As you walk between Frontierland and Fantasyland, you find yourself transported back in time to colonial America, strolling the cobblestone streets of Liberty Square.

Liberty Square Attractions

Haunted Mansion

More apt to amuse than to frighten, the mansion is full of clever special effects—at one point a ghost hitchhikes along in your doom buggy. The cast members have great costumes (including the bat-in-a-hat that ladies wear), and they add to the fun with

Hidden Mickey

Look at the arrangement of dishes on the table in the Haunted Mansion banquet scene. Do any of the place settings look like you-know-who?

their mortician-like behavior and such instructions as, "Drag your wretched bodies to the dead center of the room." The mansion is full of clever insider jokes. For example, the tombstones outside feature the names of Imagineers who designed the ride. Take a glance at the pet cemetery when you leave.

The mansion draws long lines in the afternoons, especially just before and after the parade. Try to see it midmorning, or—if you have the courage—after dark.

The Scare Factor

A significant number of kids 7 to 11 list the Haunted Mansion as one of their favorite attractions. A few families reported that kids under 7 were frightened by the setting, the opening story, and the darkness. Once they get going, they're usually okay. The attraction is richly atmospheric, but the spooks are mostly for laughs.

Liberty Square Riverboat

The second tier of this paddle-wheel riverboat offers nice views of the Rivers of America, but the 15-minute cruise is a bit of a snooze for kids. It would be fine if they could really nap, but there are few seats on the boat, so most riders stand. Board only if you have time to kill and the boat is at the dock.

The Hall of Presidents

The residents of the Hall of Presidents are so lifelike that it's a bit eerie (and Disney cast members report that this is a very "interesting" attraction to clean at night). The show opens with a film about the Constitution (otherwise known as "nap time" for the preschool set) and then moves on to the real highlight, the presidential roll call. Each chief executive responds to his name with a nod of the head or similar movement, while in the background the other presidents fidget and whisper.

The hall seats 700, with new shows every 20 minutes, and thus is a good choice during the most crowded parts of the afternoon. Ask one of the attendants at the lobby doors how long it is before the next show and amble in about 5 minutes before showtime.

Food Choices in the Magic Kingdom

Let's face it, the Magic Kingdom is *not* the fine-dining park of Walt Disney World. Even so, some options are better than others.

If you want to have a sit-down meal and see the characters, consider Cinderella's Royal Table, which is inside the castle. The "Once Upon a Time" princess breakfasts and lunches are especially popular with young girls (generally ages 10 and under) who want to meet Cinderella, Aurora, and some of the other princesses. Reservations are always snapped up months in advance, so be sure to reserve early, preferably 180 days ahead of time, by calling 407/WDW–DINE. The Royal Table is also open for dinner, but although Cinderella may greet you at the door, she doesn't mingle like at breakfast and lunch. Little girls like to wear their princess regalia when they dine in the castle, so pull out those tiaras and magic wands before you go.

Other character options include the Crystal Palace, where Winnie the Pooh and his friends circulate among diners for breakfast, lunch, and dinner. Buffets are served at all meals, so

Helpful Hint

We thought the following note from a conscientious mom of two hit the nail on the head. "The one thing we learned about the Magic Kingdom princess breakfast is not to promise this treat unless you already have advance reservations. It took us six days of getting up at 6:30 am to start trying to get through the phone line at 7 before we got lucky enough to get seats. I was already trying to figure out how to tell my then-five-year-old daughter there wasn't room for us at the castle."

you can get your food quickly, and there's plenty of variety to please picky eaters. "We love the Pooh characters, so lunch at the Crystal Palace was heaven on earth for our family," wrote a mom of two from New Jersey.

At Liberty Tavern, an all-you-can-eat dinner with down-home cooking like turkey, pork chops, mashed potatoes, and macaroni and cheese is hosted by the classic Disney characters (Minnie and pals). Character dining, no matter what the meal, requires advance reservations.

If you don't care about eating with the characters, but still want table service, check out the Plaza Restaurant and Tony's Town Square Café, both on Main Street.

In terms of fast food, your choices abound, but Cosmic Ray's Starlight Café in Tomorrowland is the largest fast-food spot in the park and the lines move fast. For snacks try the fruit cobblers at Sleepy Hollow in Liberty Square or the Dole pineapple whips at Aloha Isle in Adventureland.

One final thought. The Magic Kingdom can be a bit overwhelming, so for a true break from the hubbub and better food than you'd find anywhere in the park, visit one of the Magic Kingdom resorts. You don't have to be a guest of a resort to dine there, and it doesn't take much longer to hop the monorail to a

Insider's Secret

Closed out of the princess character meals at Cinderella Castle? Try the lesser-known princess meals in the Norway Pavilion of Epcot.

resort than it does to stay inside the Magic Kingdom and deal with the crowds.

In fact, it's easy. Exit the park, have your hand stamped for reentry, and head toward the monorail station marked "Resorts." Your first stop is the Contemporary, where at lunch the Concourse Steak House offers pasta, salads, burgers, and great smoothies. The next stop is the Ticket and Transportation Center. Sit tight. There's nowhere to eat here. Stop number three is the Polynesian and the tropical-inspired Kona Café, which has stir-fries, salads, and a dizzying selection of desserts. The final option is the Grand Floridian Café at the Grand Floridian, which offers seafood, chicken, and yummy key lime pie. After you eat, reboard the monorail, and you'll be back at the Magic Kingdom gates within minutes.

Afternoon Resting Places

- The Disney World Railroad (you can rest while you ride)
- The small park across from Sleepy Hollow in Liberty Square
- Hall of Presidents
- *Mickey's PhilharMagic*
- The Enchanted Tiki Room
- Country Bear Jamboree
- Pooh's Playful Spot or the Toontown play area (for kids to get out of the stroller and blow off steam while parents rest on benches)

Best Vantage Points for Watching the Parade

The Magic Kingdom has two basic parades: the afternoon parade (usually 3 PM), which runs daily, and the evening parade, which runs nightly in the on-season and periodically during the off-season.

On holidays and weekends during the on-season, the evening parade may run twice, once from Main Street to Frontierland and then from Frontierland back to Main Street. If you're visiting during the on-season, ask an attendant which direction the parade will be coming from and try to be near the beginning of the route. Those near the end of the route will not only have to wait an additional 20 minutes before they see their first float, but they'll also be trapped in by the exiting crowds.

One good location for afternoon parade watching is at the beginning of Main Street, along the hub in front of the Railroad Station. The parade usually begins here, emerging from behind City Hall. You do lose the vantage point of the floats coming down Main Street but it's worth it to be able to get closer to the action. Show up about 30 minutes before the parade is due to start and stake your curb space.

> **Insider's Secret**
> If you're trying to get through Frontierland during the parade, be aware that there's a second pathway that runs right along the riverbank. It's better than trying to pick your way through the crowds lining the parade route.

The crowds grow as you proceed down Main Street and are at their worst in front of Cinderella Castle. If you ignore the come-early advice and find yourself behind four layers of people on Main Street just as the parade is due to start, don't try to

fight your way up to the hub. You'll never make it. Instead, go
to the end of the route in Frontierland.

For the evening parade, come 40 minutes early and try to
get a good position on Main Street. The evening parade is pre-
ceded by a nifty little extra called Tinker Bell's Flight. Look
toward the castle and you'll see a woman dressed like Tink descend via wire from the top of the castle. The parade is followed
immediately by fireworks, which are the perfect ending to a
Disney day.

Tips for Your Last Hour in the Magic Kingdom

- Some rides—most notably Big Thunder Mountain Railroad, Cinderella's Golden Carrousel, Astro Orbiter,
  Dumbo, and Splash Mountain—are particularly beautiful
  at night.

- If you're visiting on an evening when the parade is scheduled, make sure you're stationed as close as possible to the
  beginning of Main Street. This way you can turn in your
  strollers and make a final potty run before the parade begins and make a quick exit after the fireworks end. Otherwise you risk being stuck in the exiting crowds, which can
  be really difficult to navigate, especially if you're trying to
  carry small children or push a stroller. One mother from
  Indiana wrote to us, "We got caught behind the crowd
  leaving the Magic Kingdom one night after the parade.
  (We'd watched it from Frontierland.) It was a nightmare
  because the kids were already tired, so we were trying to
  carry them down Main Street and out through the gates.
  It took us two hours between the end of the parade and
  the time we got back to our hotel room! Next time I'll
  make sure we're near the beginning of the parade route."

℮ Not watching the evening parade? It pulls almost everyone in the park to one place at one time, so about 40 minutes before the parade starts you'll notice a definite thinning of the crowds in Fantasyland and Tomorrowland. This is a great time to squeeze onto rides that had long lines earlier in the day. Just make sure you exit the park before the fireworks end . . . otherwise you'll be caught behind the departing crowd, which funnels to the shuttle and monorail stations.

Insider's Secret

The best place to watch the Magic Kingdom fireworks isn't in the Magic Kingdom at all. It's the California Grill, high atop the Contemporary Resort. The California Grill is a beautiful upscale restaurant, with some of the best cuisine in all of Orlando, if not Florida. Despite the restaurant's reputation, it isn't formal or stuffy. Kids are welcome.

To see the fireworks, reserve a time about 30 minutes before the parade is due to start. (This needs to be done before you leave home. First call 407/824–4321 to determine the evenings and times the parade is scheduled, and then reserve a table by calling 407/WDW–DINE.) Since so many guests have been showing up at the restaurant just to see the fireworks, the restaurant has been forced to implement the policy that only diners are allowed to view the show.

Once the fireworks begin, the restaurant dims its lights and pipes in the theme music from the fireworks show. You have a fabulous view of the pyrotechnic display and a bona fide magical moment.

- The rides stop running at the official closing time, but Main Street stays open for up to an hour longer. If the crowd looks bad going down Main Street you can be sure it looks even worse at the bus stop or monorail station. Stop and have a snack and wait for the crowds to thin before you exit the park.

- *Wishes,* the fireworks display in the Magic Kingdom, is absolutely beautiful and the pyrotechnics are perfectly synchronized to the musical score. *Wishes* is presented nightly at closing time, even on nights when the parade is not scheduled to run, and it's clearly visible from any location in the park.

- If you don't want to see the parade and the crowds have already begun to line up on Main Street, don't try and hack your way through the masses of people to exit. Instead, catch the train in either Frontierland or Toontown and ride to the Main Street Station. It's easy to exit from there.

Tips for Leaving the Magic Kingdom

- Upon exiting, visitors staying off-site should pause for a second and survey their options. If a ferry is in dock at your far left, that's your fastest route back to the TTC. Otherwise, queue for the express monorail back to the TTC.

- Guests of the Contemporary Resort should either take the monorail or, if stamina permits, the footpath. Guests of Wilderness Lodge and Fort Wilderness should take the water-taxi launch. Guests of the Polynesian or Grand Floridian resorts should glance down at the launch dock. If a ferry is in sight, take it back to your hotel. Otherwise, head for the resort monorail.

- Guests of other Disney hotels should return to the shuttle bus station.

CHAPTER

6

Epcot

Epcot

WORLD SHOWCASE

ITALY

AMERICAN ADVENTURE
Liberty Inn

JAPAN
Teppanyaki

MOROCCO
Marrakesh

GERMANY
Biergarten

L'Originale Alfredo di Roma

America Gardens Theater

FRANCE
Les Chefs de France

Saluting AfricaOutpost

Stroller & Wheelchair Rental

World Showcase Lagoon

CHINA
Nine Dragons

INTERNATIONAL GATEWAY

Rose & Crown

UNITED KINGDOM

NORWAY
Akershus

CANADA
Le Cellier

San Angel Inn

WORLD SHOWCASE PLAZA

MEXICO

Odyssey Center
(First Aid & Baby Care)

IMAGINATION!

TEST TRACK

Tip Board

THE LAND
Soarin'
Garden Grill

FUTURE WORLD

MISSION:SPACE

Fountain of Nations

INNOVENTIONS
East   West

THE SEAS WITH NEMO & FRIENDS
Coral Reef Restaurant

WONDERS OF LIFE

UNIVERSE OF ENERGY

SPACESHIP EARTH

Lockers

Guest Relations

Stroller & Wheelchair Rental

Entrance Plaza

PARKING

Monorail

KEY
✕ *Restaurants*
🚻 *Rest rooms*
▬ *Monorail*
🚢 *Ferry*

Getting to Epcot

Many off-site hotels and all on-site hotels offer shuttle buses to Epcot, and Epcot is also easy to reach by car. If you arrive early in the morning, you can park close to the entrance gate and forgo the tram. If you arrive a bit later, however, the trams do run quickly and efficiently. Just be sure to write down the number of the row where you parked your car.

If you're staying at the Polynesian, Contemporary, or Grand Floridian resorts, your fastest route is to take the monorail to the Ticket and Transportation Center (TTC) and then transfer to the Epcot monorail.

The Yacht and Beach Clubs, and the BoardWalk, Swan, and Dolphin resorts are connected by bridge to a special "backdoor" entrance into Epcot's World Showcase. You can get there either by water taxi or by walking.

Getting Around Epcot

As any Disneyphile can tell you, Epcot is an acronym for Experimental Prototype Community of Tomorrow. But as one of the players at the Comedy Warehouse on Pleasure Island suggests, maybe Epcot really stands for "Every Person Comes Out Tired."

Epcot is indeed sprawling—more than twice the size of the Magic Kingdom. It's composed of two circular sections, Future World and the World Showcase, which form a basic figure-eight shape. The only in-park mode of transportation is the two FriendShips that cross the World Showcase Lagoon; most of the time, you'll walk.

Tips for Your First Hour at Epcot

- If you're an on-site guest and visiting Epcot on an Extra Magic Hour morning, only a few attractions will be open, but those will have a significantly reduced wait time.

- On regular mornings, guests are usually allowed into the entrance plaza around Spaceship Earth before the rest of the park officially opens. You'll have time to get a map and entertainment schedule, and rent a stroller before the ropes drop.

- Once you're allowed into the main body of the park, get a Fastpass for either Mission: SPACE or Test Track and then ride the other. By the time you emerge from the first ride, you should be able to use your Fastpass to immediately board the second.

- If these two rides are too intense for your kids, head first to Soarin' in the Land Pavilion, then *Honey, I Shrunk the Audience* in the Imagination Pavilion.

Attractions at Epcot That Offer Fastpass

Test Track

Mission: SPACE

Honey, I Shrunk the Audience

Soarin'

Living with the Land (seasonally)

Maelstrom (seasonally)

Epcot Touring Tips

@ Take Epcot in small doses if you're traveling with young kids; four hours at a time is enough.

@ In the off-season, Epcot hours are often staggered. Future World is generally open from 9 AM to 7 PM (although Test Track and Mission: SPACE remain operative until Epcot closes) and the World Showcase is open from 11 AM to 9 PM.

@ Tour Future World in the morning and then drift toward the World Showcase in the afternoon. You can escape to the films and indoor exhibits during the hottest and busiest times of the day.

@ On entering a World Showcase pavilion that has a show or film—France, Canada, America, or China—ask the attendant how long until the show begins. If your wait is 10 minutes or less, go on inside. If the wait is longer, browse the shops or take a bathroom break and return 10 minutes before showtime. Epcot theaters are so large that even people in the back of the line can get in.

Time-Saving Tip

Avoid high-capacity shows such as *O Canada!* and the show at Universe of Energy in the morning. Your time is better spent moving among the continuous-loading attractions such as Mission: SPACE, Test Track, Body Wars, The Seas with Nemo and Friends, Soarin', and Journey Into Imagination. Save theater-style attractions for the afternoon.

@ Innoventions provides a nice break from the enforced passivity of the rides. But ride first and save the exhibits for the afternoon.

@ Check out your entertainment schedule and save time for some of the shows that take place in the pavilions of the World Showcase. Shows like *Off-Kilter* or the Chinese acrobats have major kid-appeal.

@ If you miss Mission: SPACE or Test Track in the morning, return in the evening. It's often easier to slip onto these popular rides while everyone else is eating dinner in the World Showcase or watching *IllumiNations*.

@ If you're touring off-season and plan to spend mornings in the other parks and evenings at Epcot, make your dinner reservation times early—like around 5 PM. That leaves you several hours to tour after dinner.

@ Another alternative: If the kids have had a good afternoon nap and can keep going until 11 PM, arrange your reservations for 8:45. The restaurants keep serving as the park

The Epcot Don't-Miss List

The American Adventure (in the America pavilion)
Honey, I Shrunk the Audience
IllumiNations
Innoventions
Mission: SPACE (if the kids are old enough and pass the 44-inch height requirement)
Soarin' (if the kids pass the 40-inch height requirement)
Spaceship Earth
Test Track (if the kids pass the 40-inch height requirement)
World Showcase entertainment

closes down so eating late buys you maximum hours in the park—assuming your kids can handle the schedule, that is, and assuming that you'll be seeing *IllumiNations* on another night.

@ If you're not staying for *IllumiNations,* begin moving toward the exit gates while the show is in progress.

Future World

Future World comprises nine large pavilions, each containing at least one major attraction, and is very much like a permanent World's Fair, mixing educational opportunities with pure entertainment. Most visitors are drawn first to the rides with their spectacular special effects, but don't miss Innoventions and the chance to play with the smaller interactive exhibits. These hands-on exhibits encourage young visitors to learn while doing and help kids avoid what one mother termed "audio-animatronics overload."

Future World Attractions

Spaceship Earth

Whatever their age, few travelers can remain blasé at the sight of Spaceship Earth, the most photographed and readily recognizable symbol of Epcot.

The ride inside, which coils toward the top of the 17-story geosphere, traces developments in communication from cave drawings to computers. The voice of Jeremy Irons croons in

Hidden Mickey

We all know Mickey is a star, and he actually has his own constellation in Spaceship Earth. Look for him in the starry sky at the beginning of the ride, just after you load.

your ear as you climb past scenes of Egyptian temples, a performance of Oedipus Rex, and the invention of the Gutenberg press. Even preschoolers rate Spaceship Earth highly, probably because of the excitement of actually entering the "Big Ball" and the finale, which flashes a planetarium sky above you as you slowly swirl back down through the darkness.

The Seas with Nemo and Friends

The saltwater aquarium in the Living Seas pavilion is so enormous that Spaceship Earth could float inside it. And the new ride opening in early 2007 will probably make the best-of list for preschoolers. They'll be able to board "clamobiles" and travel through a coral reef looking for Nemo of *Finding Nemo* fame. After the ride, it's on to the interactive exhibits at Sea

Insider's Secret

A program called DiveQuest lets visitors scuba dive in the aquarium, while Dolphins in Depth allows guests to meet the trainers and observe the dolphins in close quarters. For details, call 407/393–8687.

Base, and the lighthearted and funny *Turtle Talk* with Crush. The laid-back turtle interacts with kids in this fun show; encourage them to sit up front on the floor and ask Crush plenty of questions. We get tons of positive mail about this show. One father of two from Texas wrote, "*Turtle Talk* with Crush was fantastic. We rate it the sleeper hit of Epcot." And an Ohio mom wrote, "*Turtle Talk* isn't given a lot of attention at Disney— we almost couldn't find the entrance. But

Insider's Tip

Whatever is new is always hot, so the Seas with Nemo and Friends will be more crowded than most other Epcot attractions through 2007.

our kids loved it. The man who did the voice of Crush was hilarious and really joked around with all the children in the audience. Definitely worth the time!"

The Land

This cheerful pavilion, devoted to the subjects of food production and the environment, is home to three attractions, a rotating restaurant, and a fast-food court. Because there are so many places to eat here, the Land is crowded from 11 AM to 2 PM, when everyone heads in for lunch.

> ## Insider's Secret
> The Garden Grill Restaurant in the Land offers character dining at both lunch and dinner and is the perfect alternative for families who don't want to spend a morning at a character breakfast but who would still love to meet Mickey and the gang.

- *Living with the Land.* Visitors travel by boat past scenes of farming environments ending with a peek at fish farming, drip irrigation, and other innovative agricultural technologies. It's a fairly adult presentation, but it moves swiftly, so kids shouldn't be too bored. Fastpasses are seasonally available but rarely necessary.

- *Circle of Life.* This 20-minute film stars Simba, Pumbaa, and Timon from *The Lion King* and the beloved characters do a terrific job of pitching the conservation message. Simba explains how humans affect, both positively and negatively, their environment, so the show is both educational and entertaining. And because the Harvest Theater is large, with comfortable seats, *Circle of Life* is the perfect choice for afternoon.

- *Soarin'.* Soarin' promises to give you a bird's-eye view on an exhilarating flight above the beautiful state of California. It

Quick Guide to

Attraction	Location	Height Requirement
The American Adventure	World Showcase	None
Body Wars	Future World	40 inches
Circle of Life	Future World	None
Cranium Command	Future World	None
El Rio del Tiempo	World Showcase	None
Honey, I Shrunk the Audience	Future World	None
Impressions de France	World Showcase	None
Innoventions	Future World	None
Journey Into Imagination	Future World	None
Living with the Land	Future World	None
Maelstrom	World Showcase	None
The Making of Me	Future World	None
Mission: SPACE	Future World	44 inches
O Canada!	World Showcase	None
Reflections of China	World Showcase	None
The Seas with Nemo and Friends	Future World	None
Soarin'	Future World	40 inches
Spaceship Earth	Future World	None
Test Track	Future World	40 inches
Universe of Energy	Future World	None

Scare Factor
0 = Unlikely to scare any child of any age.
! = Has dark or loud elements; might rattle some toddlers.
!! = A couple of gotcha! moments; should be fine for school-age kids.
!!! = You need to be pretty big and pretty brave to handle this ride.

Epcot Attractions

Speed of Line	Duration of Ride/Show	Scare Factor	Age Range
Fast	30 min.	0	All
Moderate	5 min.	!!	6 and up
Fast	20 min.	0	All
Fast	20 min.	0	6 and up
Fast	9 min.	0	All
Fast	25 min.	!!	5 and up
Fast	20 min.	0	10 and up
n/a	n/a	0	3 and up
Fast	13 min.	!	3 and up
Fast	10 min.	0	All
Moderate	15 min.	!!	4 and up
Slow	15 min.	0	4 and up
Slow	15 min.	!!!	7 and up
Fast	20 min.	0	10 and up
Fast	20 min.	0	10 and up
Moderate	8 min.	0	All
Moderate	15 min.	!	5 and up
Moderate	15 min.	0	All
Slow	25 min.	!!!	7 and up
Slow	30 min.	!!	3 and up

works like this: you are lifted 40 feet off the ground inside a giant dome. The interior of the dome is actually an enormous screen on which are projected images of redwood forests, Napa Valley, Yosemite, and the Golden Gate bridge. You will feel like you're hang gliding as you gently climb, bank, and descend your way through the scenery. You'll even feel the wind blowing through your hair and smell orange blossoms and pine trees. One mother of three from New York raved about the ride: "Soarin' was the favorite of everyone in our family, including our 5-year-old. She is normally afraid of heights but insisted on riding it three times, and the last time she actually wanted to sit on the highest row so she could see better. It was magical!"

Helpful Hint

Like all new attractions, Soarin' draws crowds. Try to ride in the morning or use Fastpass.

Journey Into Imagination

Good news. After a brief revamp that didn't work, Figment is back. Dr. Nigel Channing (Eric Idle), the rather stuffy head of the Imagination Institute, must be broken out of his shell and taught the true meaning of imagination, and Figment is just the dragon for the job.

After the ride, stop off at the Image Works Lab where interactive exhibits allow you to distort your facial image, produce sounds by stepping on pictures of lightning and lions, or morph your face onto a sunflower or koala and e-mail the results back to your friends. It's a fresh, funny, and free way to say "Wish you were here."

Honey, I Shrunk the Audience

This is one of the best attractions in Epcot. The show is so much fun that many families report their kids want to see it more than once.

Insider's Secret

Closer is not always better, especially when it comes to a 3-D show like *Honey, I Shrunk the Audience.* For best viewing, sit about two-thirds of the way back.

Based on the movie series, the presentation begins as Dr. Wayne Szalinski (played by Rick Moranis) is about to pick up the award for Inventor of the Year. The scene quickly dissolves into mayhem when the audience is accidentally "shrunk," one son's pet snake gets loose, and the other son's pet mouse is re-

The Scare Factor

Honey, I Shrunk the Audience is highly rated by kids of all ages. If your child is afraid of snakes or mice, have him take off the 3-D glasses and either pull up his legs into the seat or sit on your lap. That way he won't see the images clearly or feel the tactile sensations.

produced 999 times. Although the 3-D images are dazzling, the effects go far beyond the visual—you actually feel the "mice" running up your legs, and the finale is a real "gotcha."

Insider's Secret

Heat getting to you? As you exit *Honey, I Shrunk the Audience,* check out Splashtacular, a fun fountain show that gives kids the chance to get wet.

Test Track

Test Track is the longest, fastest ride in all of Disney World—we're talking 34 separate turns, 50-degree banking, and speeds of 65 mph.

The cars are designed to replicate tests at the GM proving

The Scare Factor

Children must be 40 inches tall to ride. It's all about speed, with no flips or plunges, so kids 5 and up should be fine.

grounds and each vehicle is independently powered and controlled. In other words, this isn't the Tomorrowland Speedway. Thanks to an onboard computer, the cars are constantly adapting to road conditions, vehicle weight, and the location of the other 28 cars on the track.

Helpful Hint

Test Track draws some of the longest lines in all of Disney World. Fastpasses are almost always necessary, and don't wait too long to get one. At Test Track, a whole day's supply of Fastpasses is often gone by early afternoon.

You begin the ride inside, checking out how your vehicle responds to cold, heat, sharp turns, rough roads, and other stresses. The stress level of the passengers soars when you move to the impact test, break through a barrier, and then zoom outside the building to the track. Here cars reach their top speeds—well, actually, they could go higher than 65 mph, but Imagineers didn't think it would be prudent to break the Florida speed limit—as they go through a mile of curves, hills, and turns. It's one powerful ride.

Insider's Secret

Is the line for Test Track unbearably long? Fastpasses all gone? If your kids are older, consider going through the Singles Line. You won't get to ride together, but your wait time will be about one-third as long.

Mission: SPACE

Epcot's most technologically advanced thrill ride launches guests into a simulated space adventure, from the excitement of liftoff to the wonder of flight. To develop the story and design, Disney Imagineers worked with 25 space experts from NASA and the result is completely immersive and interactive.

Helpful Hint

Mission: SPACE is right beside Test Track and together they share the most crowded real estate in Epcot. Ride these two as soon as possible after arriving in the morning.

The Scare Factor

The height requirement is 44 inches, but even if your child is tall enough you should use caution when deciding whether or not to let her ride. Inside the pod, riders are instructed to keep their heads back against the seat and to look straight ahead for the duration of the ride. If your child can't follow these instructions, she may become disoriented or ill.

Mission: SPACE has sent more people to the hospital than any other Disney attraction. While most people get through the experience just fine, it's important to take Disney's safety recommendations seriously. Pregnant women, children under 7, and anyone with back, neck, high blood pressure, or motion-sickness problems should not ride.

Riders are grouped into teams of four and each person is given a crew position—Commander, Navigator, Pilot, or Engineer—and assigned the tasks that go along with their role. Once you board your pod, everything happens fast. The sensations are created by the spinning of the pod, a motion that's so rapid it feels like flight. The sustained G-forces during the launch are by far the most intense part of the ride. Before you fully recover, you're required to take on your crew role and push a few buttons (made somewhat more difficult by the gravitational pull of the ship's movement) as directed by mission control.

As you exit, there's a small Space Base crawl area for younger kids and a cool competitive group game called Space Race for older kids.

Insider's Secret

In motion simulators, you can avoid motion sickness by looking away from the screen, but on Mission: SPACE, where your cabin is actually moving, the opposite is true. If you begin to feel queasy, focus intently on the screen. Shutting your eyes is the worst thing you can do.

Also, the disorienting effects of the ride are cumulative, so just because you felt fine after your first ride doesn't mean you'll feel okay after your second. A mom from Georgia wrote, "We were in Epcot on a very uncrowded day and my kids loved Mission: SPACE so much all four of us rode it three times in a row. Big mistake! Everybody was okay with the spinning after the first couple of times but the physical effects of the ride really build up over time. One of the kids felt so sick that we had to go back to the room."

Wonders of Life

Celebrating the human body, the Wonders of Life pavilion resembles a brightly colored street fair full of hands-on exhibits. You can check out your health profile via computer, get advice on your tennis or golf swing, or test your endurance on a motorized bike. Like the Land pavilion, Wonders of Life houses three attractions.

Insider's Secret
At present, the Wonders of Life pavilion is only open seasonally and there are persistent rumors that it may be closed for good.

- ☚ *Body Wars.* Body Wars uses flight simulation technology to take riders on a turbulent high-speed chase through the human body. After being miniaturized to the size of a pinhead and injected into a patient, the crew is briefed to expect a "routine mission to remove a splinter from the safe zone just under the skin." But when one of the doctors is sucked into a capillary, you're off on a rescue chase through the heart, lungs, and brain.

The Scare Factor
The height requirement for Body Wars is 40 inches. Body Wars does have its queasy-making moments, due to the subject matter as well as the eerie accuracy of motion-simulation technology. Our readers found Body Wars considerably more intense than Star Tours, a similar motion-simulation ride at MGM.

- ☚ *The Making of Me.* This sweet 15-minute film provides a fetus-eye view of conception, gestation, and birth. Martin Short travels back in time to show his own parents as babies, then chronicles how they met and ultimately produced him. Although the film handles its subject matter directly, it's appropriate for any age.

- ☚ *Cranium Command.* One of the funniest presentations in Epcot, Cranium Command mixes audio-animatronics with film. The preshow is vital to understanding what's going on. General Knowledge taps an unfortunate recruit, Fuzzy, to pilot "the most unstable craft in the fleet," the brain of a 12-year-old boy. Fuzzy valiantly tries to guide his boy through a day of middle school without overloading his system, which isn't easy when the body parts are played by a zany all-star cast. A fun attraction for any age.

Universe of Energy

This technologically complex presentation can be enjoyed by any age on any level. The preshow features Ellen DeGeneres, Alex Trebek, and Jamie Lee Curtis. Ellen has a dream in which she's a contestant on the game show *Jeopardy,* and when she's thoroughly skunked by smarty-pants Jamie Lee, she realizes she needs to know a lot more about energy. Luckily for her, neighbor Bill Nye the Science Guy is happy to help.

The Scare Factor

Few families reported that their kids were afraid of the dinosaurs. In fact, for most kids, these huge and lifelike figures are the high point of the show.

The Disney twist comes when the 97-seat theater begins to break apart in sections that align themselves in sequence and form a train. A curtain lifts and you begin to move through a prehistoric scene that carries you back to the era when coal deposits first formed on earth. All around you are those darn dinosaurs, among the largest audio-animatronics figures Disney has ever created. After your train has once more morphed into a theater, there's a final film segment in which a newly educated Ellen gets her *Jeopardy* revenge.

Despite its proximity to the front gate, Universe of Energy is not a good choice for the morning; save it for the afternoon when you'll welcome the chance to sit down for 30 minutes.

Time-Saving Tip

When entering the Universe of Energy, ask the attendant how long it is until the next show begins, or
check the digital clock. Don't enter until it's less than
10 minutes until showtime; this is a 30-minute presentation and there's no point in wearing out the
kids before you begin. The theater can seat many
people so there's rarely a reason to line up and wait.

Innoventions

Innoventions is the arcade of the future, where you can try out
new video games before they hit the market, experience virtual reality, and play with beyond-state-of-the-art technology.
There are games, quiz shows, and interactive exhibits to
pull everyone into the action.

Helpful Hint

Don't be overwhelmed
by Innoventions. Just
wander over to a kiosk
and start playing.

Cast members are on
hand to answer questions or
help you get the hang of the
games and experiments. Exhibits change frequently,
keeping things fresh, and many of the stations are kid friendly.
Even preschoolers will find plenty to do.

Club Cool

On a hot day, check out this Coca-Cola Tasting Station where
you can sample the (sometimes unbelievably icky, at least to
American palates) flavors of soft drinks from around the world.

World Showcase

Pretty by day and gorgeous by night, the World Showcase comprises the pavilions of 11 nations: Mexico, Norway, China,
Germany, Italy, America, Japan, Morocco, France, the United

Kingdom, and Canada. The countries are like links in a chain that stretch around a large lagoon. Really large. It's a 1.2-mile trek from Mexico to Canada.

Some of the pavilions have full-scale attractions while others have only shops and restaurants. Wonderful live entertainment is also available; check your entertainment schedule for showtimes.

Each pavilion is staffed by citizens of the country it represents. Disney goes to great pains to recruit, relocate, and if necessary, teach English to the shopkeepers and waiters you see in these pavilions, bringing them to Orlando for a year and housing them with representatives from the other World Showcase nations. It's a cultural exchange program on the highest level. These young men and women save the World Showcase from being merely touristy and provide your kids with the chance to rub elbows, however briefly, with folks from other cultures.

Insider's Secret

One of the best ways to get kids involved in the World Showcase experience is by visiting the Kidcot Fun Stops. Children begin a craft project (at present it's a mask) at the first booth they visit and as they move to the next country they receive another element to add to the mask. Making the masks is a great icebreaker and gets them interacting with people from other countries. Parents report that some children get so into it that they're practically running from nation to nation. A mother of three from Wisconsin wrote, "Our daughters loved being able to add something (a feather, beads, etc.) to their masks at each craft table. They ended up with a nice (and free) souvenir, and it was a good way to keep them moving around the World Showcase."

World Showcase Attractions

O Canada!

This 20-minute Circle-Vision 360 film is gorgeous, stirring, and difficult to view with kids under 6. In order to enjoy the effect of the circular screen, guests must stand during the presentation, and no strollers are allowed in the theater. This means babies and toddlers must be held, and preschoolers, who can't see anything in a room full of standing adults, often clamor to be lifted up as well.

Impressions de France

What a difference a seat makes! Like all the Epcot films, *Impressions de France* is exceedingly well done, with lush music and a 200-degree wide-screen feel. It's easy to get in, even in the afternoon, and no one minds if babies take a little nap.

The American Adventure

This multimedia presentation, combining audio-animatronics figures with film, is popular with all age groups. The technological highlight of the show comes when the Ben Franklin robot walks up the stairs to visit Thomas Jefferson, but the entire 30-minute presentation is packed with elaborate sets that rise from the stage, film montages, and moving music.

Helpful Hint

The American pavilion becomes crowded in the afternoon but because it's at the exact midpoint of the World Showcase Lagoon, it's impractical to skip it and work your way back later. If you're faced with a half-hour wait for the show, try to catch a performance of the Voices of Liberty preshow or entertainment at the nearby Japan and Italy pavilions.

It's worth noting that some guests find the patriotism of the *American Adventure* a little heavy-handed. There seem to be two primary reactions to the show—some people weep through it and some people sleep through it. Most of our readers rate it as one of the best attractions in Epcot.

Reflections of China

Another lovely 360-degree film, this one recently revamped with lots of new footage. But again, not an easy attraction to view with young children.

Hidden Mickey

Check out the mural of Vikings in the queue line before you board Maelstrom. One of them is wearing mouse ears!

Maelstrom

In this Norwegian boat ride, your Viking Ship sails through fjords and storms, over waterfalls, and past a threatening three-headed troll—all within four minutes. Riders disembark in a North Sea coastal village where a short film is presented. A Viking ship–styled play area is to the left of the Norway pavilion and it's a good place for kids to explore while adults get a snack at the Kringla Bakeri Og Kafe.

The Scare Factor

Maelstrom sounds terrifying but the reality is much tamer than the ride description. The much-touted "backward plunge over a waterfall" is so subtle that passengers in the front of the boat are not even aware of the impending doom. The darkness and the troll put off some preschoolers but the ride is generally fine for kids 5 and up.

El Rio del Tiempo

There's rarely a wait for this little boat ride in the lovely Mexico pavilion. Reminiscent of It's a Small World in the Magic Kingdom, El Rio is especially appealing to younger riders.

Food Choices at Epcot

Epcot is *the* food park. It has an embarrassment of riches, with so many wonderful places to grab a bite that it's hard to choose.

For sit-down dining, one perennial favorite is the San Angel Inn in Mexico, which is a great place to escape on a hot sunny day. El Rio del Tiempo gurgles by and the scene is that of an evening marketplace, romantically dark even at high noon. Another popular spot is Bistro de Paris in France, which re-creates the feel of a Parisian sidewalk café with white table-cloths and bustling waiters. Le Cellier is perhaps the most popular Epcot restaurant, due to its tasty steaks and elaborate desserts.

Reservations are strongly advised and often essential for dining at Epcot's full-service restaurants. For details, see Chapter 11.

For a quick, casual sit-down meal, head for the Sunshine Seasons food court in The Land, where you can choose between healthy salads, hearty sandwiches, and a variety of well-prepared Asian and Mexican dishes at different counters. A mom from Virginia wrote to us, "I wish they had a place like Sunshine Seasons in my mall back home. They have flatbreads, Chinese and Thai food, Mexican food—and it's all cooked to order instead of sitting there forever under heat lamps. This is much better than standard fast food."

Money-Saving Tip
The average Epcot dinner for four costs about $100 without wine or beer. You can slice that bill in half if you visit the sit-down restaurant of your choice at lunch instead of dinner.

In terms of fast food, you have plenty of possibilities. The Tangierine Café in Morocco serves Mediterranean wraps, hummus salads, and tasty platters of chicken and lamb. The food is served in a pretty patio area with a perfect view of the pavilion. Don't miss the pastry counter in the back for baklava and other honeyed delights, not to mention Turkish coffee so strong that you may set a land-speed record on your next lap around the World Showcase.

Helpful Hint

If you're worried about how the kids will react to unfamiliar cuisine, not to worry. On kiddie menus, the food is a nod to the country in question—for example, skewered chicken in Morocco or fish-and-chips in the United Kingdom—but the entrées are smaller and less spicy than the adult meals and look enough like chicken nuggets and fish sticks that the kids will eat them.

While the Tangierine Café is right in the middle of the action, the Yakitori House is tucked away in the back of the Japan pavilion with a soothing view of the manicured gardens and koi ponds. Try the Kushi Yaki, broiled skewers of chicken, shrimp, and beef with rice and teriyaki sauce. Another good choice is Kringla Bakeri Og Kafe in Norway, which has wonderful open-face salmon sandwiches and delicious pastries.

Money-Saving Tip

To save both time and money stick to fast-food places for meals and make reservations at a sit-down restaurant for a truly off-time, like 3 PM or 10 PM and just have dessert. You can soak up the ambience for an investment of 30 minutes and 20 bucks.

The Yorkshire County Fish and Chips stand in the United Kingdom is always popular. Carry your food into the back garden and sit on a park bench while you listen to the British Invasion sing Beatles classics.

The Boulangerie Patisserie in France emits such phenomenal aromas of coffee and croissants that there's always a line, even though the café is in an out-of-the-way back alley. Drop by for sandwiches, quiche, and a wide selection of decadent pastries, which are so good that they make the Boulangerie a favorite with Disney cast members. *Bon appetit!*

Epcot Extras

The Magic Kingdom isn't the only place to see the characters, catch a show, watch fireworks, or buy souvenirs. Epcot provides a whole range of entertainment, but with an international spin.

Characters

The character show in the World Showcase Lagoon brings as many as 20 characters to a single spot and the crowds of kids vying for their attention are rarely as large as those at the

Insider's Secret

The princess character meals at Epcot are nearly as popular as those in the Magic Kingdom. Restaurant Akershus in Norway is the host, and the princesses show up at breakfast, lunch, *and* dinner. They only stay for about an hour though, so be sure to book your meal at the time they're slated to appear. Also note that you'll probably see Belle, Snow White, and Sleeping Beauty, but Cinderella only appears in the Magic Kingdom. Reservations are a must; call 407/WDW–DINE up to 180 days before the date you wish to attend. The earlier the better!

Magic Kingdom. Check the entertainment schedule on your map for times. If individual characters are appearing around the World Showcase—Aladdin in Morocco, for example, or Mary Poppins in the United Kingdom—the times will also be on your schedule.

Helpful Hint
The princess meals aren't just for girls. Consider this note from a mother of one in Delaware: "Even though it's somewhat geared toward girls, my seven-year-old son really enjoyed the Princess breakfast in the Norway pavilion. The waiter greeted him by calling him 'Prince' which he loved and the princesses treated him like royalty throughout the whole meal. He seemed quite smitten with them."

World Showcase Performers

Singers, dancers, jugglers, and artisans from around the globe perform throughout the World Showcase daily. Times are outlined on your entertainment schedule.

Some of these presentations are more child-oriented than others. Children especially enjoy the young Dragon Legend Acrobats in China and the remarkable living statues in Italy. Older kids can enter into the raucous action of the King Arthur skit in the United Kingdom or catch the "High Energy Progressive Celtic Music" of Off-Kilter in Canada. This translates to rock music with bagpipes, and the show is a must-see. The British Invasion, a talented '60s-style group that plays in the United Kingdom, is also popular.

The shows are set up so that you can pretty much flow from one to the other as you work your way around the World Showcase. If you're there 10 minutes before showtime you can usually get a decent seat.

A mother of two from Illinois wrote to us, "Please stress how great the World Showcase performers are. We got wonderful pictures of our children with the Living Statues, and the Chinese acrobats were so good that we went back for another show. You don't hear much about the live entertainment in the World Showcase, but we found it to be the highlight of our day at Epcot."

IllumiNations

This display of lasers, fireworks, syncopated fountains, and stirring music is a real-life fantasia and an unsurpassed Disney World classic. Very popular, very crowded, and the perfect way to end an Epcot day, *IllumiNations* takes place over the World Showcase lagoon at closing time (usually 9 PM). If you watch from the Mexico or Canada pavilion, you'll be able to beat the crowd to the exits afterward. Guests staying at the Yacht and Beach Clubs, or the BoardWalk, Swan, or Dolphin resorts and thus leaving via the "back-door" exit, can watch from the bridge between the United Kingdom and France pavilions.

Insider's Secret

The show produces a lot of smoke. Before you select your vantage point, note which way the wind is blowing. If you have a pleasant breeze in your face now, you can be sure you'll catch the full brunt of the smoke during the show.

Shopping

You'll see things in Epcot that aren't available anywhere else in Disney World: German wines, silk Chinese robes, Mexican piñatas, Norwegian sweaters, and English teas are all within strolling distance of each other. Once you've made your purchases, either have them sent to Package Pickup near the front gate and retrieve them as you exit or, if you're staying on-site, have them delivered to your hotel. Both services are free. Package Pickup does close about an hour before the park closes, so plan accordingly.

Insider's Secret

If you're intrigued by the Segways zipping around Epcot, you can sign up to learn how to ride and take a lap around the World Showcase. Call 407/393–8687 for details.

International Food and Wine Festival

Dining your way around the World Showcase is always a treat but it gets even better during one of the park's premier special events, the Epcot Food and Wine Festival. The annual festival runs for approximately a month, from mid-October to mid-November, and you can get exact dates and information about each year's events by calling 407/WDW–FEST.

Open-air booths serving the food, wine, and beer of more than 60 nations are set up around the World Showcase, offering everything from New Zealand lamb chops to Bavarian strudel. The sample-size servings range between $1 and $4 in price so you can happily nosh your way around the world, indulging in WDW's biggest buffet. If you want to learn more about what you're eating and drinking, cooking demonstrations and wine tastings are scheduled daily and are usually free.

True foodies and wine enthusiasts should consider one of the special-event dinners. The Grand Tastings, Winemaker Dinners, and Reserve Dinners are very heady events, held in secluded glamour points all around Disney property, and they sell

out months in advance. Call 407/393–3378 for a list of participants, dates, prices, and reservations.

Afternoon Resting Places at Epcot

- *The American Adventure*
- *Circle of Life* in the Land pavilion
- *Honey, I Shrunk the Audience*
- *Impressions de France*
- *The Making of Me* in the Wonders of Life pavilion
- Universe of Energy

Helpful Hint

Epcot has many shows, so if the kids need to
run off a little energy between presentations,
check out the interactive play fountains. One set
is between Mission: SPACE and the Wonders of
Life pavilion and the others are just to the right
of the bridge leading to the World Showcase.
They're a great place to cool off on a hot afternoon, especially if you bring along bathing
suits or waterproof diapers.

Tips for Your Last Hour at Epcot

- If you're staying for *IllumiNations,* find a spot around the
  World Showcase lagoon 30 minutes in advance during the
  off-season, 45 to 60 minutes in advance during the on-
  season. Have a snack to help pass the time.

- When staking out the perfect spot to watch *IllumiNations*,
  remember that much of the show takes place above you.
  If you sit beneath a tree or awning you'll have trouble seeing the fireworks in their full glory.

@ Not staying for *IllumiNations*? This is the perfect chance to swing back through Future World and ride Mission: SPACE or Test Track on your way out. Just be sure to be at the exit gates by the time the fireworks end and the onslaught of people begins.

Tips for Leaving Epcot

The lights are kept low and it's easy to lose your kids. If they're young, push your rental strollers out of the way and just carry your kids. You lose your $1 deposit on the stroller, but it's worth it not to have to push your stroller through the crowd. If they're older, make sure you all hold hands. And have a set meeting place in case you do get separated.

@ If you're not in the first wave of people to hit the exit gates (which is most likely if you watch the show from the Mexico or Canada pavilions), slow down and let the crowd pass you. Stop for a snack or shop at Mouse Gear and aim to exit about 30 minutes behind the main crowd. Transportation will keep running up to 90 minutes past the official park closing time.

CHAPTER

7

Disney-MGM Studios

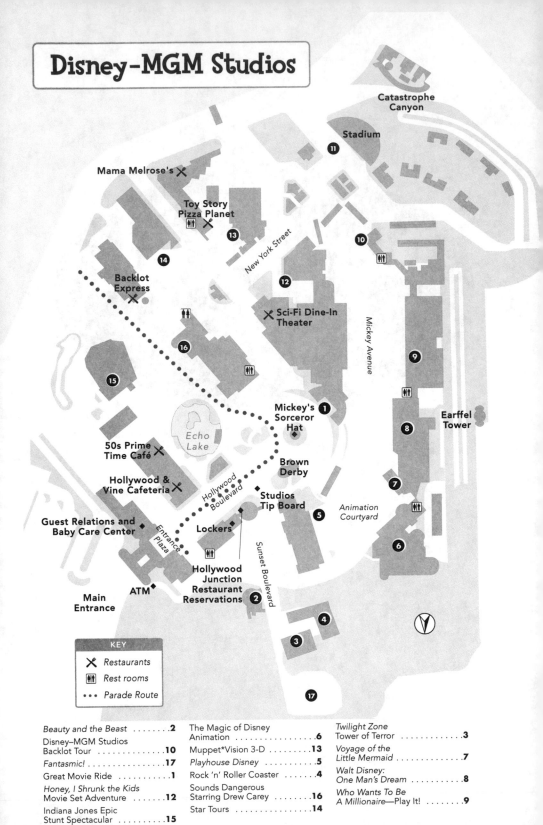

Disney-MGM Studios

Catastrophe Canyon

Stadium

11

Mama Melrose's

Toy Story Pizza Planet

13

14

New York Street

10

Backlot Express

12

Sci-Fi Dine-In Theater

Mickey Avenue

16

9

15

Mickey's Sorceror Hat

1

Earffel Tower

8

7

50s Prime Time Café

Echo Lake

Brown Derby

Hollywood & Vine Cafeteria

Hollywood Boulevard

Studios Tip Board

5

Animation Courtyard

Guest Relations and Baby Care Center

Entrance Plaza

Lockers

6

Sunset Boulevard

Hollywood Junction Restaurant Reservations

2

ATM

4

Main Entrance

3

17

KEY

- ✕ Restaurants
- 🚻 Rest rooms
- ••• Parade Route

Getting to Disney-MGM Studios

Compared with the Magic Kingdom, getting to MGM is a snap. Shuttle buses run approximately every 15 minutes from all on-site hotels. Guests staying at the Swan, Dolphin, Board-Walk, or Yacht and Beach Clubs are a 15-minute water taxi ride from the MGM gate.

If you're driving to the parks, note that the MGM parking lot is small. If you get there at opening time and park close to the entrance, then you can forgo the parking lot tram and walk to the front gate.

Getting Around MGM

MGM is a relatively small park with no trains, boats, or buses. In other words, you'll walk.

Tips for Your First Hour at MGM

  @ Pick up a map and entertainment schedule as you enter. If you need a stroller, rent one at Oscar's Super Service Station. To arrange reservations for meals, stop by the dining information booth halfway down Hollywood Boulevard.

@ If you're at MGM on an Extra Magic Hour morning, a blackboard beside the dining information booth will let you know the attractions that are operative; the whole park doesn't open early, but several major rides will be open.

@ Are your kids old enough and bold enough for a big-deal ride? Turn on Sunset Boulevard and head straight toward Rock 'n' Roller Coaster and the *Twilight Zone* Tower of Terror. Waits are usually minimal in the morning, but if it's a busy day, get a Fastpass for one attraction, then immediately board the other.

@ Have younger kids? Catch an early show of *Voyage of the Little Mermaid.*

MGM Touring Tips

@ With the exception of *Voyage of the Little Mermaid,* save theater-style presentations such as *Beauty and the Beast,* Muppet*Vision 3-D, Sounds Dangerous, and Indiana Jones for afternoon. Tour continuous-loading attractions such as the Tower of Terror, the Great Movie Ride, Rock 'n' Roller Coaster, and Star Tours early in the day.

@ Save the Backlot Tour and Animation Academy for after lunch.

@ MGM is small and easily crisscrossed, so don't feel obligated to tour attractions in any particular geographic sequence. Those 4- and 5-year-olds who may need a stroller at Epcot can do without one here.

@ The evening spectacular *Fantasmic!* is an absolute must-see. Be in place 60 minutes before showtime to make sure you have a seat.

The MGM Don't-Miss List

Rock 'n' Roller Coaster (if your kids are 8 and up)

Twilight Zone Tower of Terror (if your kids are 8 and up)

Star Tours

The Great Movie Ride

Indiana Jones Epic Stunt Spectacular

Lights, Motors, Action!–Extreme Stunt Show

Who Wants to Be a Millionaire (if your kids are 8 and up)

Playhouse Disney–Live on Stage! (if your kids are under 8)

Voyage of the Little Mermaid

Beauty and the Beast

Muppet*Vision 3-D

Fantasmic!

Attractions at MGM Offering Fastpasses

Rock 'n' Roller Coaster

Twilight Zone Tower of Terror

Star Tours

Muppet*Vision 3-D

Voyage of the Little Mermaid

Indiana Jones Epic Stunt Spectacular

Lights, Motors, Action!–Extreme Stunt Show

Who Wants to Be a Millionaire

MGM Attractions

On Sunset Boulevard

Twilight Zone Tower of Terror

The *Twilight Zone* Tower of Terror combines the spooky ambiance of a decaying, cobweb-covered 1930s-style Hollywood hotel with sheer thrills. For the clever preshow, Imagineers spliced together clips from the old *Twilight Zone* TV series, bringing back the long-deceased Rod Serling as narrator.

The story begins on a dark and stormy night in 1939 when five people—a movie star and starlet, a child actress and her nanny, and a bellboy—board a hotel elevator. The hotel is struck by lightning, the elevator drops, and the five passengers are transported into the Twilight Zone. One of the cast members who works at the attraction reports that the most common questions people ask her are "Is this a real hotel?" and "Am I going to die?" (The answer to both is no.)

After the creepy preshow, you file through a dark basement queue at the end of which you board a freight elevator much like the ill-fated one that disappeared years earlier. Your seat has a lap bar and each "elevator" holds about 25 people.

Your car moves out of its elevator shaft and through a hallway with holographic images before eventually settling into a second elevator shaft. (This is all drawn out with agonizing slowness.) Then the doors of your elevator car open to reveal a panoramic view of the park from nearly 150 feet in the air, then you free fall.

Hidden Mickey

During the preshow, take note of the child actress boarding the elevator. She's holding a Mickey Mouse toy.

When the ride first opened, you only dropped once, but Imagineers have since introduced a random drop pattern, which means that computers controlling the ride select from several

The Scare Factor

The Tower of Terror has a 40-inch height requirement, which means that many preschoolers are tall enough to ride. Nonetheless, our suggestion is 8 and up, both because of the spooky setup and the drop. The expanded drop sequence means you're bouncing around in the shaft for a good 20 to 30 seconds, which can feel like forever to a terrified child.

possible drop sequences. You may be hauled up and dropped as many as seven times, and the trip up is as exhilarating as the trip down.

Rock 'n' Roller Coaster

The Rock 'n' Roller Coaster is one of the best rides in Disney World. The soundtrack, featuring Aerosmith, is perfectly synchronized to the movements of the coaster and the volume is cranked to the max.

Hidden Mickey

As you walk through the rotunda area before boarding check out the floors; two Hidden Mickeys are in the tiles.

The premise is simple. You play the part of fans that have shown up at an Aerosmith taping but, unfortunately, the group is in the process of leaving for a concert. They insist you come along to the show, so you're boarded into 24-passenger stretch limos, which their manager promises are "real fast," and you're off on a rock-and-roll trip through the highways of L.A.

Time-Saving Tip

Lines for both Rock 'n' Roller Coaster and Tower of Terror are long in the afternoon. Use Fastpass.

Quick Guide to

Attraction	Location	Height Requirement
Beauty and the Beast— Live on Stage!	Sunset Blvd.	None
Disney-MGM Backlot Tour	Mickey Ave.	None
Fantasmic!	Sunset Blvd.	None
The Great Movie Ride	Hollywood Blvd.	None
Honey, I Shrunk the Kids Movie Set	New York St.	None
Indiana Jones Epic Stunt Spectacular	Hollywood Blvd.	None
Lights, Motors, Action! Extreme Stunt Show	New York St.	None
The Magic of Disney Animation Tour	Animation Courtyard	None
*Muppet*Vision 3-D*	New York St.	None
Playhouse Disney—Live on Stage!	Animation Courtyard	None
Rock 'n' Roller Coaster	Sunset Blvd.	48 inches
Sounds Dangerous Starring Drew Carey	Hollywood Blvd.	None
Star Tours	Hollywood Blvd.	40 inches
Twilight Zone Tower of Terror	Sunset Blvd.	40 inches
Voyage of the Little Mermaid	Animation Courtyard	None
Walt Disney: One Man's Dream	Mickey Ave.	None
Who Wants to Be a Millionaire— Play It!	Mickey Ave.	None

Scare Factor
0 = Unlikely to scare any child of any age.
! = Has dark or loud elements; might rattle some toddlers.
!! = A couple of gotcha! moments; should be fine for school-age kids.
!!! = You need to be pretty big and pretty brave to handle this ride.

MGM Attractions

Speed of Line	Duration of Ride/Show	Scare Factor	Age Range
Fast	30 min.	0	All
Fast	35 min.	!	5 and up
Fast	25 min.	!!	3 and up
Fast	25 min.	!	5 and up
Slow	n/a	0	2 and up
Fast	30 min.	!	All
Moderate	25 min.	!!	All
Moderate	35 min.	0	All
Fast	20 min.	!	2 and up
Moderate	15 min.	0	All
Moderate	3 min.	!!!	8 and up
Slow	15 min.	!!	7 and up
Moderate	10 min.	!!	5 and up
Moderate	10 min.	!!!	8 and up
Slow	20 min.	!!!	6 and up
Moderate	20 min.	0	8 and up
Slow	60 min.	0	8 and up

Takeoff is amazing—0 to 60 in 2.8 seconds—and then you're quickly thrown into your first total flip. The mazelike track will make a total of three inversions and at one point you rip through an "O" in the HOLLYWOOD sign. The coaster is smooth and fast and offers uneasy riders one comfort: since the whole ride takes place inside a building you never go very high, so there's no plunging sensation. Rock 'n' Roller is more about speed than big drops.

The Scare Factor
Loud, fast, and wild, especially at takeoff, this coaster is for older kids and teens. With a 48-inch height requirement, suffice it to say that Rock 'n' Roller will be much too much for kids under 8.

Beauty and the Beast—Live on Stage!
The Theater of the Stars is modeled on the Hollywood Bowl and it's the perfect setting for this 25-minute Broadway-caliber show. The costuming, choreography, and production are first-rate. The story is told a little out of sequence, but since approximately 99.9% of the audience have seen the movie, it's really not a problem. *Beauty and the Beast* is a good choice for afternoon. The theater is covered and large enough to seat 1,500, so if you show up 20 minutes before showtime you should get a seat without a problem.

Fantasmic!
Fantasmic! may be the best show in any Disney park. It has everything—lasers, fireworks, lighting effects, music, fountains, a 6,900-seat amphitheater, 1.9 million gallons of water, 45 cast members, and a 50-foot fire-breathing dragon. The show plays at closing every night, and twice nightly on busy days.

Helpful Hint
Sit at least 15 rows from the front to avoid being sprayed with water.

Insider's Secret

Fantasmic! is always packed, but one surefire way to make sure you get in and get a decent seat is to purchase a *Fantasmic!* Dinner Package. The package includes a prix-fixe meal at one of three MGM restaurants (the Brown Derby, Mama Melrose, or Hollywood & Vine) plus access to a priority-seating area of the *Fantasmic!* theater. The price of the package depends on the restaurant you choose and ranges from $23.99 to $36.99 for adults, and $10.99 to $11.99 for kids ages 3 to 9. Prices don't include park admission, tax, gratuity, or drinks (except at Hollywood & Vine, where nonalcoholic drinks are part of the buffet).

Plan to eat early—maybe two or three hours before the show. After dinner, as you pay, you're given a voucher that lets you into the priority-seating area. Don't arrive at the last minute though—you aren't guaranteed a specific seat, just a seat within a specific area. For one of the best spots, you should arrive 40 to 60 minutes before the show. Without the dinner package, you need to arrive 60 to 90 minutes early. That extra 20 minutes saved can make a world of difference if you're traveling with tired and antsy children. Book the package by calling 407/939–3463 (407/WDW–DINE) or stop by Guest Relations as you enter MGM in the morning to see if reservations are available. They often are. One caveat: *Fantasmic!* is an outdoor show and if the weather is truly inclement it can be cancelled at the last minute. You still get your dinner, but you're not reimbursed for losing out on the preferred seating for the show.

The Scare Factor

Every Disney villain you can think of shows up for the cartoon Armageddon and the middle scenes of the show are emotionally wrenching for preschoolers. Of course, Mickey does ultimately rally to save the day, and most children, no matter what their age, rate the show very highly. The noise level is also quite high, which frightens some babies.

Mickey performs in his role as the Sorcerer's Apprentice, fighting off a horde of evil Disney characters with a variety of special effects, including the projection of film images onto a screen of water. For awhile it looks like the bad guys are winning, and these dark scenes are upsetting for some children. In due time, however, Mickey's imagination is able to conjure up images of happiness, love, and friendship, and the good-guy characters show up in force. It's surprisingly moving, even for adults.

On Hollywood Boulevard

The Great Movie Ride

Beginning in the Chinese Theater at the end of Hollywood Boulevard, the Great Movie Ride is a bone fide classic. Disney's largest ride-through attraction, it loads steadily and fairly swiftly, and is best toured either midmorning or in the last hour before the park closes.

The Scare Factor

You'll encounter the Alien from *Alien*, the Wicked Witch from *The Wizard of Oz*, and any number of no-gooders on your trip. Some of the scenes are too startling for preschoolers, but the fact that your tram driver disappears and reappears does underscore the fact that it's all "just pretend."

Your tour guide provides an amusing spiel as you glide past soundstage sets from *Casablanca, Alien, The Wizard of Oz*, and other great films. The audio-animatronics figures of Gene Kelly, Julie Andrews, and Clint Eastwood are among Disney's best. But things suddenly turn ugly as your car stalls and the movie scenes come to life. Depending on which car you've boarded, you're about to be overrun by either a Mafia-style gangster or a Western desperado. Your tram will be taken hostage, but don't fret too much. In a later scene, drawn from *Indiana Jones and the Temple of Doom*, justice prevails. Was there ever any doubt there would be a happy ending?

Insider's Secret
Most of the waiting area is inside the Chinese Theater; if you see a line outside, you can be sure that there are hundreds more tourists waiting inside. Return during the parade or in the evening.

Afternoon Parade
A theme parade runs every afternoon and the exact time and route are outlined on your map. Stake out curb space 30 minutes in advance during the on-season. Because the parade route is so short, the crowds can be 8 to 10 people deep, and no vantage point is significantly less crowded than another. Although not as elaborate as those in the Magic Kingdom, the afternoon parades are well done and full of clever jokes.

On Echo Lake

Star Tours
Motion-simulation technology and a jostling cabin combine to produce the real feel of flight in Star Tours. With the hapless Captain Rex at the helm you're off for what is supposed to be a routine mission to the Moon of Endor. "Don't worry if this is your first flight," Rex comforts visitors, "it's my first one, too."

The Scare Factor

Most kids love Star Tours and find it's like being inside a very exciting, very authentic video game. There's a 40-inch height requirement. One warning: Although not as wild as the similar Body Wars at Epcot, Star Tours can cause motion sickness.

One wrong turn later and you're ripping through space at hyperspeed, headed toward combat with the dreaded Death Star.

George Lucas served as creative consultant and the ride echoes the charming as well as the terrifying elements of the *Star Wars* series. The chatter of R2-D2, C3PO, and assorted droids makes even the queues enjoyable. Star Tours is the best of both worlds—visual effects so convincing that you'll clutch your arm rails but actual rumbles so mild that only the youngest children are eliminated as passengers.

Lines move at an agreeable pace, but it's still best to ride in the morning if you can. Fastpass is available.

Sounds Dangerous Starring Drew Carey

In Drew Carey's spy spoof, you wear headphones and listen as Drew upends a jar of killer bees, drives a car, has a haircut, and visits the circus. The show is a crash course on behind-the-scenes sound production.

The Scare Factor

For long periods of the show you sit in total darkness to accentuate the sound effects and this unnerves some young kids. At nearly every performance at least one toddler is shrieking, which obviously undercuts the enjoyment of everyone in the theater, not to mention the terrified child. For kids with no fear of the dark, the show is an entertaining introduction to the lost world of radio, where sound told the story.

Helpful Hint
Sounds Dangerous is a good choice for afternoon. It's rarely crowded and you can sit for a while.

Indiana Jones Epic Stunt Spectacular
This stunt show is loud, lively, and full of laughs. Audience volunteers are a key part of the action and your odds of being tapped improve if you show up early and are near the front of the line. Professional stunt people re-create daring scenes from the Indiana Jones movies, and this 30-minute show is a great chance to see how some of those difficult and dangerous stunts actually wind up on film. The finale is spectacular.

Lines can look daunting, but the 2,200-seat theater is so huge that even people in the back are usually seated. That said, if you're visiting on a truly crowded day, you could always use Fastpass or wait until the less crowded evening shows.

The Scare Factor
For most people *Indiana Jones* is funny not scary, but the sudden explosions and gunfire can startle some kids. Consider this report from an Ohio father of four: "It didn't occur to me that the Indiana Jones show would be frightening for a young child but we sat near the front and not only was it extremely loud but we could even feel the heat from the explosions. I moved to the back of the theater with our younger child, who was beginning to get upset, and let the older ones stay up front with my wife. I don't think sitting up close at a show with a young child is a good idea."

In Animation Courtyard

Voyage of the Little Mermaid

Using puppets, animation, and live actors to retell the story of Ariel and Prince Eric, *Voyage of the Little Mermaid* remains one of the most popular shows at MGM. Either come early or use a Fastpass.

The special effects in this 20-minute show are among the best Disney has to offer. You'll feel as if you're really underwater and the interplay between the animation, puppetry, and live actors is ingenious.

The Scare Factor

Voyage of the Little Mermaid does have some frightening elements. The storm scene is dark and loud, and Ursula the Sea Witch is one big ugly puppet. That said, most kids have seen the movie and know enough to expect a happy ending, so they usually make it through the dark scenes without becoming too upset.

The Magic of Disney Animation

The Magic of Disney Animation has been revamped to make it more family friendly and the new version is a lot of fun. It opens with a fast and funny show starring Mushu, the pint-size dragon from *Mulan* with the voice of Eddie Murphy, and a live Disney animator. The animator describes how a character evolves in the animation process, and Mushu learns, to his horror, that he originally wasn't destined to be a dragon at all.

After the show, it's on to the interactive exhibits. These are designed to be fun for all ages and you can stay as long as you like. "You're a Character," a quiz that tells you which Disney character is most like you, will save you years of money spent on therapy. (Don't like your character? Try the test again!) Or you can insert your own voice into clips of animated classics, digitally color a cartoon, or meet the stars of Disney's latest film.

The best part of the attraction for older kids is the Animation Academy, where you can learn to draw a Disney character. Your drawing becomes a great free souvenir that you can take home. Many kids like to have the character they drew autograph the picture the next time they see him or her in the park. Or you can buy a frame for your masterpiece as you exit the attraction. If you get hooked and want to draw more than one character, you can reenter the Animation Academy later without going back through the entire attraction.

Playhouse Disney—Live on Stage!

Younger kids love this stage show where they sing, dance, and play along with Bear and his pals from other Disney Channel shows. The performance space holds large crowds, with the children (largely preschoolers) grouped on the floor where they can participate in the show. Performers are skilled at drawing even the youngest and the shyest of children into the action.

Although the show is simple, it's a big hit with toddlers and preschoolers and substantial lines begin forming about 30 minutes before showtime. Visit whenever your kids are at their happiest and most rested.

Walt Disney: One Man's Dream

This is more of an exhibit than an attraction, but it does remind you that almost everything in Disney World sprang from the extraordinary vision of a single man. There are plenty of artifacts and memorabilia, as well as a film about Walt Disney's life.

On Mickey Avenue

Backlot Tour

The Backlot Tour begins with a stop at the special-effects water tank, where audience volunteers help film a naval battle scene. Then you stroll through the props department before boarding a tram that scoots you through the wardrobe department

The Scare Factor

The shaking and splashing of Catastrophe Canyon only lasts about 30 seconds and most kids find it fun. Fine for all ages.

and past huge outdoor sets representing a typical small town and a large city. Finally, the tram stops in Catastrophe Canyon where riders are caught in an earthquake and flash flood. (If you're sitting on the left side, prepare to get wet.) After the rumbles subside, you ride behind the canyon to see how the disasters were created.

Who Wants to Be a Millionaire–Play It!

Theme park guests vie for the chance to sit in the hot seat and play for prizes. The show runs continuously in a studio that's a replica of the TV show set, complete with lighting, sound effects, and an engaging emcee. Anyone who can answer the questions can play the game. If a child makes it to the hot seat, a parent can come along to help. Just as on the show, the contestant gets three lifelines. "Ask the Audience" and "50-50" work as you'd expect, but "Phone a Friend" has become "Phone a Complete Stranger." If a contestant opts to use that lifeline, a red telephone rings outside on Mickey Avenue and the attendant hands it to the nearest adult passing by. That person has

Helpful Hint

Every member of the audience has an equal shot of making it to the hot seat, but even if you don't win the Fastest Fingers question, you're still not out. Continue to play along, because when the player in the hot seat falters, the audience member with the highest score takes over.

60 seconds to help the contestant answer the question and the results can be pretty funny.

Contestants get Millionaire pins, caps, polo shirts, and games as they climb the question ladder. The ultimate million-point prize is a Disney Cruise vacation for four.

On New York Street

Honey, I Shrunk the Kids

This playground is based on the popular film of the same name. "Miniaturized" guests scramble through a world of giant

> ## Insider's Secret
> Stay alert inside *Honey, I Shrunk the Kids*. When a child enters a tunnel or climbs to the top of a slide, it's often difficult to judge exactly where she'll emerge. For that reason, the attraction could be called "Honey, I Lost the Kids."

LEGOs, 9-foot Cheerios, and spiderwebs three stories high. It's the perfect place for kids to blow off steam and very popular with the under-10 set. The only complaint is that it needs to be about four times larger!

Children 2 to 5 have a special area of their own, with a downsized maze and slide where they can play in safety away from the rougher antics of the older kids.

> ## Helpful Hint
> *Honey, I Shrunk the Kids* can get very hot on a summer afternoon. Bring water bottles with you and make sure the children stay well hydrated.

Muppet*Vision 3-D

The Muppets combine slapstick and high wit, so everyone from preschoolers to adults will find something to make them laugh.

Helpful Hint
The 3-D effects are more convincing if you sit near the center toward the back of the theater.

Kids love the 3-D glasses and the eye-popping special effects. And the preshow is nearly as clever as the 20-minute main show. This is a good choice for midmorning, when you've ridden several rides and would like to just sit and laugh for a while.

The Scare Factor
Although Muppet*Vision 3-D tested highly among kids ages 2 to 5, some parents reported that children under 2 were unnerved by the sheer volume of the finale.

Lights, Motors, Action!–Extreme Stunt Show

Based on the popular *Moteurs . . . Action!* Stunt Show Spectacular at Disneyland Paris, this show, opened in 2005, features special cars, motorcycles, and Jet Skis built to blow up, split in half, and perform other high-octane stunts. When the show starts you've been transported to a movie set where the director is filming chase scenes and other daring feats with a cast and crew of 50. The show is fast, furious . . . and a great addition to the Backlot area, which is getting a general sprucing up. New cityscapes, including San Francisco and Chicago, will be joining the Backlot's existing New York City skyline.

Helpful Hint
Remember, what's new is always hot, so try to catch one of the earlier *Lights, Motors, Action!* shows and be there 30 minutes in advance. Showtimes will be listed on your entertainment schedule and the tip board on Hollywood Boulevard.

"The *Lights, Motors, Action!* stunt show was incredible," wrote one mother of two from Massachusetts. "We saw it twice. It's

The Scare Factor
The volley of engines is very loud and may startle babies and toddlers.

an especially good show for boys since some of the other shows at MGM are a little girly."

Meeting the Characters at MGM

MGM is a great place to meet the characters. Consult your map or the tip board, which is midway down Hollywood Boulevard, for times and places they'll appear and check out these locations.

- A variety of characters greets visitors at park opening and returns to the entrances around 3 PM.

- The classic characters can be found in their trailers on Mickey Avenue. Mickey greets visitors in his cushy digs at the end of the street and the well-monitored line makes sure you have time for a photo, autograph, and hug.

- The *Toy Story* crowd—Buzz, Woody, and Jesse—hangs out at Al's Toy Barn in the Backlot area.

- Periodically the *Star Wars* crew can be found outside the Star Tours ride.

Food Choices at MGM

The Hollywood Brown Derby is one of the best restaurants inside a Disney theme park. Although it has gourmet cuisine and a beautifully urbane setting, it's still casual and friendly enough to take the kids. The menu changes seasonally and is frequently updated, but one thing that's always available is the signature Cobb salad.

Other MGM restaurants offer big doses of fun for kids. The '50's Prime Time Café plunks you down in the middle of a television sitcom and serves comfort food like meat loaf, milk shakes, and mac and cheese. TVs play nonstop, you're seated in replicas of baby-boomer kitchens, and the waitress pretends to be your mom. Before the meal is over, everyone gets into the act; Mom is likely to inspect your hands for cleanliness before she'll feed you or she may force the kids to finish their green beans using the dreaded airplane technique.

Helpful Hint

It's always a good idea to make reservations for sit-down restaurants, but if you arrive at MGM without a reservation, drop by the dining information booth on Hollywood Boulevard and see what's left. If you're willing to eat at an off time like 4 PM, you may still get in.

Equally campy is the Sci-Fi Dine-In Theater Restaurant, where you eat in cars as if you were in a drive-in movie. Your waiters are carhops, the film clips are unbelievably cheesy, and the waiters add to the fun by presenting your bill as a speeding ticket. (Kids are often "driving" so they're usually presented with the bill. If they can't pay they may have to wax the car.) Drinks even come with glow-in-the-dark ice cubes. Oh yeah, and in the midst of all the action, the Sci-Fi manages to serve pretty decent food.

Due to its out-of-the-way location near Muppet*Vision 3-D, Mama Melrose's is definitely the least crowded and the fastest of the sit-down places. The pizzas and salads are very good; the veal saltimbocca and penne alla vodka are excellent.

If you just want a quick nosh, the Backlot Express lives up to its name and serves burgers and salads fast. The ABC Com-

Helpful Hint
Villains in Vogue is the perfect place to shop for Halloween costumes because all the bad guys (and girls) are represented. Rather go as a princess? Check out In Character near *Voyage of the Little Mermaid*. If there's a Wookiee in the party, head to Tatooine Traders, just outside of Star Tours, to find costumes of your favorite *Star Wars* characters.

missary has a fairly unusual menu for a fast-food place, with some Mexican and Chinese dishes mixed in with the sandwiches and salads. If your party can't agree on what to eat, head for the open-air food court called the Sunset Ranch Market on Sunset Boulevard. You can each go in different directions for pizza, hot dogs, turkey legs, ice cream, and fruit, then all meet back at your table.

Tips for Your Last Hour at MGM

- To guarantee yourself a seat for *Fantasmic!*, you'll need to enter the stadium at least an hour in advance, 90 minutes during the on-season. That's quite a wait, so you may want to eat dinner while you hold your seat. The stadium sells hot dogs and such, but if you want a more elaborate meal, you can buy fast food from anywhere in the park and carry it in. You can save 20–30 minutes' worth of waiting if you buy the *Fantasmic!* dinner package, which includes a meal at one of MGM's sit-down restaurants plus reserved seating (in a specific part of the theater, not in specific seats).

- If you're not watching *Fantasmic!*, the last hour before closing is a great time to hit any attraction you missed early in the day or to revisit favorites. Just be sure to be out of the park before the show wraps up. The big fire-works salvo at the end is your cue to get moving toward the exits.

Tips for Leaving MGM

@ Although a terrific show that more than justifies any in-convenience, *Fantasmic!* draws virtually everyone in the park to one spot at closing. Ergo, exiting afterward is a nightmare. Try to sit in the Mickey section so you'll have the best shot at getting out fast and beating the crowds to the buses, trams, or water taxis.

@ If you're sitting near the water or in one of the sections to the extreme right or extreme left of the stadium, you've got no choice but to deal with the crowd. One option is to sit tight and wait for the stadium to at least partially empty then eat or shop your way though the park, allowing most of the people to exit ahead of you. If you do decide to exit with the group, be sure to carry or hang on to your kids. The exit is by far the scariest part of the show.

CHAPTER

8. The Animal Kingdom

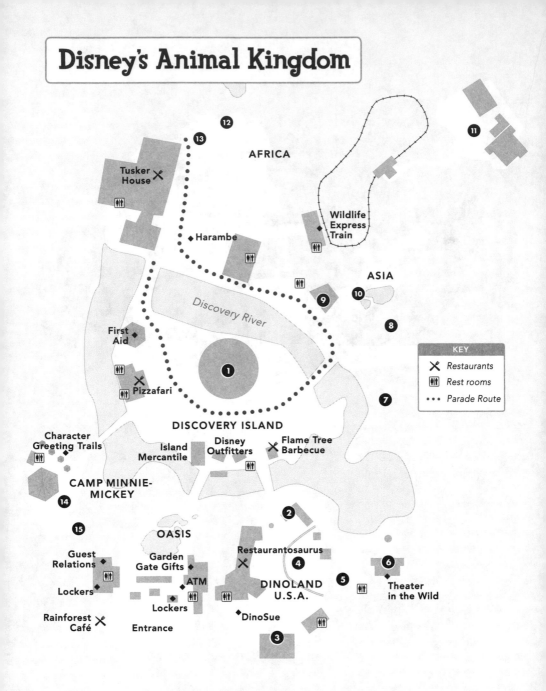

Disney's Animal Kingdom

AFRICA

Tusker House ✕
🚻

12
13

Harambe ♦

Wildlife Express Train
🚻

🚻

ASIA

9
10
8

Discovery River

First Aid ♦

1

✕ Pizzafari
🚻

7

DISCOVERY ISLAND

KEY	
✕	Restaurants
🚻	Rest rooms
•••	Parade Route

Character Greeting Trails ♦
🚻

Island Mercantile

Disney Outfitters
🚻

✕ Flame Tree Barbecue

CAMP MINNIE-MICKEY

14
15

OASIS

Guest Relations ♦
🚻

Garden Gate Gifts ♦

ATM

Restaurantosaurus
✕

2

4

6

Lockers ♦

Lockers
🚻

DINOLAND U.S.A.

5
🚻

Theater in the Wild

Rainforest Café ✕

Entrance

♦ DinoSue
🚻

3

Africa

Kilimanjaro Safaris **13**

Pangani Forest
Exploration Trail **11**

Rafiki's Planet Watch **12**

Asia

Expedition: Everest **7**

Flights of Wonder **9**

Kali River Rapids **8**

Maharajah
Jungle Trek **10**

Camp Minnie-Mickey

*Festival of the
Lion King* **14**

*Pocahontas and
Her Forest Friends* **15**

DinoLand U.S.A.

Boneyard **2**

Dinosaur **3**

Primeval Whirl **5**

*Finding Nemo –
the Musical* **6**

TriceraTop Spin **4**

Discovery Island

Tree of Life – It's Tough
to be a Bug! **1**

Getting to the Animal Kingdom

The Animal Kingdom parking lot is relatively small; all on-site hotels run direct shuttles and many off-site hotels do as well. If possible, arrive by bus. If you're coming by car, try to arrive early, before the main parking lot is filled. Otherwise, you're directed to an auxiliary lot.

Getting Around the Animal Kingdom

With more than 500 acres, technically the Animal Kingdom is the largest of all Disney parks, but most of the space is earmarked for animal habitats, such as the huge 100-acre savanna featured in Kilimanjaro Safaris. The walkable part of the park is relatively compact—a good thing since the only real means of getting around is on foot. The layout is basically circular, with the 14-story Tree of Life in the center. This may sound like the Animal Kingdom is easy enough to navigate, but in the middle of the day the area around the main entrance can become so crowded that it's nearly impassable. If you're trying to move around the park, your best bet is to cut through the Asia section, essentially going behind the Tree of Life. It looks like you're going out of your way (and you are), but the traffic flow works more in your favor.

At Disney World it's easy to fall into the trap of thinking "the faster you go, the more you'll see," but at the Animal Kingdom, the opposite is true. Slow your pace a little, because this park is designed for savoring. There are more than 1,700 live animals representing more than 250 species in the Animal Kingdom, and the park is also a botanical marvel, showcasing more than 3,000 species of plants. So, relax and enjoy the incredible natural beauty of the park and the many small-animal habitats tucked along the way.

Tips for Your First Hour in the Animal Kingdom

- On Extra Magic Hour mornings, only a few attractions will be operative during the first hour, but they will be indicated on a sign as you enter.

- The Oasis is the entry area, much like Main Street in the Magic Kingdom, and it often opens 30 minutes before the stated entry time. Characters are usually on hand to keep the kids entertained.

Insider's Secret

When the park opens, attendants are usually standing near the Tree of Life, directing guests toward attractions. Because they're on walkie-talkies with the operators of the rides, these cast members can give you approximate wait times and save you from hotfooting it to a ride only to find a 40-minute wait. The tip board in front of the Tree of Life also lists upcoming showtimes and the approximate wait time for major attractions.

    ☾ The animal habitat areas in the Oasis are charming, but don't visit them in the morning. You'll be stampeded by the people behind you hustling to get to the big rides . . . not to mention the fact you need to hustle to the big rides yourself. It's better to visit the Oasis in the afternoon or evening, on your way out of the park. That way it's not a big deal if you stand there 20 minutes waiting for the three-toed sloth to move.

    ☾ Head first to Expedition Everest. If the wait is less than 20 minutes, ride.

    ☾ Next, ride Kilimanjaro Safaris.

Attractions at the Animal Kingdom Offering Fastpasses

Dinosaur

Expedition Everest

It's Tough to Be a Bug!

Kali River Rapids

Kilimanjaro Safaris

Primeval Whirl

Animal Kingdom Touring Tips

    ☾ Because of the relatively small number of attractions, you can tour the Animal Kingdom in about five or six hours. The park is often mobbed between 10 AM and 2 PM, but usually begins to clear out by mid-afternoon. If you can't be there first thing in the morning, consider arriving after lunch.

    ☾ Don't feel that you have to see all the live shows, which may be too much sitting for young children. *Festival of the Lion King* is a must-see, but read the descriptions of the

Quick Guide to

Attraction	Location	Height Requirement
The Boneyard	DinoLand	None
Character Greeting Area	Camp Minnie-Mickey	None
Dinosaur	DinoLand	40 inches
Expedition Everest	Asia	44 inches
Festival of the Lion King	Camp Minnie-Mickey	None
Finding Nemo—the Musical	DinoLand	None
Flights of Wonder	Asia	None
Gorilla Falls Exploration Trail	Africa	None
Pocahontas and Her Forest Friends	Camp Minnie-Mickey	None
Kali River Rapids	Asia	38 inches
Kilimanjaro Safaris	Africa	None
Maharajah Jungle Trek	Asia	None
Primeval Whirl	DinoLand	48 inches
Tree of Life— *It's Tough to Be a Bug!*	Safari Village	None
TriceraTop Spin	DinoLand	None
Wildlife Express to Rafiki's Planet Watch	Africa	None

Scare Factor
0 = Unlikely to scare any child of any age.
! = Has dark or loud elements; might rattle some toddlers.
!! = A couple of gotcha! moments; should be fine for school-age kids.
!!! = You need to be pretty big and pretty brave to handle this ride.

Animal Kingdom Attractions

Speed of Line	Duration of Ride/Show	Scare Factor	Age Range
n/a	n/a	0	All
Moderate	n/a	0	All
Moderate	10 min.	!!!	7 and up
Moderate	10 min.	!!!	8 and up
Moderate	25 min.	0	All
Moderate	30 min.	0	All
Fast	25 min.	0	All
Moderate	n/a	0	All
Fast	12 min.	0	All
Moderate	7 min.	!	4 and up
Moderate	20 min.	!	6 and up
Fast	n/a	0	All
Slow	7 min.	!!	5 and up
Slow	10 min.	!	All
Slow	4 min.	!	All
Fast	20 min.	0	All

Insider's Secret

In your dash to get to the rides and shows, don't forget that the Animal Kingdom is really all about the animals. The Maharajah Jungle Trek and Gorilla Falls Exploration Trail are major attractions, as well designed as any zoo, and there are other small enclaves of animal habitats around the Tree of Life.

others and choose the ones that sound the most interesting or age appropriate.

@ Because of their proximity, consider combining a morning visit to the Animal Kingdom and an afternoon visit to Blizzard Beach. The parks are five minutes apart by car and many hotel buses make stops at both.

@ The Animal Kingdom closes early (between 5 and 7 PM depending on the season) and has no closing show.

Animal Kingdom Attractions

The attractions may be few in number, but they're powerful in impact. Most of the rides and shows are designed for the whole family to enjoy together.

On Discovery Island

Tree of Life—*It's Tough to Be a Bug!*
This state-of-the-art 3-D film is a real highlight for all ages. First of all, it's shown inside the Tree of Life, which is an absolutely amazing edifice with 325 animals carved seamlessly into its trunk. Perfect for pictures.

The show combines visual, sensory, and tactile effects and the cast of characters, including an accurately named Stinkbug, is so funny that everyone leaves the attraction laughing. The best effect of all is at the very end of the show.

The Scare Factor

It's Tough to Be a Bug! is a huge hit with most kids, but the soundtrack is very loud and there are a couple of scary scenes. At one point, large spider puppets drop down from the ceiling and dangle over your heads. Later the theater goes dark, you hear the sounds of swarming wasps, and there's the chance that the back of your seat might give you a small electrical zap, indicating you've been stung. (Not into pain? Simply lean forward in your seat.) The majority of children seem to find Flik and friends to be great fun, but there's usually at least one child crying in the audience. If your kids are scared of the dark or bugs, skip the show.

Mickey's Jammin' Jungle Parade

This cute 15-minute parade, featuring the characters "on safari," runs every afternoon, usually at 4 PM. (Check the tip board to confirm showtime and your map to confirm the parade route.) Expect beautiful animal puppetry, amazing stilt-walkers, and a lot of wacky visual humor in the parade. Although crowds don't get as thick as those at the Magic Kingdom parades, it's a good idea to stake your space at least 15 minutes before showtime.

In Africa

Kilimanjaro Safaris

This is the Animal Kingdom's premiere attraction, a ride that simulates an African photo safari. The animals have a great deal of open space around them and in fact appear to be running free—although cleverly incorporated water and plant barriers ensure that the cheetahs don't meet up with the ostriches and graphically illustrate the circle of life in front of the tourists.

Your guide helps you tell the impalas from the gazelles and at times your vehicle (called a lorry) comes startlingly close to the wildlife. The story line is that you're helping the reserve's game warden look for poachers who have abducted a baby elephant, Little Red.

Because the animals do have so much room to roam along the 2-mile route, some safari trips yield more sightings than others do. Safari drivers say that the animals are often active in the morning, but that you have a better chance of seeing cheetahs, rhinos, and warthogs later in the day. And because of the attraction's mammoth and unpredictable animal cast, Kilimanjaro is in essence a different adventure every time. You could go on one safari in the morning and return in the afternoon for a whole new show. Consider this report from a grandmother of seven: "Because we live near Orlando we visit Disney World often and never tire of the Animal Kingdom. We have found the best time to see lots of animals on Kilimanjaro Safaris is on a rainy, drizzly

Time-Saving Tip
Want to ride twice? Get a Fastpass.

The Animal Kingdom Don't-Miss List

Dinosaur (if your kids are 7 or older)
Expedition Everest (if kids are 8 or older and at least 44 inches tall)
Festival of the Lion King
Gorilla Falls Exploration Trail
It's Tough to Be a Bug!
Kali River Rapids
Kilimanjaro Safaris
Maharajah Jungle Trek

day. If you can time your visit for just after a shower, you'll see plenty of animals walking around enjoying the cool fresh air."

Gorilla Falls Exploration Trail

Near the exit of Kilimanjaro Safaris is a self-guided walking trail. The highlight is seeing the jungle home of Gino, the silverback gorilla, and his harem. (The dominant male in a gorilla troop is called the silverback because he is ordinarily older than the other males and often has gray hairs mixed in with the black.) Along the trail you also pass everything from mole rats to hippos to birds in an enclosed aviary, but children seem to especially enjoy the warthogs and meerkats in the savanna exhibit. Trail Guides are on hand to answer questions and help point out the animals.

Rafiki's Planet Watch

If you're interested in learning more about how Disney cares for the animals in the park, this attraction will answer many of your questions.

You board a nifty train called the Wildlife Express for a five-minute ride to Rafiki's Planet Watch. Along the way, you'll see where the animals sleep at night—a cool peek behind the scenes that older kids appreciate. Passengers disembark at Rafiki's Planet Watch, an utterly out-of-the-way station in the farthest-flung section of the park. There you'll find any number of exhibits on the subjects of conservation and animal endangerment. Kids especially enjoy touring the veterinary

> **Helpful Hint**
> Save Rafiki's Planet Watch for early afternoon, when you've toured most of the major attractions.

> **Helpful Hint**
> The actual conservation station is a 10-minute walk from where the train lets you out.

Helpful Hint

A character greeting area is to the right just before you cross the bridge into DinoLand. A sign tells you which characters you'll find waiting inside.

labs where newborns and sick animals get a lot of attention and the Affection Station, where they can pat and touch the friendly goats, llamas, and sheep. Rafiki is often on hand to do autographs, pictures, and hugs. Check your entertainment schedule for times he is due to appear.

In DinoLand

Dinosaur

Guests are strapped into "high-speed" motion vehicles and sent back in time to the Cretaceous period to save the gentle, plant-eating iguanodon from extinction.

The Scare Factor

Dinosaur combines atmospheric scariness with a wild-moving vehicle. The height requirement is 40 inches, which means that plenty of preschoolers qualify to board; nonetheless, based on the realism of the dinosaurs, we say wait until kids are at least 7 to ride, and even then consider whether they're brave enough to handle very big, very loud dinosaurs jumping out at them while the car takes steep drops. "As much as our young son (age 7) loves dinosaurs, this ride proved to be too much for him," wrote a mom of two. "We are planning another trip to Disney this year and he still reminds us that he is not going on the dinosaur ride again. The size and closeness of the effects just proved to be too much."

It's a noble mission, but it ain't easy. Along the way, Disney throws everything it has at you: asteroids, meteors, incoming pterodactyls, and ticked-off people-eating dinosaurs. The dinosaurs are extremely lifelike and in some cases, extremely close. The jeeps bounce around like mad, so Dinosaur can be a bit rough—but it's also a powerfully fun ride.

Finding Nemo—the Musical

After seven years of *Tarzan Rocks!* shows at the Theater in the Wild, Tarzan has finally hung up his loincloth to make way for a new attraction set to open in late 2006. This time Disney has taken an animated film, *Finding Nemo,* and transformed it into an original musical production with puppets, dancers, acrobats, and special effects, all choreographed to bring guests into Nemo's big blue world. The basic story remains the same as in the movie—Nemo and his father Marlin go on separate journeys that ultimately teach them how to understand each other—but the addition of music and state-of-the-art puppetry gives the tale a twist. Expect multigenerational humor and Broadway- and pop-inspired tunes.

Time-Saving Tip

Because of the proximity of the two attractions, *Finding Nemo* is a good place to take younger kids while older siblings wait in line and ride Expedition Everest. Arrive at the theater 40 minutes ahead of showtime to get a good seat.

The Boneyard

A great attraction for kids 7 and under, the Boneyard is a playground designed to simulate an archaeological dig site. Kids can dig for "fossils," excavate "bones," and play on mazes, bridges, and slides. The playground is visually witty—where else can you

Helpful Hint
The good news is that kids can lose themselves in the Boneyard and happily play there for an hour or longer. The bad news is that parents can lose their kids as well. The Boneyard is sprawling, so keep your eyes on young children at all times, especially when they're playing on the slides. When they enter at the top, it's often hard to tell what chute they're in or where they'll emerge.

find slides made from prehistoric animal skeletons?—and has fun surprises, such as a footprint that roars when you jump on it.

Visit the Boneyard after you've toured the biggies and the kids are ready to romp for a while. The play area is largely exposed to the sun and can get very hot on a Florida afternoon, however, so remember the sunscreen and water bottles.

Hidden Mickey
In the woolly mammoth dig site, there's a Hidden Mickey formed with two hard hats and a fan.

TriceraTop Spin

Two years ago, Disney opened a new miniland, Chester and Hester's Dino-Rama, a tribute to the owners of the campy T-shirt and trinket shop near the exit to Dinosaur. The miniland is a dino-theme roadside fair with traditional midway games and a pair of we-guarantee-you'll-learn-nothing-here rides.

The first is the kid-friendly TriceraTop Spin, a circular ride similar to Dumbo, except that

The Scare Factor
If they loved Dumbo, they'll love TriceraTop Spin.

Helpful Hint
The Boneyard and TriceraTop Spin are a good place for parents to take younger kids while their older siblings ride Dinosaur.

you fly in dinosaurs, naturally. The beasts tilt back and forth as you climb or descend.

Primeval Whirl
The second ride in Chester and Hester's Dino-Rama is Primeval Whirl, a crazy mouse–style coaster with spinning cars, hairpin turns, and numerous dips.

The Scare Factor
A bit surprisingly, Primeval Whirl has a 48-inch height requirement. The ride is faster than it looks and has many spins. Most kids over 5 (assuming they make the height requirement) love it, but if you have any doubts, watch it make a cycle or two before joining the queue.

Time-Saving Tip
Primeval Whirl is a slow-boarding, low-capacity ride and can draw major lines. If you're visiting on a busy day, use Fastpass.

Lucky
DinoLand is also home to Lucky, Disney's first-ever free-roaming audio-animatronics creation. Lucky walks about DinoLand interacting with guests and even signing autographs. He can laugh,

sneeze, bray, and even hiccup, and he represents the absolute latest in audio-animatronics technology.

In Camp Minnie-Mickey

Character Greeting Area

Camp Minnie-Mickey is the Animal Kingdom equivalent of Toontown. You can find separate greeting areas where you can line up to meet the characters, all adorably decked out in safari gear. The greeting areas are especially busy just after a showing of *Festival of the Lion King*.

Festival of the Lion King

This is one of the best attractions in the Animal Kingdom, and one of the best shows in all of Disney World.

Festival of the Lion King features what you might expect—singers, dancers, the characters—as well as acrobatic "monkeys" twirling fire batons, and "birds" that dramatically take flight. The costuming is incredible, the music is wonderful, and the finale is guaranteed to give you goose bumps.

The performers interact directly with the audience and at one point small children from the crowd are invited to join in a simple circular parade. Children sitting near the front are more apt to be tapped.

Festival of the Lion King is very popular. Showtimes are printed on your entertainment schedule; be there at least 30 minutes beforehand to assure yourself a seat, 45 minutes if you'd like to be near the front.

Pocahontas and Her Forest Friends

This sweet little show is a good choice for younger kids (ages 9 and under). Pocahontas, Grandmother Willow, and live animals team up to deliver a gentle lesson about protecting our wildlife. Although the animals featured vary, you might see an armadillo, a skunk, snakes, and birds. The theater is small so you can sit quite close to the stage—and the animals.

Showtimes are indicated on your entertainment schedule and it's rarely necessary to show up more than 10 minutes early. Visit in the afternoon when the rest of the park is crowded and you'll enjoy resting a bit. The animal training shows, with times indicated on your entertainment schedule, are more interesting to preteens.

In Asia

Kali River Rapids

For this water ride, you board an eight-passenger raft for a descent down a meandering river through rapids, geysers, and waterfalls. Expect to get very wet, possibly soaked, depending on where you're sitting in the raft. (And since the rafts are circular and constantly turning throughout the ride, it's impossible to predict which seats will catch the most spray.) Stow cameras and other water-sensitive valuables in lockers before you board, and bring your trusty poncho.

Helpful Hint

On Kali River Rapids, be sure to keep your feet up on the center bar. A wet fanny is an inconvenience, but wet shoes and socks can lead to blisters and ruin your whole day. Also consider bringing a change of clothes. One mom said her soaking wet child burst into tears and had to be taken back to the hotel to change. Here are comments from another: "They aren't kidding when they say you'll get wet on Kali River Rapids. We rode first thing in the morning, expecting to get splashed, and we really got soaked. It was so uncomfortable we had to go back to our room to change clothes. Now we know to ride it later in the day, preferably just as we're about to leave the Animal Kingdom."

The Scare Factor

The height requirement has been lowered from 42 inches to 38 inches, reflecting the fact that Kali River Rapids is a very mild ride, with only one sizable descent along the way. It's fine for anyone who isn't afraid of getting wet.

Insider's Secret

Are some of your kids too young or too short to ride? Let them man the water cannons on the bridge as you approach the ride; there they can take aim against their older siblings as they pass in the rafts below. Revenge is sweet! And to be honest, shooting absolute strangers can be fun, too.

Maharajah Jungle Trek

Another lovely walking path, this one goes through habitats of Asia. The Bengal tigers are the undisputed stars of the show but you'll also encounter Komodo dragons, gibbons, and, most intriguing of all, giant fruit bats. Take time along the path to appreciate the glorious landscaping and the beauty of the architecture.

Hidden Mickey

The Maharajah Jungle Trek is Hidden Mickey city. There are several in the drawings on the ruins just as you enter the tiger habitat.

Flights of Wonder

The Caravan Stage is home to this lovely display of birds in free flight. The show's premise is a bit silly—the story is about a tour guide who has lost his tour group and is afraid of birds—but you can count on seeing falcons, vultures, hawks, and toucans demonstrating their unusual talents. Several members of the audience, includ-

Insider's Secret

The Animal Kingdom provides interactive entertainment throughout the park. Cast members are stationed with animals throughout the park and kids are welcome to ask questions and have up-close encounters with the bugs, birds, reptiles, and small mammals. At the Dawa Bar in the Africa section you'll find storytellers, music, African drumming, and the amazing Karuka Acrobats.

And keep an eye out for DeVine, a moving human topiary, who can often be found literally hanging around the park. She blends in so well with the vegetation that she's been known to startle some guests.

ing kids, are invited onstage to interact with the birds. Showtimes are noted on your entertainment schedule; be there 10 minutes before showtime to assure a good seat. *Flights of Wonder* is a good choice for the most crowded times of the afternoon.

Expedition: Everest

Opened in spring 2006, this roller coaster is the Animal Kingdom's most popular ride. The premise is that your mountain train is chugging up the snowy mountainside when it suddenly encounters a break in the track. Uh-oh. The trip back down not only involves wild plunges and even wilder speeds but

The Scare Factor

Although Expedition: Everest doesn't have the corkscrews and flips that are at Rock 'n' Roller Coaster, the yeti is indeed slightly more frightening than Steven Tyler. Also, the train moves at almost twice the speed of Space Mountain, which means the ride will probably be too intense for kids under 8.

Helpful Hint

Come immediately upon entering the park in the morning, or use Fastpass.

you'll also meet up with the yeti that lives in the mountain, and rumor has it he's not in a good mood. Your train races both forward and backward through bamboo forests and glacier fields as you attempt to escape his rage.

Food Choices in the Animal Kingdom

Since the Animal Kingdom closes the earliest of all the parks—usually between 5 and 7 PM, depending on the season—people rarely eat dinner there. Thus, there's only one sit-down restaurant, the Rainforest Café, which is just as you enter the park. It's a chain, but kid friendly and open for breakfast, lunch, and dinner.

Outstanding fast-food places include the Tusker House in Africa, which serves vegetables that are cooked fresh every 15 minutes, as well as rotisserie chicken, soups, and salads. Or try the chicken stir-fry at the Chakranadi Chicken Shop in Asia. Flame Tree Barbecue, near the entrance to DinoLand, is another good lunch choice.

All of these restaurants have outdoor patios where you can take your food, find a pretty view, and really relax. All these lush, shady eating areas in the Animal Kingdom help blur the line between fast-food and sit-down dining. The Dawa Bar, adjacent to the Tusker House patio, offers entertainment in the afternoon, such as authentic African music and dance.

The Animal Kingdom also hosts a character breakfast at Restaurantosaurus in DinoLand. Donald and his friends play the roles of student paleontologists on a dig site and there's plenty of wacky humor. Make reservations before you leave home by calling 407/WDW–DINE.

Tips for Your Last Hour
in the Animal Kingdom

@ Why is there no big closing show at the Animal Kingdom? Most evening shows require fireworks, lasers, and
other pyrotechnics, and all that noise and light would
scare the animals.

@ Since there's no closing show, midday crowds drift out of
the Animal Kingdom throughout the afternoon and early
evening, and leaving isn't a problem. Return to the parking lot or bus station whenever it suits your schedule.

CHAPTER

9

The Disney World Water Parks

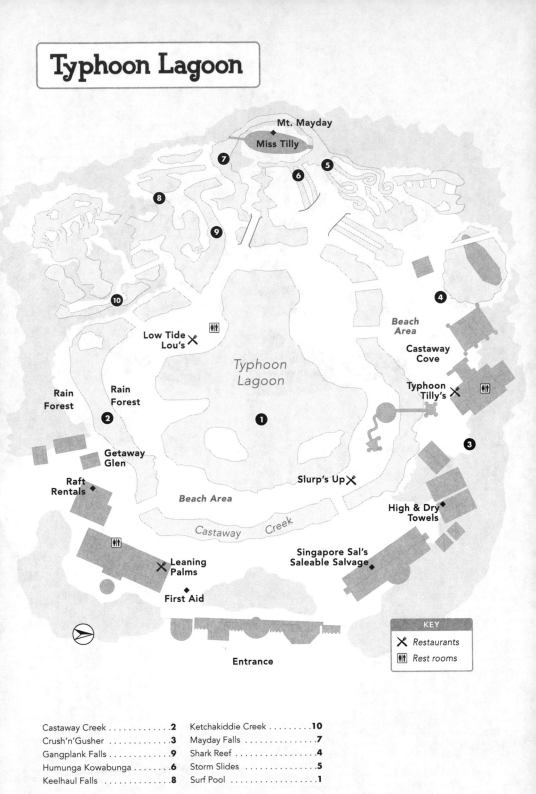

Typhoon Lagoon

Mt. Mayday

Miss Tilly

7

6

5

8

9

10

Low Tide Lou's

Typhoon Lagoon

Beach Area

4

Castaway Cove

Typhoon Tilly's

3

Rain Forest

Rain Forest

2

1

Getaway Glen

Slurp's Up

Raft Rentals

High & Dry Towels

Beach Area

Castaway Creek

Leaning Palms

Singapore Sal's Saleable Salvage

First Aid

KEY

✗ Restaurants

🛉 Rest rooms

Entrance

Getting to the Water Parks

On-site visitors can take the bus to both Typhoon Lagoon and Blizzard Beach, but expect a long commute. Getting to Typhoon Lagoon may involve sitting through three stops at Downtown Disney, and getting to Blizzard Beach often involves a stop at the Animal Kingdom. Plus, guests of the Magic Kingdom resorts (the Grand Floridian, Contemporary, Wilderness Lodge, and Fort Wilderness) have to go to the TTC and then transfer to a water park bus. In other words, bus travel can be a headache. If you have a car, drive to the water park.

Try to arrive about 20 minutes ahead of the stated opening times for the parks, particularly if you're visiting in summer or during a major holiday. During midday and afternoon hours in peak seasons, the parking lots often fill to capacity.

Water Park Touring Tips

- Girls should buy a one-piece swimsuit before going. More than one bikini top has been lost coming down a waterslide.

- The water parks draw a rowdy preteen and teenage crowd, which means young kids and unsteady swimmers may get dunked and splashed more than they like. If your children are very young, stick to the kiddie sections (Ketchakiddee Creek in Typhoon Lagoon and Tike's Peak at Blizzard Beach), which are off limits to older kids.

- Always crowded, the parks are extra packed on weekends, because they're popular with locals as well as tourists.

- Summer afternoons in Florida often mean thunderstorms, and even a rumble of distant thunder can lead to water park closings. If you're visiting in summer and want to make sure you have time to try everything, visit the water parks first thing in the morning.

- Bring your own towels. There are plenty of lockers ($5 small, $7 large, with a $2 refundable deposit), and the locker keys come on rubber bands that slip over your wrist or ankle, so you can keep them with you while you're in the water.

- If you arrive in the morning when a swarm of guests enters at once, getting a locker can be quite a hassle, with the rental lines sometimes 20 minutes long and the area around the lockers packed. Some families skip locker rentals altogether and keep vitals such as room keys, charge cards, and a bit of cash in one of those flat plastic holders you wear around your neck. (They sell them in the water park gift shops for about $5.) That way they can grab the best lounge chair locations and dash straight to the rides while everyone else is still trying to get a locker.

Helpful Hint

Bring rubber beach shoes with nonskid bottoms if you have them. They'll protect your soles from the hot sidewalks, and you don't have to take them off for the rides.

@ You can also borrow life vests for free, although you have to leave your driver's license or a credit card as a deposit. Snorkeling equipment can be picked up for no charge at Hammerhead Fred's near the Shark Reef at Typhoon Lagoon.

@ Because you're climbing uphill all day, half the time dragging a tube or mat behind you, the water parks are extremely exhausting. If you spend the day at a water park, plan to spend the evening in films or shows. Or take the night off.

@ There are fast-food restaurants at both water parks as well as places to picnic.

@ The Lost Kids Stations at both parks are so far away from the main water areas that it's unlikely your children will find their own way. Instruct your children, should they look up and find themselves separated from you, to approach the nearest person wearing a Disney name tag. A cast member will escort the kids to the Lost Kids Station, and you can meet them there. Because both of the parks are full of meandering paths with many sets of steps and slides, it's easy to get separated from your party. Set standard meeting places and times for older kids.

Helpful Hint

Trying to decide which water park to visit? We agree with this statement from a father of two from Michigan: "Last year with our extended family we visited both water parks and concluded that Typhoon Lagoon was the favorite of the adults and the younger children because it's very pretty with nice beaches and shallow places for little ones to swim. Family members age 10 to 25 preferred Blizzard Beach because of all the big slides."

@ If you're visiting in summer, consider dropping by both Typhoon Lagoon and Blizzard Beach. They're very different experiences. Typhoon Lagoon has the better beaches and pools and is more relaxing, although the new Crush'n'Gusher has definitely upped the thrill factor. Blizzard Beach is the *POW!* park, focusing on slides.

@ Typhoon Lagoon and Blizzard Beach are often closed for refurbishing in January and February, although it's rare for both to be closed at once unless the weather is truly cold or inclement. If you're planning a winter trip, call 407/824–4321 to see which will be open during the time you're visiting.

@ Ride the slides and flumes in the morning and save the pools for the afternoon. Lines for the slides reach incredible lengths by midday.

Insider's Secret

Whichever water park you choose, be sure to visit it early in your Disney World visit. Several families reported that they saved this experience until late in their trip and then found it was the highlight of the whole vacation for their kids. "If we'd known how great it was, we would have come several times," lamented one father. "As it turns out we only went to Blizzard Beach once—on the morning of the day we were due to fly out."

Typhoon Lagoon

Disney calls its 56-acre Typhoon Lagoon "the world's ultimate water park," and the hyperbole is justified. Where else can you float through caves, take surfing lessons, picnic with parrots, and swim (sort of) with sharks? Typhoon Lagoon is the perfect replica of the perfect tropical isle—and the perfect place for a vacation-weary family to relax. Older kids can hit the thrill slides, younger kids can splash in the bays and dig in the sand, and parents can relax (at least in shifts) under a palm tree with a piña colada in one hand and a best seller in the other.

For anyone with a Water Parks and More option, entrance to Typhoon Lagoon is free. Otherwise, admission is $34 for adults and $28 for children 3 to 9, not including sales tax.

Typhoon Lagoon Attractions

Crush'n'Gusher

The Lagoon's newest thrill ride combines flumes, spillways, and steep drops, but the real kick is that you're hit so hard with pulsating streams of water that at one point in the ride your two-person raft is actually propelled back uphill. The concept behind

> ### The Scare Factor
> The Crush'n'Gusher provides major thrills and is not for the nervous. The height requirement is 48 inches; even if they're tall enough, you should probably warm them up on Keelhaul Falls before tackling Crush'n'Gusher.

the ride is that you're lost in an abandoned fruit-processing facility. There are three paths out—the Banana Blaster, Coconut Crusher, and Pineapple Plunger—each about 420 feet long with plenty of twists and turns along the way.

Humunga Kowabunga

With three enclosed waterslides that drop you a stunning five stories in a matter of seconds, Humunga Kowabunga is definitely a thrill. Riders reach speeds of up to 30 mph!

> ### Helpful Hint
> Women and girls should wear one-piece swimsuits. According to the cast members who work at Humunga Kowabunga, at least one woman per hour loses her swimsuit top during the descent.

The Scare Factor

This is an intense ride, one that fully deserves its height requirement of 48 inches. Part of the scare factor is certainly the drop, but the fact that you're also falling in complete darkness adds to the thrill. Nonetheless, once people ride it and get over that initial trepidation, they usually climb right back up to do it again.

Storm Slides

Although just as fast as Humunga Kowabunga, the Storm Slides are curvier and thus a little tamer than a straight plunge down the mountain. Each of the three slides offers a slightly different route, although none is necessarily wilder than the others.

The Scare Factor

Kids of any age can ride, but they need to be fairly good swimmers. Although the pool you land in at the bottom isn't deep, you do hit the water with enough force to temporarily disorient a nervous swimmer. Most kids 7 to 11 love these zesty little slides, and, if they're good swimmers, some kids even younger can handle the Storm Slides.

Mayday Falls and Keelhaul Falls

A Disney employee helps you climb into your inner tube and begin your winding journey down a white-water stream. The journey is fast, giggle inducing, and has enough turns that you often feel like you're about to lose your tube.

The Scare Factor

Keelhaul Falls is slightly milder than Mayday, so let children try it first. Cast members can provide some smaller inner tubes with built-in bottoms. Kids as young as four have reported loving this ride.

Gangplank Falls

You weather these white-water rapids in four-passenger rafts. Slower and calmer (but much bumpier) than Mayday or Keelhaul, Gangplank is a good choice for families with kids who are nervous about tackling a white-water ride on their own. Gangplank Falls does load slowly, however, and the ride is short, so hit it early in the morning before the line becomes prohibitive.

Surf Pool

In this huge and incredible 2.5-acre lagoon, guests can ride machine-made waves up to 6 feet high. The waves come at 90-second intervals and are perfectly sized for tubing and bodysurfing. A foghorn blast alerts you to when a big one is on its way; if you're bobbing around with young kids, stay in the shallow areas where the swells won't be too overwhelming and you can avoid the surfers.

Toddlers and preschoolers can safely splash around in two small, roped-off coves called Blustery Bay and Whitecap Cover.

Castaway Creek

Castaway Creek is a meandering 2,000-foot river full of inner tubes. You simply wade out, find an empty tube, and climb aboard. It takes about 30 minutes to lazily circle the rain forest, with a bit of excitement at one point when riders drift under the waterfall. There are numerous exits along the creek, so anyone who doesn't want to get splashed can hop out before the falls. In fact, Castaway Creek serves as a means of transporta-

Insider's Secret

Families with teens should consider the surfing lessons that are given in the Typhoon Lagoon wave pool before the park opens in the morning. The instructors are top-notch and since you're learning to surf in a controlled environment, it's safe and almost everyone manages to catch a wave by the end of the class. The cost is $135 per person—pricey, but our readers say it's worth it. For details or reservations, call 407/939–7529 (407/WDW–PLAY).

tion around the park; savvy guests who don't want to burn their feet on hot pavement or waste energy walking around, often hop in and float their way from attraction to attraction.

The Scare Factor

Castaway Creek is a fun, relaxing ride appropriate for any age. The water is 3 feet deep throughout the ride, however, so keep a good grip on young kids or those who can't swim.

Shark Reef

An unusual attraction, Shark Reef is a saltwater pool where snorkelers swim "among" exotic marine life, including sharks. The sharks are behind Plexiglas and are not too numerous, so anyone expecting the *Jaws* experience will be disappointed.

Disney provides the snorkeling equipment and a brief orientation on how to use it. Only official Disney equipment is allowed in the pool, so don't bother packing your own masks.

The Scare Factor
Kids must be 10 or older to enter Shark Reef. Younger siblings can watch from an underwater viewing area that gives you a good view of the marine life and the snorkelers.

Ketchakiddee Creek

This is a water playground designed for toddlers and preschoolers, with geysers and waterspouts in the shapes of crocodiles and whales, as well as pint-size slides, a grotto with a waterfall, and a small white-water raft ride. No kids over 48 inches are allowed inside, which keeps the area safe for the younger kids.

Blizzard Beach

Blizzard Beach may have the most clever theme of any Disney park. The tropical ambience of Typhoon Lagoon seems natural for a water park, but who could have predicted a melting ski lodge?

Blizzard Beach is built on the tongue-in-cheek premise that a freak snowstorm hit Orlando and a group of enterprising businesspeople built Florida's first ski resort. The sun returned in due time, and for a while it looked like all was lost—until someone spied an alligator slipping and sliding down one of the slushy slopes. Thus Blizzard Beach was born. The snow may be gone but the jumps, sled runs, and slalom courses remain, resulting in a high-camp, high-thrill ski lodge in the palms. The motif extends into every element of the park: There are Plexiglas snowmen, a chalet-style restaurant, even ski marks running off the side of the mountain. And the original skiing alligator, Ice Gator, is the park mascot.

At the center of Blizzard Beach is "snowcapped" Mt. Gushmore. You can get to the top via ski lift (long line, short

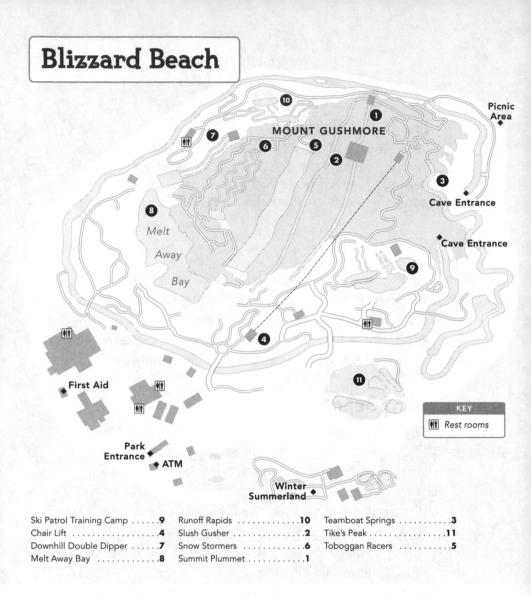

Blizzard Beach

Picnic Area

MOUNT GUSHMORE

Cave Entrance

Cave Entrance

Melt Away Bay

First Aid

Park Entrance

ATM

Winter Summerland

KEY

Rest rooms

ride) or a series of stairs (big climb, short breath), but how you get down is up to you. The bold descend via Summit Plummet or Slush Gusher, but there are medium-intensity flumes, tube rides, and white-water raft rides as well.

Blizzard Beach was built in response to Typhoon Lagoon's popularity and has since become the more popular of the two. There are big crowds in the morning, but showing up early is the only way you can ensure you'll get in at all. Like Typhoon Lagoon, Blizzard Beach is included in the Water Parks and

More; otherwise, admission is $34 for adults and $28 for children 3 to 9, not including sales tax.

Blizzard Beach Attractions

Summit Plummet
The icon of the park, Summit Plummet is 120 feet tall, making it twice as long as Humunga Kowabunga at Typhoon Lagoon. From the outside, it looks like Summit Plummet riders are

The Scare Factor
The height requirement for Summit Plummet is 48 inches. Although it's a very short experience—less than four seconds from top to bottom—the drop may be the most intense sensation in all of Disney World. In short, this flume is not for the faint of heart.

shooting out of the side of the mountain into midair. And in reality the ride is nearly as intense, with a 60-degree, 60 mph drop. That's considerably faster than the top speed at Space Mountain—and here you're not even riding in a car.

Slush Gusher
This is another monster slide, but with a couple of bumps to slow you down. Akin in intensity to Humunga Kowabunga at Typhoon Lagoon, Slush Gusher is so much fun that many kids insist on doing it more than once, despite the climb to the top and the long line.

Insider's Secret
Don't forget to cross your legs tightly as you descend. Your bathing suit will still ride up, but at least you'll have some protection against the Mother of All Wedgies. And, women and girls should wear one-pieces unless they want their tops up by their ears as they land.

Runoff Rapids

You take a separate set of stairs up the back of Mt. Gushmore to reach these three inner-tube rides. To start, you get to choose between tubes that seat one, two, or three people. Just remember, the heavier the raft, the faster the descent, so don't assume that by piling all the kids in one raft you're toning down the experience. The rapids are great fun, and each of the slides provides a slightly different thrill so you can try it over and over. The only downside is that you have to carry your own raft up the seven zillion stairs (157, to be exact); visit early in the morning before your stamina fails.

Snow Stormers

This is a mock slalom run that you descend on your belly as you clutch a foam rubber "sled." The three slides are full of twists and turns that splash water back into your face, and if you'd like, you can race the sledders on the other two slides to the bottom. It's so much fun that hardly anyone does it just once.

Toboggan Racers

Eight riders on rubber mats are pitted against one another on a straight descent down the mountain. The heavier the rider, the faster the descent so the attendant at the top of the slide will give kids a head start over adults. Not quite as wild as Snow Stormers, Toboggan Racers lets kids get used to the sensation of sliding downhill on a rubber sled.

Teamboat Springs

In one of the best rides in the park, the whole family can join forces to tackle the white water as a group. The round boats, which you board at the top of Mt. Gushmore, can carry up to six people, and the ride downhill is zippy, with lots of splashes and sharp curves. Teamboat Springs draws an enthusiastic thumbs-up from all age groups, from preschoolers to grandparents. It's much longer, wilder, and more fun than Gangplank Falls, the comparable white-water ride at Typhoon Lagoon.

Downhill Double Dipper

On this individual tube ride, you race the rider in the other chute, going through water curtains and freefalls during your descent. At one point in the ride, you're completely airborne. The Double Dipper is fun and addictive, albeit a bit more jarring than some of the other rides at Blizzard Beach. Test the kids on nearby Runoff Rapids before you tackle it.

The Scare Factor

Downhill Double Dipper is a bit rougher than it looks and has a 48-inch height requirement.

Ski Patrol Training Camp

This special play area is designed for kids 5 to 11 who are too old for Tike's Peak, but not quite ready for the big-deal rides. They can walk across icebergs, swing from T-bars, test their mountaineering skills, and ride medium-intensity slides.

Tike's Peak

This is where the toddlers and preschoolers gather to play on small slides and flumes, in igloo-style forts, and in a wading pool that looks like a broken ice-skating rink. No kids over 48 inches tall are allowed to play.

Chair Lift

The Chair Lift offers direct transportation to the top of Mt. Gushmore where Summit Plummet, Slush Gusher, and Teamboat Springs await. It's also a fun little diversion in itself, but lines can grow unbelievably long in the afternoon. Hiking up the steps is a lot faster.

Melt Away Bay

Unlike the huge Surfing Lagoon at Typhoon Lagoon, this swimming area is relatively small and offers mild swells instead of big waves. Fed by "melting snow" waterfalls, the pool is perfect for young kids and unsteady swimmers. There are plenty of chairs and shady huts nearby for relaxing, but these tend to be claimed early in the day.

CHAPTER
10
The Rest of
the World

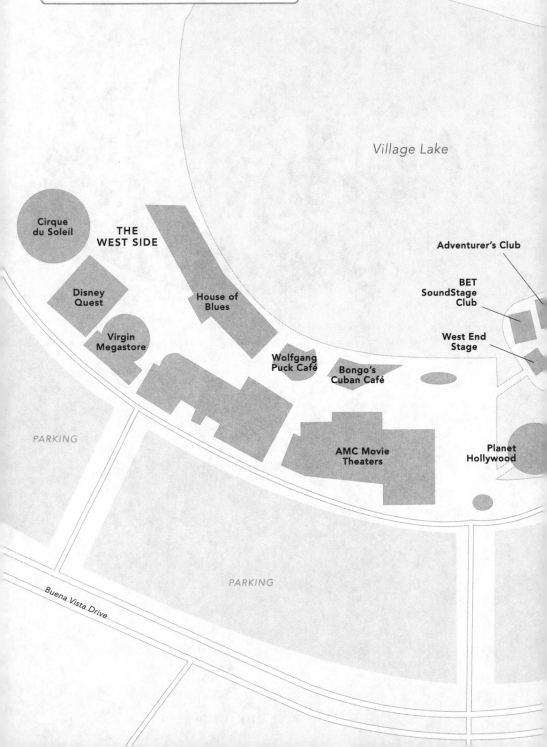

Downtown Disney & Pleasure Island

Village Lake

Cirque du Soleil

THE WEST SIDE

Disney Quest

Virgin Megastore

House of Blues

Wolfgang Puck Café

Bongo's Cuban Café

Adventurer's Club

BET SoundStage Club

West End Stage

AMC Movie Theaters

Planet Hollywood

PARKING

PARKING

Buena Vista Drive

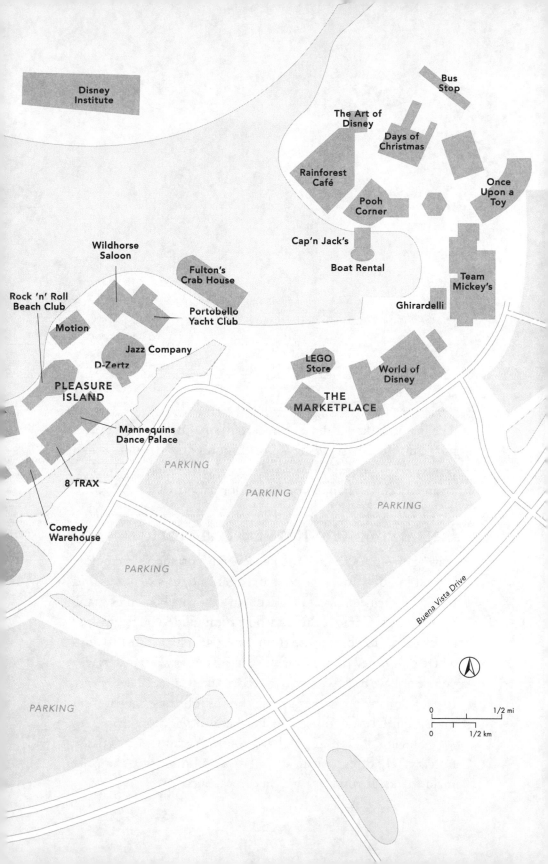

Beyond the Major Parks

The major parks get most of the attention, but many guests report that their best Disney World moments—from racing a Mouse Boat around the Seven Seas Lagoon to settling back at a comedy club—happen in the minor parks of Disney World.

Getting to the Rest of the World

Staying on-site? Although the Disney transportation system does a good job of shuttling guests between the on-site hotels and the major theme parks, it breaks down a bit when it comes to the minor parks. Consult the transportation guide you're given at check-in for the best route from your particular resort to anywhere on Disney property. If the trip involves two transfers and you don't have a car with you, consider taking a cab. They're easy to get from any on-site resort and the cost of being hauled from one end of Disney property to another is never more than $20.

Staying off-site? If you have your own car, use it. Off-site hotels rarely offer shuttle service to anything other than the major parks. If you don't have a car, call a cab.

Getting to Downtown Disney

On-site hotels have direct bus service to Downtown Disney. The buses make three stops: at the Marketplace, Pleasure Island, and West Side. Those staying at Port Orleans, Saratoga Springs, or Old Key West have boat service directly to the Marketplace, a pleasant way to get there.

In addition, on-site and off-site guests can drive directly to Downtown Disney. There's no charge for parking, but if the parking lot is full, as it sometimes is at night, consider valet parking ($8).

Getting to the Wide World of Sports

The fastest route is to drive your own car. Otherwise, buses are an option, but few run to this out-of-the-way location. Check your transportation guide for the best route from your resort; if more than two transfers are involved, take a cab.

Getting from One Resort to Another

Your simplest option is to use the theme park that is closest to you as a transfer station. For example, if you're staying at the Grand Floridian and have dinner reservations at the Board-Walk, take the monorail to the Magic Kingdom and catch a bus to the BoardWalk from there.

Helpful Hint
Transportation options are always subject to change. To assure the best route to get somewhere, consult the transportation guide you're given at check-in or consult a concierge at the Guest Services desk of your hotel.

The Don't-Miss List for the Rest of the World

Character Breakfasts (if you have kids under 9)

Cirque du Soleil

DisneyQuest (if you have kids over 10)

Downtown Disney

Pleasure Island (for an adult night out)

Downtown Disney

The enormous entertainment, dining, and shopping complex known as Downtown Disney has three major sections: the Marketplace, Pleasure Island, and West Side. The three sections are linked by walking paths, shuttle buses, and ferry service. Not surprisingly, Downtown Disney is packed at night, when the restaurants and clubs are going full force. Families who'd like to visit Downtown Disney when there are fewer crowds should show up in the afternoon and eat dinner relatively early, like at 5 PM.

"We didn't want to buy a ticket for our first day, since we were landing in Orlando around noon," reported one woman who visited with her husband and 14-year-old sister. Instead we went to Downtown Disney, and we thought it was a great introduction to Disney World. We picked up our tickets at Guest Relations, so we were all set for the following day, then we kicked off our vacation with a great meal at Fulton's Crab House and some shopping at World of Disney."

For information about upcoming Downtown Disney activities, call 407/939–2648.

Downtown Disney Marketplace

The Marketplace section of Downtown Disney, not surprisingly, is full of shops. A good place to start is the World of Disney, the largest Disney store on Earth. You can find a bit of everything here.

Another must-see is Once Upon a Toy, the ultimate shop for Disney-theme toys. (It goes without staying that this can be an expensive stop on your tour!) Kids also enjoy Team Mickey's Athletic Club, which sells sporting equipment and clothes, and the Days of Christmas. The LEGO Store is just amazing, with enormous LEGO sea serpents, spaceships, and life-size people scattered around the lagoon, as well as a play area where kids can build their own models.

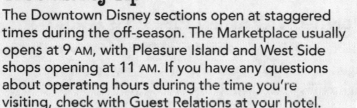

Time-Saving Tip
The Downtown Disney sections open at staggered times during the off-season. The Marketplace usually opens at 9 AM, with Pleasure Island and West Side shops opening at 11 AM. If you have any questions about operating hours during the time you're visiting, check with Guest Relations at your hotel.

If money is no object, visit the Art of Disney, where you can find limited-edition cels and other collectibles. Scrapbook hobbyists will enjoy Disney's Wonderful World of Memories next door, which offers Disney scrapbook supplies.

The Rainforest Café is great fun because birds and fish (real) and rhinos and giraffes (fake) surround your table while you eat. Check out the bar stools with their flamingo and zebra legs. Long waits are standard at the Rainforest Café, but you can put in your name and shop while you wait.

Hidden Mickey

Look closely at the fountains near the entrance to the Marketplace. Does the shape look familiar?

The Marketplace has a small play area with a few simple rides and neat interactive splash fountains to keep younger kids entertained. You can also find the world's largest—and possibly only?—perikaleidoscope (a cross between a periscope and a kaleidoscope). Or venture down to the dock and rent one of the zippy Mouse Boats.

Insider's Secret

Downtown Disney is a great spot for the first night of your vacation. It doesn't require a ticket, but it still has plenty of Disney spirit.

Downtown Disney Pleasure Island

At Pleasure Island, the motto is "It's New Year's Eve every night!" The island comes alive at 7 PM each evening when seven nightclubs open their doors. A featured band puts on an outside show, winding down just before midnight, when the street party culminates in the New Year's Eve countdown.

Children under 18 are welcome if accompanied by a parent or guardian, except at Mannequins and the BET Sound-Stage. Although Pleasure Island is geared to adults, some families do bring the kids. This is a wholesome, Disneyesque nightclub environment, which means no raunchy material at the comedy club and no barroom brawls. Security is tight and disorderly conduct is not permitted. A mom from Maine wrote to us about taking her children there: "Some people say Pleasure Island isn't for kids, but our 10-year-old and 12-year-old loved the Comedy Warehouse."

Money-Saving Tip

The $20.95 admission gives you unlimited access
to all the clubs, and if you bought the Magic Plus
Pack option, you're entitled to free admission to
Pleasure Island. Periodically there are discounts
that drop the price of admission lower or increase
the number of evenings you can visit. Note that if
you just want to visit the shops and restaurants of
Pleasure Island, there's no admission charge until
7 PM, when the clubs open.

If you choose Pleasure Island for parents' night out and
want to make a real evening of it, get an in-room sitter for the
kids. Most hotel services close down at 11 PM or midnight, and
if you want to stay at PI for the street party, you won't be back
until after that. With an in-room sitter, the kids can go to bed
at their usual hour.

Pleasure Island Touring Plan

@ Arrive around 8 PM. Take in the Comedy Warehouse first.
(The dance clubs don't gear up until later.) These 30-
minute shows, a mix of skits and improv, are proof that
comedians don't have to be profane to be funny. Because
much of the material is improvised, you can return to the
Comedy Warehouse several times in an evening, seeing an
essentially different act each time. This is also the best
Pleasure Island club for teens and kids.

@ For something completely different, try the Adventurer's
Club, a lavish, eccentric hideaway based on British hunt-
ing clubs of the 1930s. You won't be in the bar for long before you realize that some of your fellow patrons are

actors—and that the bar stools are sinking and the masks on the walls are moving.

@ At 8 Trax, polyester and disco are still king. It's fun to watch the fortysomethings sitting in their beanbag chairs, valiantly pretending that they don't remember the lyrics to ABBA and Bee Gees tunes.

@ Divide your remaining time between the four dance clubs: The Rock 'n' Roll Beach Club offers a live band and an informal pool-shooting, beer-drinking, resort-style ambience. Mannequins is darker and wilder with a DJ, light effects, and a revolving dance floor. At Motion the music is Top 40 and dancers are surrounded by videos on oversize screens. The BET club plays soul, R&B, and hip-hop music. Sometimes there are concerts featuring contemporary BET artists: call 407/939–2648 for details.

@ Be back outside for the street party (sometimes 11 PM, sometimes midnight) and countdown to New Year's.

Downtown Disney West Side

The West Side is home to a variety of shops and restaurants, a 24-screen AMC theater, and a Virgin Megastore, which sometimes has concerts out front. You can also find two of Disney World's hottest attractions: DisneyQuest and Cirque du Soleil.

Bongos Cuban Café offers an Americanized version of Cuban dishes, a wild tropical decor, and throbbing Latin music. The House of Blues serves up Cajun and Creole cooking along with live jazz, country, and blues music. The Gospel Brunch from 10:30 AM to 1 PM on Sunday is an especially good choice for families. The price is $31 for adults and $16 for kids 3 to 9. Tickets can be purchased by calling 407/934–2583 (407/934–BLUE).

Wolfgang Puck Café serves terrific pizzas and sushi downstairs. Request the upstairs dining room for tonier adult dining.

Insider's Secret

Few Downtown Disney restaurants accept advance reservations and the restaurants can get very packed. You can always put your name in and browse the shops while you wait, or plan to have dinner around 5 PM before the crowds show up.

The giant blue globe of Planet Hollywood holds props from a variety of movies, and even the menus—printed with high school graduation pictures of stars—are entertaining. Film clips run constantly on giant screens and the atmosphere is loud and cheerful.

DisneyQuest

Most people call DisneyQuest an arcade simply because there isn't another name that could identify this totally new type of play environment. Within its five levels, you will indeed find all the classic arcade games, but also high-tech interactive experiences that almost defy description. Favorites include Pirates of the Caribbean, where you literally take the deck to battle phantom buccaneers, and Virtual Jungle Cruise, an exhausting river-raft ride in which riders paddle through the rapids of a prehistoric world. During your stay you can also battle comic book villains, rescue settlers from an uprising on a foreign planet, shoot foam

Time-Saving Tip

DisneyQuest can become overwhelmingly crowded in the evening, on weekends, and on rainy days. To make sure you have the chance to try out everything, visit at opening time on a weekday morning.

balls at your competitors in a bumper-car war, and become a human joystick in a hockey-style pinball game.

The centerpiece attraction of DisneyQuest is CyberSpace Mountain. Bill Nye the Science Guy helps you design your own virtual roller coaster. You can build in as many flips, spirals, and hills as time and distance allow; program in the speed of the car; and even get to name the sucker. When you're finished your coaster is given a scariness rating from 1 to 5, meaning that you can either design a gentle, rolling, grade-1 coaster suitable for kids or a flip-you-over, slam-you-down, grade-5 coaster. (If you end up with a coaster too mild or too wild, you can always redesign it.) Then you enter a booth where you're strapped into a capsule, and you ride a virtual re-creation of the coaster you just designed, complete with spins and flips.

Helpful Hint

DisneyQuest is large and loud, and each play zone has steps leading to other levels. In other words, it's easy to lose your kids. If you're going to let older kids and teens explore on their own, pick a designated time and place to regroup—perhaps the Cheesecake Factory, an upstairs restaurant, for a snack.

Needless to say, preteens and teens can get hooked on this stuff very fast, and DisneyQuest is primarily designed for the 10–20 set. (Some parents drop off teens at the arcade while they relax at one of the West Side restaurants.) But there's entertainment for younger siblings as well, and any age can enjoy the gentle arcade games like Skeeball or the Create Zone where you can design your own toy or learn to draw a Disney character.

DisneyQuest usually opens at 10:30 AM during the on-season and 11:30 AM during the off-season. A single entry price ($34 for adults, $28 for kids 3 to 9) lets you play as long and as

Helpful Hint

No strollers are allowed inside DisneyQuest, and there are a lot of stairs. Plan accordingly.

much as you like—an alarming thought for the parents of a 12-year-old boy. Admission is also included with the Magic Plus Pack option.

Cirque du Soleil

After a week at Disney World, probably the last thing you're itching to do is to buy an expensive ticket to watch an acrobatic show. But the Cirque du Soleil show *La Nouba* positively wowed the families we surveyed.

Cirque du Soleil has a three-tiered pricing structure. General tickets are $75 for adults and $56 for kids ages 3 to 9, but you can upgrade to premium tickets in the centrally located seats for $87 for adults and $65 for kids 3 to 9. During the off-season specially priced tickets are sometimes available for $59 for adults and $44 for kids 3 to 9. The 90-minute show normally runs Tuesday through Saturday twice daily (usually at 6 PM and 9 PM). For reservations, details, and specific pricing for the dates you'll be visiting, visit www.cirquedusoleil.com or call 407/939–7600.

Although the athleticism and agility of the troupe will amaze you, it's their ability to use props, sets, costumes, and their bodies to set a mood and tell a story that makes the Cirque du Soleil experience so unique. Don't expect any elephants or people being shot out of cannons—Cirque performances are more like theater than traditional circuses. Cirque du Soleil can best be appreciated by kids ages 8 and up.

Helpful Hint

It can take quite a long bus ride to get to Downtown Disney West Side where Cirque du Soleil is located, even from an on-site hotel. Since the resorts often share buses to Downtown Disney, and since the West Side stop is last once you get there, you'll have to sit through several stops before you arrive. The moral? Drive if you can, but if you're taking a bus to Cirque du Soleil leave your hotel an hour and a half before showtime.

BoardWalk and the ESPN Club

Not up for the sprawl of Downtown Disney? At night, the shops, restaurants, and nightclubs in front of the BoardWalk Resort take on a whole new glitter. You can find plenty of low-key entertainment—face painting, hair braiding, midway games, and sometimes comics and magic acts—along the waterfront. Eat dinner at the Flying Fish Café if you're feeling fancy, then rent a surrey bike ($18 to $24 for 30 minutes, depending upon size) for a lap around the lagoon.

The ESPN Club is a good stop for sports enthusiasts. The center contains a broadcast and production facility (meaning celebrity athletes are sometimes on hand) and serves up—and I quote—"the best ballpark cuisine from around the country." This bold claim translates into sandwiches, salads, and burgers, all sized for hearty appetites.

Two BoardWalk clubs are open strictly to adults 21 and older. The Atlantic Dance Club changes format frequently but is presently offering DJ-spun Top 40 dance music without a cover charge. (For details, call 407/939–2444.) Jellyrolls is a sing-along piano bar with lots of audience participation. (On weekends there may be a cover charge of $5 to $10.) Either club is a good alternative to Pleasure Island if you'd like a bit of

Insider's Secret

If you're at Disney World during football season, drop by the ESPN Club. The place is always mobbed with fans from all across the country cheering on their teams and it feels like Super Bowl every Sunday. Seventy TVs make sure you don't miss a single play—TVs even hang inside the stalls in the bathroom! Be sure to pack your team jersey.

adult entertainment but don't have the stamina for full-throttle club hopping.

The fact that the BoardWalk is not as vast and crowded as Downtown Disney appeals to many visitors; you can have a good meal and some entertainment without getting back into the mouse race. And at night, with the glowing Yacht and Beach Clubs visible across the water and the fireworks of Epcot in the distance, the BoardWalk ranks as one of the most beautiful spots in Disney World. Pull up a rocker and let the world go by.

On-site guests can take monorails or buses to any theme park and then transfer to the BoardWalk bus. If you're staying at the Yacht and Beach Clubs, the Swan, or the Dolphin, just walk. Off-site guests can either park in the BoardWalk lot or pay for the $8 valet parking, which is worth it on weekend evenings when the regular lot is crowded.

Disney Extras

Dinner Shows and Character Breakfasts

Book any dinner shows you would like to attend before you leave home by calling 407/939–3463 (407/WDW–DINE). Reservations are accepted up to two years in advance and are especially important for the popular Hoop-Dee-Doo Musical

Revue, which requires a lot of hoop-dee-doo just to get tickets. The on-site dinner shows include the following:

- The Hoop-Dee-Doo Musical Revue plays three times nightly (at 5, 7:15, and 9:30 PM) at Pioneer Hall in Fort Wilderness campground. You can dine on ribs, fried chicken, and strawberry shortcake while watching a lovably hokey show that includes lots of audience participation. The cost is $49 for adults and kids 12 and up, $25 for children 3 to 9.

- The Spirit of Aloha is presented seasonally in the open-air theater in Luau Cove at the Polynesian Resort. You can enjoy authentic hula dancing, traditional music, Lilo and Stitch, and a Polynesian feast. The cost is $49 for adults and kids 12 and up, and $25 for children 3 to 9.

- Mickey's Backyard Barbecue is presented seasonally at Fort Wilderness and features a country band, line dancing with the characters, and picnic food such as barbecued chicken and corn on the cob. The price is $38 for adults and kids 12 and up, $25 for children 3 to 9. The barbecue is decidedly rowdier than other Disney dinner events. A mother of four from New York wrote, "The closest we came to a never-again moment was Mickey's Backyard Barbecue. It was a free-for-all with characters and kids running loose on the dance floor. On the other hand, the Polynesian luau was a delight, with plenty of entertainment for the kids but a much calmer atmosphere."

If you're staying off-site and don't want to return to Disney World in the evening or if you've waited too late to book a Disney show, be advised that Orlando is chock-full of family-style dinner shows, many of which can be booked on the same day you want to attend. Pick up a free local Entertainment Guide (www.entertainment.com) at your hotel to check out what's playing. (The entertainment guides have discount coupons as well.)

Character Dining

The character meals are time-consuming and expensive, but families with kids 9 and under give them very high marks. It's not about the food, which is usually fine—it's about the chance to have the characters actually visit your table so that there's plenty of time for pictures, hugs, and autographs. Prices run $19 to $29 for adults and $11 to $13 for children, with the more elaborate Sunday brunches being slightly more expensive. Reservations can be arranged 180 days in advance by calling 407/939–3463 (407/WDW–DINE).

Insider's Secret
Since dining will take about two hours, try to book the first character breakfast of the day. Families who have scheduled character breakfasts on the last day of their visits have also noted that a long breakfast coincides well with the usual 11 AM check-out time at most Orlando hotels.

At present Disney is offering the following character meals, but note that times, places, and prices change often so call to confirm the information before you book the meal. (Note: Kids' prices are for children ages 3 to 9. And any character meal that takes place inside a theme park requires theme park admission.)

In the Resorts
- Cape May Café, Beach Club Resort—Seaside picnic breakfast buffet with Goofy and friends ($19 adults, $11 kids).

@ Chef Mickey's, Contemporary Resort—Party with Mickey and other classic characters ($19 adults, $11 kids for breakfast; $29 adults, $11 kids for dinner).

@ My Disney Girl's Perfectly Princess Tea Party—For the ultimate princess experience, pull out your wallet, take a deep gulp, and head to the Grand Floridian for the Perfectly Princess Tea Party. Held daily from 10:30 to noon, the tea party includes a meet-and-greet with Princess Aurora from *Sleeping Beauty,* plus storytelling, sing-alongs, and a princess parade. (Needless to say, all little girls wear their princess gear for this one.) Tea party guests receive a My Disney Girl collectible doll, ribbon tiara, bracelet, and special princess scrapbook. The cost for one child is $200, additional children are $135 each, and adults are $65. Reservations can be made at 407/939–3463 (407/WDW–DINE).

@ 1900 Park Fare, Grand Floridian—Circus-theme breakfast with Mary Poppins characters ($19 adults, $14 kids). Dinner is with Cinderella characters ($29 adults, $14 kids).

@ Ohana's, Polynesian Resort—Luau breakfast with Mickey and friends ($19 adults, $11 kids).

Insider's Secret

If you're going to a princess character breakfast, it's only fitting that little girls wear their full princess regalia for the event.

In the Magic Kingdom

@ Cinderella's Royal Table in Cinderella Castle—Once Upon a Time medieval banquet breakfast with princess characters ($22 adults, $12 kids).

Insider's Secret

The "Once Upon a Time" princess breakfast at Cinderella's Royal Table is so popular with swooning little girls that it's nearly impossible to book. For dates in summer, it often sells out within minutes of the reservation line opening. Your best bet is to call *exactly* 180 days in advance at *precisely* 7 AM. Call 407/939–3463 (407/WDW–DINE). For less busy times of the year, calling 90 days in advance is sometimes enough. Otherwise consider the equally regal princess-theme buffet at Akershus in the Norway pavilion at Epcot.

@ Crystal Palace   Three meals a day with Pooh and friends ($19 adults, $11 kids for breakfast; $21 adults, $11 kids for lunch; $28 adults, $11 kids for dinner).

@ Liberty Tree Tavern—Traditional Thanksgiving dinner with Minnie and friends ($28 adults, $11 kids).

In Epcot

@ The Garden Grill Restaurant in the Land Pavilion— Country cooking with Mickey and the gang ($22 adults, $12 kids for lunch; $22 adults, $12 kids for dinner).

@ Akershus in Norway—Breakfast, lunch, and dinner buffets in a castle setting with Belle, Jasmine, and other princess characters ($22 adults, $12 kids).

Helpful Hint

If you like to spend your mornings in the theme parks, plan your character meal for lunch or dinner, when you'll welcome the chance to rest during a leisurely meal.

In the Animal Kingdom

- @ Restaurantosaurus in DinoLand—Donald and other paleontology students help guests "Dig into Breakfast" ($19 adults, $11 kids).

Mickey's Very Merry Christmas Party

Disney World is at its most magical during the holidays. Hours are extended, special parades and shows debut, and the parks and hotels are beautifully decked. If you fantasize about seeing it snow on Main Street, this is your chance. (We're talking real snow here—generated from the rooftops along Main Street and billowed down on the crowd below.)

Tickets for Mickey's Very Merry Christmas Party, a holiday celebration with shows and parades held in the Magic Kingdom on selected evenings, should be purchased well in advance by calling 407/934–7639 (407/W–DISNEY). Disney World often offers special holiday packages in late November and early December, and these usually include tickets to Mickey's Very Merry Christmas Party.

The week between Christmas and New Year's is the absolute busiest of the year at WDW, but it's possible to celebrate the holidays at Disney without being caught in the crush. Decorations go up just after Thanksgiving and the special shows and parades debut shortly thereafter; the first two weeks of December are among the least crowded of the year and thus the perfect time to celebrate Christmas at Disney (assuming, of course, that your child's school schedule can accommodate the trip).

Each resort puts up its own theme decorations as well—a nautical tree for the Yacht Club, seashell ornaments at the Beach Club, Native American tepees and animal skulls for the Wilderness Lodge, the enormous Victorian dazzler at the Grand Floridian. The resort-theme decorations, in fact, are so

Helpful Hint

While Mickey's Very Merry Christmas Party and Not-So-Scary Halloween Party are great fun, they are such crowded events that it's not a particularly good time to try out the rides. Ride another day, and spend your party evening focusing on the special activities and shows.

gorgeous that holiday tours of the Disney hotels are popular among Orlando locals.

Mickey's Not-So-Scary Halloween Party

On selected evenings during the last two weeks of October, the Magic Kingdom hosts Mickey's Not-So-Scary Halloween Party. As the name implies, this celebration is geared toward younger kids, with fortune-tellers, face painters, and trick-or-treating throughout the park; parades featuring the characters in costume; and a special fireworks finale. Be sure to bring along everyone's Halloween costumes.

Insider's Secret

If you have preteens and teens who are up for a gorier scene, check out the super scary Halloween Nights event at Universal Studios.

Helpful Hint

Advance tickets for Mickey's Not-So-Scary Halloween Party are a must, so call 407/934–7639 (407/W–DISNEY) before you leave home. The party runs several times during the weeks before Halloween but the October 31 party always sells out first.

Tours for Kids and Families

Most of Disney's behind-the-scenes tours require that guests be 16 and up to participate, but there are three programs at the Grand Floridian that are created specifically for kids and one tour in the Magic Kingdom that is designed for families with children of all ages.

These programs are not only great fun for the kids, but also a bargain at $28 per child, which includes lunch and an hour or two of child care. At present prices you'd pay $16 for two hours of child care (not to mention there's a four-hour minimum for most services) and about $5 for a child's lunch, so the program is pretty much a gimme. Most importantly, children love the programs so much that they're being offered on more days of the week to accommodate the demand. Reserve your child's place before you leave home, preferably at the same time that you make reservations for your meals.

Disney's Pirate Adventure

This rollicking two-hour boat tour takes kids on a treasure hunt across the Seven Seas Lagoon with stops at all the Magic Kingdom resort marinas. Counselors help kids collect clues and complete a map that ultimately leads them to buried treasure. It's a good choice for active kids in the 4 to 10 age range. Lunch is served on the pontoon boat after the last stop and everyone leaves with a goody bag of treasure. "My six-year-old son loved the Pirate Adventure at the Grand Floridian," reported one mom from New York. "It's very reasonably priced and since I'm a single parent I have to confess it was wonderful to just have an hour to lie by the pool while he was on tour."

The Adventure currently departs the Grand Floridian marina at 10 AM on Monday, Wednesday, and Thursday. Kids ages 4 to 10 may participate in this child-only event that costs $28. For reservations, call 407/939–3463 (407/WDW–DINE) 90 days in advance.

Wonderland Tea Party

Kids join two characters (generally Alice in Wonderland and the Mad Hatter) for a tea party held at 1900 Park Fare in the Grand Floridian. The table is festively decorated and a full lunch is served, but this is a tea party in reverse, so naturally the children start with dessert. Afterward, the characters lead them in a variety of games and each child leaves with a souvenir photo of him- or herself with the characters.

The Wonderland Tea Party is served weekdays from 1:15 to 2:30 PM for kids ages 4 to 10 (no moms!) and the cost is $28. For reservations, call 407/939–3463 (407/WDW–DINE) 90 days in advance.

Grand Kid Adventures in Cooking

In order to start things off on an appropriately messy note, the children decorate their aprons and chef hats by dipping their hands in different colors of paint and then pressing them on their costumes. After a cleanup session, a restaurant chef helps them make a special treat such as chocolate chip muffins or strawberry shortcake. When the food is finished, the kids, in their chef hats and aprons, parade to the Grand Floridian lobby to serve their fellow guests, including their parents, samples of what they've baked.

Adventures in Cooking is a child-only event for kids ages 3 to 10 and is held Tuesday and Friday from 10 to 11:45 AM. The cost is $28. For reservations call 407/939–3463 (407/WDW–DINE) 90 days in advance.

Family Magic Tour in the Magic Kingdom

Everyone gets into the act on this tour; while the activities are geared to kids ages 3 to 10, parents

Insider's Secret

Looking for a way to kill an hour or two while the kids participate in one of the Grand Floridian programs? The spa is just around the corner.

and both younger and older siblings can come along. The only rule is that you have to be willing to act silly.

Your tour guide meets you at Guest Relations in the Magic Kingdom and sets up the premise of the tour. Perhaps Peter Pan has stolen Captain Hook's favorite hook and the captain is so furious that his band of buccaneers is threatening to take over the whole Magic Kingdom. In order to stop him, you must follow a map that takes you around the park—hopping, skipping, hiding, and keeping an eye out for each new clue.

At the final stop of the tour you can meet up with a character or two and have a special closing surprise. For example, if you get Peter Pan out of trouble, he'll appear and thank you by being your personal tour guide on Peter Pan's Flight. (Peter Pan is presently the star of the tour, but there have been different scenarios in the past and probably will be in the future, so don't make any specific promises to the kids.) The tour is a great option for families who have been to the Magic Kingdom several times and are looking for a new spin.

The Family Magic Tour is held weekdays from 10 AM to noon and the cost is $25 per person, regardless of age. Call 407/939–8687 (407/WDW–TOUR).

That Sportin' Life: on Water

Most on-site hotels have lovely marinas with a variety of watercraft for rent; for off-site guests, a fleet awaits at the Buena Vista Lagoon in Downtown Disney Marketplace.

But the major water recreation area of WDW is the Seven Seas Lagoon in front of the Magic Kingdom. Marinas at the Grand Floridian, Polynesian, Contemporary, Fort Wilderness, and Wilderness Lodge all service the lagoon, and you don't have to be a guest of the resort to rent watercraft. (Although you will need to show either a driver's license or a resort ID.)

Reservations are a good idea, especially in the on-season,

and it also never hurts to confirm prices before you go. Call 407/939–7529 (407/WDW–PLAY) for more information.

Water sport options include the following:

Boat Rental

The Disney fleet includes Mouse Boats ($28 for 30 minutes), canopy boats ($30 for 30 minutes), sailboats ($27 for 60 minutes), pontoons ($40 for 30 minutes), pedal boats ($10 for 30 minutes), and canoes ($9 for 30 minutes). The marina staff can help you decide which watercraft best fits your needs.

The most popular are the Mouse Boats, those zippy little two-passenger speedboats you see darting around the Buena Vista and Seven Seas Lagoons. Drivers must be at least 14 years old and 5 feet tall, although kids of any age will enjoy riding along beside Mom and Dad.

Insider's Secret
By far the best place to rent Mouse Boats in all of Disney World is the Seven Seas Lagoon. You have plenty of room to explore and can really pick up some speed. The boats are for rent at the marinas in the Contemporary, Polynesian, and Grand Floridian resorts or Wilderness Lodge.

Waterskiing

Ski boats complete with instructors and full equipment can be rented at the Contemporary Resort marina. The cost is $150 an hour for up to five guests and reservations can be made 180 days in advance by calling 407/939–7529 (407/WDW–PLAY).

Fishing

Fishing equipment is for rent at Downtown Disney, Coronado Springs, Fort Wilderness, and the Port Orleans Resort, Riverside section. If you'd like a bit more action than simply dropping a line, two-hour fishing tours for parties of up to five people depart from numerous water locations throughout WDW, including special excursions for kids 6 to 12. Reservations can be made up to 180 days in advance; call 407/939–7529 (407/WDW–PLAY) for exact times, locations, and prices.

Surfing

Surfing lessons are offered at Typhoon Lagoon on select mornings before the park opens. Participants must be at least 8 years old and strong swimmers. For those up to the challenge, this clinic ($155 per person) is one of the most fun things to do in all of WDW. Because the waves are controllable and the instructors are top-notch, almost everyone can ride a wave by the end of the class. Call 407/939–7529 (407/WDW–PLAY) for details.

Parasailing

Another high-thrill activity is parasailing. Excursions leave daily from the Contemporary Resort marina and the 10-minute flights cost $85 for one person or $170 for two riders in tandem. At your top height of 500 feet above the lake you can see all four parks. The Sammy Duvall Watersports Center also offers wakeboarding and tubing. For more information call 407/939–0754.

Specialty Cruises

Two of the greatest ways to spend an evening in Disney World are watching the Magic Kingdom fireworks or the pyrotechnics of *IllumiNations* at Epcot. And there's no classier viewing spot than aboard your private boat. At present, there are three separate ways to rent watercraft for an evening cruise, but the cruises are so popular that Disney may be adding more options soon. You can reserve a boat 180 days in advance by calling 407/939–7529 (407/WDW–PLAY).

The *Grand 1* is a 45-foot Sea Ray that holds up to 12 people; even though it's moored at the Grand Floridian marina, it can pick up guests at any of the Magic Kingdom resorts. Cruise parties head out to the middle of the Seven Seas Lagoon for a perfect view of the Magic Kingdom fireworks. The cost is $350 an hour and the price includes a captain and deckhand.

If you'd rather view *IllumiNations* up close, consider the open-air motorboat called *The Breathless,* which departs from the Yacht and Beach Club marina. *The Breathless* holds up to 7 people, and rents for $235 an hour, including captain.

The final option is the pontoon boats, which are available for both Magic Kingdom and Epcot viewing. While a little less posh than the first two options, the view is exactly the same. You can seat up to 10 people for $235 an hour, which includes a driver.

When you factor in how many people can participate in the experience, the specialty cruises are actually a pretty cost-effective way to create a memorable evening for the whole family. Just be sure to reserve well in advance.

That Sportin' Life: on Land

Biking

Bikes are for rent at most on-site hotels at a cost of $10 an hour or $28 a day; helmets are free.

Golf

There are six courses on WDW grounds with greens fees running anywhere from $60 to $200 for Disney World resort guests and $75 to $225 for day guests. With such pricey fees, anyone planning to try out all the courses should consider a package that includes unlimited golf. The WDW Golf Studio offers private instruction and clinics for both adults and juniors. Call 407/939–4653 (407/WDW–GOLF) for details.

Health Clubs and Spas

The Contemporary, Grand Floridian, Swan, Dolphin, Yacht and Beach Clubs, BoardWalk, Animal Kingdom Lodge, Coronado Springs, Old Key West, and Saratoga Springs resorts all have health clubs. The rates range from $12 to $17 a day, with reduced length-of-stay rates. The most complete workout facility is at Saratoga Springs.

There are full-service spas at the Grand Floridian, Saratoga Springs, and Animal Kingdom Lodge. "My seven-year-old daughter had her first manicure at the Grand Floridian spa and was in heaven," a mom from New York wrote. "She felt very grown up and the manicurist was the sweetest cast member I've ever met—even at Disney World where everybody is nice!"

Horseback Riding

Guided trail rides leave the Fort Wilderness grounds four times a day. Children must be at least 9 to ride; the horses are gentle and the pace is slow. The cost is $35 for a 45-minute tour and reservations can be made up to 30 days in advance by calling 407/939–7529 (407/WDW–PLAY).

Younger kids can ride the ponies at the Fort Wilderness Petting Zoo while older siblings are on the trail ride.

Helpful Hint

Fantasia Fairways is much too tough for kids under 10, and even Fantasia Gardens is a fairly difficult course. Winter Summerland is a better choice for the preschool and grade school set.

Miniature Golf

Fantasia Gardens, just across from the Disney-MGM Studios, is real eye candy—an 18-hole minigolf tribute to the movie *Fantasia* with dancing hippos, orchestrated fountains, and the

Sorcerer's Apprentice running the whole show. A second course, Fantasia Fairways, is a miniature version of a real golf course, with sand traps, water hazards, and roughs. Although you play with a putter, the holes are 100 feet long and difficult enough to drive a veteran golfer to curses.

The second miniature golf complex at Disney World is Winter Summerland (located beside Blizzard Beach), where you're greeted with the question "Would you like to play in snow or sand?" Your first clue that there's strange weather ahead is that Santa, his sleigh pulled by flamingos, has crash-landed on the roof and skidded through a snowbank/sandbank into the wackiest campground on earth. You can opt to play either the icy white "greens" of the winter course, where you can find a hockey rink, a snow castle, and slalom ski runs, or the sandy shores of the summer course, where the Beach Boys serenade you amid pools, waves, and barbecue pits.

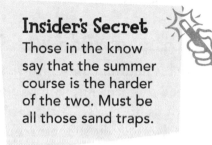

Insider's Secret
Those in the know say that the summer course is the harder of the two. Must be all those sand traps.

Rates at Fantasia Gardens, Fantasia Fairways, and Winter Summerland are $12 for adults, and $10 for kids 3 to 9. Reservations are not necessary, but to verify opening hours during the time you'll be visiting, call 407/939–7529 (407/WDW–PLAY).

Running

Trails cut through the grounds of nearly every Disney resort. Consult Guests Services for ideas on the best route around your particular hotel. Wilderness Lodge, with its invitingly shady trails, is an especially good choice if you're visiting in summer when even morning runs can be steamy.

Tennis

Several on-site resorts (the Contemporary, the Grand Floridian, the Yacht and Beach Clubs, BoardWalk, Old Key West, Saratoga Springs, the Swan, and the Dolphin) have tennis courts, and the Contemporary also offers daily clinics for guests 10 and older. There's considerable variation in rental rates and reservation policies, so call 407/939–7529 (407/WDW–PLAY) for details.

Disney's Wide World of Sports

This multimillion-dollar sports complex hosts competitions and tournaments, with facilities to accommodate 25 different kinds of sports. It's the spring training camp of the Atlanta Braves and the summer training camp of the Tampa Bay Buccaneers. You can also find a branch of the All Star Café, a huge sports bar with multiple screens and interactive games.

Activities at the Wide World of Sports vary widely, so call 407/939–4263 or visit www.disneyworldsports.com before you leave home to find out what will be going on during your visit. If there's something that catches your fancy, admission is $10 for adults, $7 for kids 3 to 9. Getting to the Wide World of Sports is tricky. There's no direct bus service, so the trip, with transfers, can take about 90 minutes each way. Drive if you can; if you don't have a car, consider calling a cab.

CHAPTER

11

Dining at Disney

Full-Service Restaurants at Disney

You've come to ride, but you also need to eat. The good news is that the variety and quality of the on-site restaurants has vastly improved in the 17 years I've been doing this guide. The bad news is that the size of the crowds has also increased, making it more of a hassle to get into the restaurants.

Unless you want to eat fast food for every meal, you should make your dining reservations before you arrive, preferably when you book your hotel. Sure, there's a chance you can get a last-minute reservation *if* you're visiting during the off-season, and *if* you're not picky about the time and the place, and *if* you reserve early enough on the day of, but who wants to waste precious morning time—the best time of day to ride the rides—trying to navigate the reservations system? Your best bet is to make advance reservations so you don't have to think about where you're eating every night.

Making Reservations

Disney finally abandoned the awkward phrase "priority seating" and changed it to "advance reservations." Although the language is different, the system is still much the same, and works like this: a reservation doesn't hold the restaurant to a specific time for seating you but rather guarantees you the next available table after you arrive.

Let's say you made advance reservations for four people at 7 PM. When you show up at 7, your table won't be waiting with your name on it, but you will be given the next available table for four. Waits average between 10 and 30 minutes under the system, but it's still far better than walking in with no prior arrangement.

So how do you make reservations? You call 407/939–3463 (407/WDW–DINE) up to 180 days in advance of the day for which you want reservations. Admittedly, this requires some planning. Ideally, you'll sketch out a general schedule for each day and evening of your vacation, so you'll know that on Tuesday you're having dinner at Epcot and on Saturday you're having a character breakfast.

Helpful Hint

If you really can't plan out your schedule ahead of time, take the safe route and book your dinners at restaurants in your on-site hotel. That way you'll be ready for an early bedtime and an early morning the next day. If you get a last-minute reservation at another restaurant, you can always cancel your first reservation or simply not show up.

Insider's Secret

You can make multiple reservations for different restaurants at the same time, although it's bad form not to cancel the others once you've made up your mind which restaurant to attend. Also, there's no penalty for not showing up for a reservation, except at some experiences like the Once Upon a Time character meals, where a credit card deposit is required. As a rule, it's better to overbook than underbook, especially if you're traveling at a busy time.

If you've arrived at Disney without dining reservations, you can try to get last-minute slots by calling 407/WDW–DINE as soon as you know where to eat. Don't hesitate to call using your cell phone while you're waiting in line for a ride. If you're staying at an on-site hotel, you can also press the dining button on your hotel room phone. You won't get Saturday night seating at California Grill by waiting until you get there, but if you're pretty flexible about where you eat and when you eat, finding last-minute reservations is possible.

You can also try to reserve in person at the restaurants or at dining reservations booths throughout the parks. At MGM drop by the reservations booth at the corner of Sunset Boulevard and Hollywood Boulevard. At the Animal Kingdom, none of the restaurants allow advance reservations except for character meals. To see if there are any openings for Donald's Breakfast at Restaurantosaurus, check with AK Guest Relations. At the Magic Kingdom, go to the restaurant itself or City Hall. At Epcot, which offers the best shot of getting into a restaurant at the last minute thanks to the sheer number of them, go to Guest Relations at Innoventions Plaza, to the left of Spaceship Earth as you enter. At Downtown Disney, go directly to the

Helpful Hint

If you're worried that the kids will get antsy during a full-service dinner, rest assured that Disney is all about getting the food out fast. The kiddie menus have games and puzzles, and waiters will bring out crayons, crackers, and drinks with lids to keep the kids busy while you wait.

restaurant where you want to dine, or stop by Guest Relations. If you're staying off-site and would like to dine at a restaurant inside a Disney resort, let the concierge or front desk staff at your own hotel handle it, or call 407/939–3463 (407/WDW–DINE) once you arrive in Orlando.

Best Fast-Food Restaurants for Families

IN THE MAGIC KINGDOM:
COSMIC RAY'S STARLIGHT CAFÉ

There's plenty of seating, the line moves fast, and they have sandwiches and salads in addition to the usual hamburgers and chicken fingers.

AT EPCOT: SUNSHINE SEASONS

Several cuisines are served at various counters, so each family member can choose a completely different meal and then meet up at the same table.

AT DISNEY–MGM STUDIOS:
TOY STORY PIZZA PLANET

Good pizza, fast service, and an arcade combine to keep the kids happy.

IN THE ANIMAL KINGDOM: TUSKER HOUSE

The most health-conscious counter-service eatery in Disney World, with plenty of flavor to boot.

Best Character Meals

AKERSHUS PRINCESS STORYBOOK MEALS

All the princesses except Cinderella (who stays in her castle) show up at breakfast, lunch, and dinner here. You get to meet Snow White, Ariel, Belle, Aurora, Jasmine, Mulan, Alice, and more.

CHEF MICKEY'S

The best character meal for kids who want to meet the classic Disney characters like Mickey and Donald.

THE CRYSTAL PALACE

Pooh fans love to meet Tigger, Piglet, and, of course, Winnie the Pooh, at this Magic Kingdom restaurant.

Best Restaurants for a Parents' Night Out

CALIFORNIA GRILL

Real foodies love this romantic restaurant in the Contemporary Resort with a view of the Magic Kingdom fireworks show.

JIKO

Exquisite contemporary African food paired with fabulous South African wines make this Animal Kingdom Lodge restaurant one of the best in Orlando.

VICTORIA AND ALBERT'S

Pure elegance and flawless cuisine make this posh restaurant in the Contemporary Resort perfect for a special celebration.

Finding Healthy Food

Restaurants that serve meals meeting the low-fat standards set by the American Heart Association are indicated with a red heart on your theme park map. Chefs at most full-service restaurants are willing and able to adapt recipes, serving sauces on the side or leaving out forbidden ingredients.

Fruit stands are throughout all four parks and they make it easier for families on the move to select grapes instead of chips or juice instead of the omnipresent soft drink.

Many of the fast-food counters offer salads and sandwiches as alternatives to burgers and pizza. A mother of three from New York noted, "It was great to find out that Disney offers pre-packaged kosher meals of hamburgers, hot dogs, and chicken nuggets at Cosmic Ray's in the Magic Kingdom. The meals were $8.95 each and they also had a kosher microwave."

> **Helpful Hint**
> Eating on the run? Information about fast food is found within each theme park chapter.

> **Helpful Hint**
> Restaurant hours are sometimes changed or shortened during the off-season, but signature restaurants are always open.

Rating the Disney Restaurants

The restaurant descriptions that make up the bulk of this chapter cover only full-service sit-down restaurants. Let's face it, most fast-food places are pretty similar and there's only so much you can say about burgers, fries, and soft-serve ice cream. Therefore, we decided not to overwhelm you with full descriptions of all of the 100-plus food service venues throughout Walt Disney World and to focus this chapter on the full-service restaurants, where you're apt to be spending more time and more money and will thus have higher expectations.

Definition of Quick-Guide Ratings

Food Quality

★★★   Exceptionally good

★★   Tasty food

★   Okay in a pinch

Price for an Adult Meal Comprising a Main Course and an Appetizer

$$$ Expensive; about $20 and up

$$ Moderate; about $15

$ Inexpensive; about $10

Advance Reservations

Not Offered: This restaurant does not accept advance reservations unless you have a party of 10 or more. You can show up at an off-time and get a buzzer—a big, flat beeper that vibrates when your table is ready—and shop nearby while you wait for your table.

Recommended: This restaurant draws average-size crowds. In high season, it'll fill to capacity, so you should make reservations at least several days in advance. If you're touring in the off-season or dining at off-hours, you should be able to walk in and get a table.

Necessary: This is a popular restaurant. If you haven't made advance reservations, you'll probably be closed out.

Suitability for Kids

High: The restaurant is informal, with food choices designed to appeal to kids. There may be some sort of entertainment going on or perhaps the setting itself is interesting.
Moderate: This restaurant is casual and family oriented.
Low: This is one of WDW's more adult restaurants with sophisticated menu choices and leisurely service.

Meals Served

B is for breakfast, *L* is for lunch, and *D* is for dinner.

Magic Kingdom Restaurants

The Crystal Palace ★★★

The Crystal Palace buffets are particularly good, including even those most elusive of all WDW foods—vegetables. Winnie the Pooh and friends circulate among diners. Because buffets allow even the pickiest of eaters to find something they like and because of the presence of the characters, the Crystal Palace is perfect for families. There's even an ice-cream sundae bar where kids can make their own gooey creations. Consider this report from a Texas mother of two: "In general I dislike buffets, but the food here was far better than I expected, and our children absolutely loved the sundae bar. (Even though things got so messy that we did have to change their shirts after lunch!) The Crystal Palace would be a good choice even if it didn't have the Pooh characters."

Advance reservations are necessary unless you're eating at an odd time, like 3 PM.

Quick Guide to Full-in the Magic

Restaurant	Description	Location
Cinderella's Royal Table	Dine in the castle with the princess characters	Fantasyland
The Crystal Palace	Buffet dining with Winnie the Pooh and friends	Main Street
Liberty Tree Tavern	Thanksgiving-style feast with the characters	Liberty Square
The Plaza Restaurant	Don't miss the sundaes	Main Street
Tony's Town Square Restaurant	*Lady and the Tramp* theme and Italian classics	Main Street

Cinderella's Royal Table ★★

High amid the spires of Cinderella Castle in Fantasyland, this restaurant is the most glamorous in the Magic Kingdom. Prime rib is one of the specialties and all the dishes, even at lunch, are whimsically presented.

Cinderella appears downstairs at various times throughout the day to greet diners. (Ask what times she is scheduled to appear when you make reservations.) This restaurant is also the home of the extraordinarily popular "Once Upon a Time" princess character breakfasts and lunches. Remember to book early. A mother of two from Virginia reported, "It took us three days to get through the phone line for the princess breakfast in the Magic Kingdom, but it was well worth it! My four-

Service Restaurants Kingdom

Rating	Price	Advance Reservations	Suitability	Meals Served
★★	$$$	Necessary	High	B, L, D
★★★	$$	Necessary	High	B, L, D
★★	$$	Recommended	High	L, D
★★	$$	Recommended	Moderate	L, D
★★	$$	Recommended	High	L, D

year-old daughter wore her Cinderella dress, and she loved all the special attention she received. It was a year ago and she still talks about it."

Liberty Tree Tavern ★★

In Liberty Square and decorated in a style reminiscent of colonial Williamsburg, the Tavern serves salads, sandwiches, and New England clam chowder at lunch. The evening menu is an all-you-can-eat Thanksgiving-style feast with turkey and stuffing, flank steak, mac and cheese, and other family favorites. The Disney characters, dressed in cute Revolutionary War–era garb, visit with guests in the evening.

The Plaza Restaurant ★★

The salads, sandwiches, and burgers served at the Plaza are very filling. The restaurant is also known for its wide selection of ice-cream treats, which are trotted over from the Sealtest Ice Cream Parlor next door.

Tony's Town Square Restaurant ★★

Located in the Main Street Hub, this thoroughly enjoyable restaurant is dedicated to *Lady and the Tramp*, with scenes from the film dotting the walls and a statue of the canine romantics in the center. The cuisine, like that of the café where Tramp wooed Lady, is classic Italian, and the portions are generous.

Epcot Restaurants

Akershus ★★★

The Norwegian buffet at Akershus (which one parent described as "all the herring you can eat") never really caught on, so this lovely castlelike restaurant in the Norway pavilion is shifting its buffet menu to include more American staples.

Even better, Akershus has princess-theme character dining at breakfast, lunch, and dinner. This should take some of the pressure off the unbelievably popular "Once Upon A Time" breakfast in the Magic Kingdom, but you'll still need to make reservations months in advance.

Bistro de Paris ★★★

The Bistro is quieter, calmer, and more elegant than its sister, Les Chefs de France, located below it. It's also a tad too civilized for kids under 12. Expect classic French cuisine, a wonderful wine selection, and Continental service.

Les Chefs de France ★★

Modeled after the sidewalk cafés of Paris, this restaurant is as romantic as they get. It has a classical French menu and you can gaze out at the World Showcase action. Adults and older kids will appreciate it best.

Le Cellier ★★★

Le Cellier is one of the most popular restaurants in Epcot, perhaps because there are relatively few steak houses in Disney World. The steaks here are excellent, as is the salmon, and the desserts are as big as the prairies of Alberta.

Coral Reef ★★

One whole wall of this restaurant is glass, giving diners a remarkable view of the Living Seas tank. Watching the fish keeps the kids entertained while parents browse the menu, which features, naturally, upscale seafood dishes.

The Garden Grill ★★

Easily recognizable American dishes, served family style, make this a good choice for younger children. The restaurant is on a revolving platform, allowing diners to observe scenes from the Living with the Land boat ride below. Best of all, the characters (dressed like farmers) circulate among the diners.

L'Originale Alfredo di Roma Ristorante ★★

The Alfredo in question is the gentleman who created fettuccine Alfredo, the specialty of the house. All pasta is made on the premises and the trompe l'oeil paintings make this one of the most visually interesting restaurants in Epcot.

Quick Guide to Full-

Restaurant	Description	Location
Akershus	Authentic Norwegian cuisine and princess character buffets	Norway
Biergarten	Rousing, noisy atmosphere and live entertainment	Germany
Bistro de Paris	Classic French cuisine— very elegant, very adult	France
Coral Reef	Great views of the Living Seas tank	Living Seas pavilion
Garden Grill Restaurant	American dishes and the Disney characters	Land pavilion
Le Cellier	Great steaks, excellent salmon, huge desserts	Canada
Les Chefs de France	Like a Paris sidewalk café	France
L'Originale Alfredo di Roma Ristorante	House specialty is fettucine Alfredo	Italy
Marrakesh	Exotic food and surroundings, belly dancers	Morocco
Nine Dragons	Cuisine representing every region in China	China
Rose & Crown Dining Room	Pub atmosphere and live entertainment	United Kingdom
San Angel Inn	Beautiful, romantic setting	Mexico
Teppanyaki	Dining room chefs slice and dice before your eyes	Japan

Service Restaurants at Epcot

Rating	Price	Advance Reservations	Suitability	Meals Served
★★★	$$	Necessary	High	B, L, D
★	$$	Recommended	High	L, D
★★★	$$$	Necessary	Low	D
★★	$$$	Necessary	High	L, D
★★	$$	Recommended	High	L, D
★★★	$$$	Recommended	Low	L, D
★★	$$$	Necessary	Moderate	L, D
★★	$$$	Necessary	Moderate	L, D
★★	$$	Recommended	Moderate	L, D
★★	$$	Recommended	Low	L, D
★★	$$	Recommended	Moderate	L, D
★★	$$	Recommended	Moderate	L, D
★★	$$$	Necessary	High	L, D

Marrakesh   ★★

Ready for exotic surroundings and unusual entertainment? Kids enjoy the belly dancers and the ladies sometimes invite them to enter into the act. The unfamiliarity of the food may pose a problem, but if the kids can be persuaded to give it a try, they can find that roasted chicken tastes pretty much the same the world over.

Nine Dragons   ★★

There isn't much entertainment in the dignified Nine Dragons, which has food from every region of China. But the staff is quite happy to accommodate youngsters' special requests such as, "Can you hold the sweet-and-sour sauce on the sweet-and-sour chicken?"

Rose & Crown Dining Room   ★★

This charming bar and restaurant has live entertainment, friendly service, and pub grub such as fish-and-chips and meat pies. If you opt to eat outside on the patio, you have a great view of the World Showcase Lagoon.

San Angel Inn   ★★

A beautiful location inside the Mayan pyramid of the Mexico pavilion, with the Rio del Tiempo murmuring in the background, makes this restaurant a charming choice. The service is swift and friendly and older kids can browse among the market stalls of the pavilion or even ride El Rio del Tiempo while waiting for their food.

Teppanyaki Dining Room   ★★

In the Japan pavilion, Teppanyaki offers grilled specialties at large tables, in front of which the chefs slice and dice in the best

Benihana tradition. It's terrifically entertaining for the kids—the chefs often jazz up the presentation even more in their honor—and the stir-fried, simply prepared food is a hit with all ages. A father of four from Ohio wrote a rave review: "Japan is a good choice if you want to eat out in Epcot with kids. The chefs toss food and catch it in their hats, make silly jokes like throwing the butter and saying 'butterfly,' and one time when we were in they had a lady making origami animals for the children. Plus, since they cook at the table, you get your food a lot faster than at most Epcot restaurants."

Biergarten ★

There's plenty of room to move about in this German beer hall where yodelers and an oom-pah-pah band get the whole crowd involved in singing and dancing. The all-you-can-eat buffet features traditional Bavarian dishes such as bratwurst, spaetzle, and salads.

Restaurants at Disney-MGM Studios

The Hollywood Brown Derby ★★★

A signature Cobb salad as well as veal, pasta, and fresh seafood are served at the Derby, where, just as you'd expect, caricatures of movie stars line the walls. The food is quite sophisticated considering that you're inside a theme park, and the restaurant itself is elegant and lovely, like stepping back into Hollywood at its heyday. The price for the *Fantasmic!* Dinner Package is $36.99 for adults, $10.99 for kids 3–10, not including drinks.

50's Prime Time Café ★★

With its kitsch decor and ditzy waitresses dressed like June Cleaver, this restaurant is almost an attraction in itself. Meat loaf, macaroni, milk shakes, and other comfort foods are served

Quick Guide to Restaurants

Restaurant	Description
50's Prime Time Café	Want to star in a 1950s sitcom?
Hollywood & Vine	Large, attractive buffeteria
Hollywood Brown Derby	Elegant and lovely with upscale cuisine
Mama Melrose's Ristorante Italiano	Good food, good service, wacky ambience
Sci-Fi Dine-In	Campy; you eat in cars at a drive-in theater

in a 1950s-style kitchen, while dozens of TVs blare clips from classic shows in the background.

"Hi kids," says your waitress, pulling up a chair to the Formica-top table. "You didn't leave your bikes in the driveway, did you? Let me see those hands." Assuming you pass her clean-fingernails inspection, "Mom" will go on to advise you on your food choices. "I'll bring peas with that. Vegetables are good for you." The camp is lost on young kids, but they nonetheless love the no-frills food and the fact that Mom brings around crayons and coloring books, then hangs their artwork on the front of a refrigerator with magnets. But it's the baby-boomer parents, raised on the sitcoms that the restaurant spoofs, who really adore this restaurant. "You just have to get in the mood of the place," advised a mother of one from Illinois. "The whole rou-

Full-Service at MGM

Rating	Price	Advance Reservations	Suitability	Meals Served
★★	$$	Recommended	High	L, D
★★	$	Recommended	High	L, D
★★★	$$$	Recommended	Low	L, D
★★	$$	Recommended	Moderate	L, D
★★	$$	Recommended	High	L, D

tine about being on a TV show is very corny and very funny and the servers are great. We liked the food (chicken, pot roast, steak, salads, potatoes, the basics), but when we left my eight-year-old daughter said 'That was a good show' and I think that's exactly the way you need to think of it."

Hollywood & Vine ★★

This large, attractive, art deco "buffeteria" offers a wide variety of classic American and Continental dishes at breakfast, lunch, and dinner. Because the lines move steadily, this restaurant is fairly easy to get in to without advance reservations. The price for the *Fantasmic!* Dinner Package is $23.99 for adults, $11.99 for kids 3–10, including fountain drinks.

Mama Melrose's Ristorante Italiano ★★

This restaurant is tucked away near the Muppet*Vision 3-D plaza and the out-of-the-way location means that you can sometimes squeeze in without advance reservations. Expect a casual New York feel and quick service. The restaurant serves gourmet flatbreads from a wood-burning oven and a wide variety of pasta dishes; the Penne alla Vodka is a favorite. The price for the *Fantasmic!* Dinner Package here is $29.99 for adults, $10.99 for kids 3–10, not including drinks.

Sci-Fi Dine-In Theater Restaurant ★★

At least as campy as the 50's Prime Time Café, the Sci-Fi seats diners in vintage cars while incredibly hokey movie clips run on a giant screen. Food offerings range from drive-in staples

Quick Guide to Full-in the Animal

Restaurant	Description
Rainforest Café	Animal Kingdom's only full-service restaurant

like milk shakes and popcorn all the way to seafood and St. Louis–style ribs. Kids adore the setting and the funny waiters; in fact they often get so absorbed in the old movie clips that they sit quietly while parents relax in the backseat. (Be sure to ask about the light-up ice cubes. At the Sci-Fi, even the Cokes are happening!)

Animal Kingdom Restaurants

Rainforest Café ★★

The jungle motif and large aquariums make the Rainforest Café great fun for kids. The food is nothing special, but tasty enough, with an emphasis on appetizers, like spring rolls and veggie wraps, and other simple meals, like burgers, sandwiches, and huge salads. There are locations at both the Animal King-

Service Restaurants
Kingdom

Rating	Price	Advance Reservations	Suitability	Meals Served
★★	$$	Not accepted	High	B, L, D

dom and Downtown Disney. The latter doesn't accept advance reservations; take a buzzer and shop while you wait.

Restaurants in the WDW Hotels

Artist Point   ★★

The most upscale of the Wilderness Lodge eateries, Artist Point offers excellent Pacific Northwest–theme food in a casual, almost rustic, setting. The salmon is the house specialty, and the wine list highlights excellent selections from the Pacific Northwest.

Big River Grille & Brewing Works   ★

WDW's only on-site brewpub is a good place to sample new beers and a couple of specialty ales. The food—mostly sand-wiches and salads—is pedestrian, but the pleasant patio allows you to take in the action of the BoardWalk while you sip your beer.

bluezoo   ★★

Famed chef Todd English brought this sleek, upscale seafood restaurant to the Dolphin. Although it's far too tony in atmos-phere and eclectic in menu for most kids, bluezoo is a good spot for drinks or a parents' night out. The menu changes reg-ularly but tends to feature unusual seafood dishes, such as the butter-poached Maine lobster with truffle-potato ravioli.

Boatwright's Dining Hall   ★

The only full-service restaurant in Port Orleans is this casual dining hall in the Riverside section. The Cajun cooking is very tame and classic American dishes round out the menu. The room is not walled, located beside the food court, and thus al-ways noisy.

Boma ★★★

This large family restaurant in the Animal Kingdom Lodge offers one of the best breakfast buffets in all of WDW. You can find the usual American classics, like eggs and pancakes, plus excellent grilled sausage, sometimes made with unusual African game, and an outstanding selection of breads and pastries. The dinner buffet features African-inspired dishes, including wonderful grilled meats. You get plenty of value for your money. "This is by far the best deal in Disney World," agreed a mom from Georgia. "The food was fresh and beautifully prepared and we stuffed ourselves. Both the kids and the adults loved it."

California Grill ★★★

Widely acknowledged to be the best restaurant in all of Disney World, the California Grill is very popular and always crowded. (One clue to the quality: Disney executives dine here.) Not only is the food excellent and stylishly presented, but the views from the top of the Contemporary are unparalleled, especially during the Magic Kingdom fireworks.

Cape May Café ★★★

Our readers give high marks to this bright and airy eatery in the heart of the Beach Club. It has an excellent seafood buffet at dinner, featuring shrimp, clams, mussels, and a couple of land-lubber choices. The breakfast buffet, during which the characters dressed in adorable old-fashion bathing attire circulate among the diners, is very popular. Consider this report from a grandmother of four from Ohio: "We wouldn't consider it a trip to Walt Disney World without a stop at the Beach Club's Cape May Café. It's a family tradition and the food is wonder-

Quick Guide to Full-
in the

Restaurant	Description	Location
Artist Point	Fine dining in a rustic setting	Wilderness Lodge
Big River Grille & Brewing Works	Casual restaurant and brewpub	BoardWalk
bluezoo	Fine seafood in a sleek, upscale setting	Dolphin
Boatwright's Dining Hall	Southern dishes and tame Cajun	Port Orleans, Riverside
Boma	African-inspired buffet and great breakfasts	Animal Kingdom Lodge
California Grill	The best of all	Contemporary
Cape May Café	Character dining at breakfast, clambakes in the evening	Beach Club
Chef Mickey's	Character dining while the monorail zooms by	Contemporary
Citricos	Gourmet cuisine and an outstanding wine list	Grand Floridian
Concourse Steakhouse	Excellent burgers and steaks	Contemporary
Coral Café	Buffets in the evening	Dolphin
ESPN Club	The perfect place to watch the big game	BoardWalk
Flying Fish Café	Excellent seafood and steaks	BoardWalk
Grand Floridian Café	Great variety, southern classics	Grand Floridian
Gulliver's Grill at Garden Grove	Whimsical décor, basic food	Swan

Service Restaurants WDW Hotels

Rating	Price	Advance Reservations	Suitability	Meals Served
★★	$$$	Recommended	Low	D
★	$$	Not accepted	Moderate	L, D
★★	$$$	Necessary	Low	D
★	$$	Recommended	Moderate	B, D
★★★	$$	Recommended	Moderate	B, D
★★★	$$$	Necessary	High	D
★★★	$$	Recommended	High	B, D
★★	$$	Necessary	High	B, D
★★★	$$$	Necessary	Low	D
★★	$$$	Recommended	Moderate	B, L, D
★	$$	For large parties only, recommended	Low	B, L, D
★	$	Not accepted	Moderate	L, D
★★★	$$$	Necessary	Low	D
★★	$$	Recommended	Moderate	B, L, D
★★	$$	Recommended	Moderate	B, L, D

(continued)

Quick Guide to Full-
in the

Restaurant	Description	Location
Jiko	African-influenced cuisine, South African wines	Animal Kingdom Lodge
Kimonos	Sushi in an elegant setting	Swan
Kona Café	Pacific Rim food with a tropical emphasis	Polynesian
Maya Grill	Latin American–inspired cuisine	Coronado Springs
Narcoossee's	Great fresh seafood; view of MK fireworks	Grand Floridian
1900 Park Fare	Buffet-style character dining	Grand Floridian
'Ohana	Family-friendly, with island entertainment	Polynesian
Palio	Gourmet Italian in a colorful setting	Swan
Shula's	Linebacker-size steaks in a dignified atmosphere	Dolphin
Shutters	Casual island fare	Caribbean Beach
Spoodles	Tapas and pizza in a casual setting	BoardWalk
Victoria and Albert's	The most elegant restaurant on Disney property	Grand Floridian
Whispering Canyon Café	Comfort food, family-style service	Wilderness Lodge
Yacht Club Galley	Cheery and bright—a cut above a coffee shop	Yacht Club
Yachtsman Steakhouse	One of the premier steak houses in Disney World	Yacht Club

Service Restaurants
WDW Hotels

Rating	Price	Advance Reservations	Suitability	Meals Served
★★★	$$$	Recommended	Moderate	D
★★	$$	For large parties only, recommended	Low	D
★★	$$	Recommended	Moderate	B, L, D
★	$$	Recommended	Low	B, D
★★	$$$	Recommended	Low	D
★★	$$$	Necessary	High	B, D
★★	$$	Recommended	High	B, D
★★	$$$	Recommended	Moderate	D
★★★	$$$	Recommended	Low	D
★	$$	Recommended	Moderate	D
★	$$	Recommended	Moderate	B, D
★★★	$$$	Necessary	Low	D
★★	$$	Recommended	High	B, L, D
★★	$$	Recommended	Moderate	B, L, D
★★	$$$	Recommended	Low	D

ful. We always leave the theme parks in the afternoon to take a nap, and Cape May is the perfect place to eat dinner before you go back into Epcot to see *IllumiNations.*"

Chef Mickey's ★★

The Contemporary Resort is one of the best places in Disney World for a character breakfast or dinner. As Mickey and the crew wander among the diners, the monorail whisks by overhead. The buffet has classic American breakfast food in the morning and family-pleasing standards like pasta, chicken, and roast beef in the evening, plus a sundae bar for the kids. A father of three from New Jersey echoed the reports of many of our readers: "Chef Mickey's is definitely the way to go if you want to see the basic old-fashioned Disney characters like Mickey and Goofy. The buffet was great and the characters spent plenty of time with our sons."

Citricos ★★★

Citricos offers southern French cuisine in the Grand Floridian and the restaurant is known for its outstanding wine list. Up to 20 labels are available by the glass, with a specific wine paired with each appetizer and entrée on the menu. A real treat for a parents' night out.

Concourse Steakhouse ★★

The Steakhouse, in the cavernous lobby of the Contemporary Resort, offers all the beef you'd expect, as well as chicken and pasta. It's a nice getaway spot for lunch if you're in the Magic Kingdom—the burgers are outstanding.

Coral Café ★

With breakfast and dinner buffets as well as an à la carte menu, the Coral Café is the largest restaurant in the Dolphin Resort. Picture an upscale coffee shop with long hours and casual food and you have the idea.

ESPN Club ★

Anchoring one end of the BoardWalk, the ESPN Club is better known for broadcasting sports events than for its food. "Our teenaged sons loved going to the ESPN Club on a Sunday during football season," wrote one mom of three from Pennsylvania. "The place was packed with people from all over the country, all wearing jerseys and screaming for their teams. We should have packed our Eagles jerseys—next time we'll know!" Menu choices include buffalo wings, burgers, nachos, and, of course, plenty of beer. There's an arcade next door to entertain the kids. Of course, the Club is packed on weekends when big games are broadcast.

Flying Fish Café ★★★

The zany art deco decor is by Martin Dorf, who also designed the California Grill and Citricos. The menu is updated frequently but generally includes wonderful seafood, delicious steaks, and excellent risottos. If you haven't made reservations, you can always dine at the bar and watch the chefs at work.

Grand Floridian Café ★★

If you'd like a good solid meal of traditional favorites, simply served, with a pretty view of the Grand Floridian grounds, this café is for you. The menu tilts a bit to the south—fried chicken, local fish, and key lime pie.

Gulliver's Grill at Garden Grove ★★

This is the largest restaurant in the Swan and it has a bit of a split identity. In the morning and at lunch, it's an upscale coffee shop. In the evening it becomes Gulliver's Grill, with more elaborate dining and characters on hand to entertain the kids.

Jiko ★★★

Jiko (Swahili for "cooking place") is the flagship restaurant of the Animal Kingdom Lodge, and the menu features contemporary African cuisine with an emphasis on fresh vegetables, grains, and game. Two wood-burning stoves simulate the effect of cooking in the open bush. The interesting wine list is exclusively South African. "Very exotic with wonderful food and a lovely setting," reported a father of two from New York. "Our server was extremely knowledgeable about the South African wines. We'll be back!"

Kimonos ★★

If you love sushi and sashimi, you'll adore this elegant restaurant in the Swan Resort. The food is fresh and delicious, and karaoke keeps things lively in the evenings.

Kona Café ★★

The Kona Café offers Pacific Rim food with a tropical emphasis. The crab cakes are delicious, and the desserts alone make the Kona worth the trip.

Maya Grill ★

The Maya Grill serves steak, pork, chicken, and seafood with a nuevo Latin touch. Many of the entrées are grilled over an open fire.

Narcoossee's ★★

Inside the white octagonal building on the water at the Grand Floridian, Narcoossee's offers exceptionally pretty views as well as fresh seafood. You get a pretty good view of the Magic Kingdom fireworks from here.

1900 Park Fare ★★

This large, pleasant Grand Floridian restaurant is appealing to families because it offers character dining and large buffets with kid-pleasing food. Alice in Wonderland and her friends are on hand to greet the kids. Be forewarned—this place is always loud, even when the characters aren't in attendance.

'Ohana ★★

A fun, family-friendly place—the name, in fact, means "family" in Hawaiian—in the Polynesian Resort, 'Ohana specializes in skewed meats, teriyaki- and citrus-base sauces, and tropical fruits and vegetables. The food is prepared in a large, open fire pit, and there is often some sort of activity, such as limbo contests, to keep the kids entertained. "This place is a blast," a mom from North Carolina wrote to us. "The food is good and they get it out fast, but the really nice thing is all the activities for the kids, like crazy relay races and hula lessons. We sat down at the table, ordered some of those big tropical umbrella drinks, and just relaxed and watched the kids have a ball. The only bad thing was that there was so much going on our youngest son never got around to eating his dinner. The nice waitress said this happened all the time and boxed it for him to take back to the room."

Palio ★★

The Swan is home to this trattoria, which serves wonderful pasta in a pleasant, open setting. *Palio* is Italian for "flag," and, indeed, many brightly colored flags hang from the rafters.

Shula's ★★★

The Dolphin's swankiest steak house is owned by former Miami Dolphin coach Don Shula. (Nice tie-in!) The restaurant is quite dignified, despite the football theme, and you'll need an NFL-size appetite to finish the 48-ounce Porterhouse or 4-pound lobster. Note: This is not, repeat not, a family restaurant. The menu pointedly says "No children's menu available."

Shutters ★

Shutters, in the Caribbean Beach Resort, is a casual island-theme restaurant serving prime rib, lamb chops, and jerk chicken. If you just can't go to Florida without sampling a big, fruity rum drink, this is your kind of place.

Spoodles ★

Although it was a family favorite for years, at this writing we've received numerous bad reviews about both the tapas-style cuisine and the service at Spoodles. We'll reevaluate the restaurant for the next edition, but until then we recommend selecting one of the other BoardWalk restaurants.

Victoria and Albert's ★★★

Extraordinarily elegant cuisine and special attention to details, such as personalized menus, harp music, and roses for the ladies, are the hallmark of this lovely restaurant. The only AAA five-diamond restaurant in WDW (and the most expensive), V&A is the ultimate spot for a parents' night out.

Whispering Canyon Café ★★

Kids can saddle up and ride stick ponies to their table at this family-style eatery in the Wilderness Lodge. All-you-can-eat barbecue dinners are brought to the table in cast-iron buckets, or you can order à la carte. If you like home cooking in a casual atmosphere where the kids can get a bit rowdy, Whispering Canyon is a good bet.

Yacht Club Galley ★★

This restaurant, off the main drag in the Yacht Club Resort, serves up fish, chicken, and beef in a pleasant nautical-theme room. The breakfast buffet offers hearty eaters the chance to load up for a day of touring.

Yachtsman Steakhouse ★★

I'm not sure how a yachtsman gets his hands on so much good beef, but this Yacht Club restaurant is one of the premier steak houses in Disney World. You can find a full selection of hand-cut steaks and chops with your choice of sauces, served up in a clubby dining room.

Restaurants in the Rest of the World

All-Star Café ★★

This sports bar is the only full-service restaurant at Disney's Wide World of Sports complex. TVs broadcast sporting events from every wall and the mood is loud, cheerful, and raucous, with plenty of games for the kids. Expect pasta, pizza, sandwiches, and burgers.

Quick Guide to Full-in the Rest

Restaurant	Description	Location
All-Star Café	Ultimate sports bar with cool games for the kids	Disney's Wide World of Sports
Bongos Cuban Café	Americanized versions of Cuban dishes	Downtown Disney West Side
Fulton's Crab House	Fine dining on a riverboat	Pleasure Island
House of Blues	Cajun and Creole cooking with live music	Downtown Disney West Side
Planet Hollywood	Always fun, film clips run constantly	Downtown Disney West Side
Portobello Yacht Club	Northern Italian cuisine	Downtown Disney Pleasure Island
Raglan Road	Irish Pub with music and dance	Pleasure Island
Rainforest Café	Fun and funky atmosphere	Downtown Disney Marketplace
Wolfgang Puck Café	Terrific salads, pizza, and sushi	Downtown Disney West Side

Service Restaurants of the World

Rating	Price	Advance Reservations	Suitability	Meals Served
★★	$$	Not accepted	Moderate	L, D
★	$$	Not accepted	Moderate	L, D
★★★	$$$	Recommended	Low	L, D
★★	$$	Not accepted	Moderate	Sunday brunch, L, D
★★	$$	Recommended	High	L, D
★★	$$	Recommended	Low	D
NA	$$	Recommended	Low	L, D
★★	$$	Not accepted	High	B, L, D
★★★	$$$	Only upstairs, recommended	Moderate	L, D

Bongos Cuban Café   ★

Created by Gloria Estefan, Bongos delivers an Americanized version of Cuban dishes, such as black bean soup and grilled pork, a wildly tropical decor, and loud Latin music.

Fulton's Crab House   ★★★

Fulton's, on the moored *Empress Lilly* riverboat, offers seafood flown in fresh daily from all over the world. The raw oysters are always a treat.

House of Blues   ★★

Dan Aykroyd's House of Blues serves up Cajun and Creole cooking while a nightclub attached to the restaurant serves up the jazz, country, rock and roll, and, yes, blues music. The Gospel brunch on Sunday is an especially good choice for families. To find out who's playing or to purchase tickets call 407/934–2583 (407/934–BLUE).

Planet Hollywood   ★★

Planet Hollywood's giant blue globe holds numerous movie props, including the bus from *Speed,* which hovers menacingly overhead while you dine. Film clips run constantly and even the menus, which are printed with the high school graduation pictures of stars, are entertaining. Planet Hollywood is always loud and often packed, especially on weekends.

Portobello Yacht Club   ★★

Come here for classic Northern Italian cuisine, including veal, pasta, grilled chicken, and gourmet flatbreads. The desserts are a force to be reckoned with, and the patio is especially pleasant in spring and fall.

Raglan Road   Not yet rated

A life-size bronze statue of Irish poet Patrick Kavanaugh sitting lost in thought on a bench greets you outside this Irish pub in Pleasure Island. Inside are four, huge, wooden bars that were crafted in Ireland in the 19th century. As for the food, the classics go upscale, with Angus-beef shepherd's pie, and Colorado lamb in a sophisticated port wine sauce. A dive bar this is not— a pint of Guinness will cost you $6.50.

Rainforest Café   ★★

This sister restaurant to the Animal Kingdom location serves casual food in a jungle-theme atmosphere. Most kids love the Rainforest Café, but the music can get very loud, which may bother babies and toddlers. Waits can be long in the evening and advance reservations are not presently available, so take a buzzer and shop around the Marketplace while you wait.

Wolfgang Puck Café   ★★★

There are three parts to this restaurant—the ultracasual Express, which offers salads, sandwiches, and such; the inside restaurant, which provides Puck's signature pastas and pizzas, as well as outstanding sushi; and, upstairs, the formal dining room, serving the best Puck has to offer. Needless to say, the first two locations work best for families, and the latter is best reserved for a parents' night out.

CHAPTER

12

Disney
After Dark

Disney World After Dark with the Kids

Is there life in Disney World after 8 PM? Sure there is. The crowds thin, the temperature drops, and many attractions are especially dazzling in the dark. During peak seasons the major theme parks run extra-long hours, so it's easy to have fun at night. But, needless to say, the particular kind of fun you'll have depends on whether the kids are with you.

Evening Activities for the Whole Family

The Evening Parade in the Magic Kingdom

Disney's ever-popular evening parades blend lasers, lights, and fireworks for a dazzling display. Tinker Bell's Flight begins a few minutes before the parade, so be sure to look to the castle to watch her descent. Then, just after the parade, the fireworks begin.

The parade runs every night during the on-season and twice a night during the busiest weeks of the year. In the off-season it runs only on selected evenings, so plan your schedule to ensure you'll be in the Magic Kingdom on one of the nights it's slated to run. If you miss the parade, you can still get to see

Insider's Secret
On evenings when SpectroMagic runs twice, the 11 PM parade is rarely as crowded as the 9 PM one.

the *Wishes* fireworks since it always closes the evening. Times and dates are listed on your entertainment schedule; you can get this information in advance by calling Guest Relations at your hotel or visiting www.disneyworld.com.

Fantasmic!
This nightly closing show at MGM is a must-see. The combination of fantastic music, live actors performing cool stunts, lasers, fireworks, water screens, and favorite Disney characters makes for one spine-tingling show.

IllumiNations
At the risk of sounding like a broken record, *IllumiNations* fully ranks with *Fantasmic!* and SpectroMagic as a fantastic closing show that appeals to all ages. It can be viewed nightly from anywhere around the World Showcase Lagoon at Epcot closing time.

The Electrical Water Pageant
If you're staying on-site, the Electrical Water Pageant may actually float by your hotel window, because it's staged on the Seven Seas Lagoon, which connects the Polynesian, Contem-

Helpful Hint
Electrical Water Pageant times vary with the season, so contact Guest Services for the exact time the parade is scheduled to float by your resort. If you're not staying at a Magic Kingdom resort but would like to see the parade, plan to have dinner at one of the resorts in question, then wander out to the beach area at showtime.

porary, Grand Floridian, and Wilderness Lodge resorts. A much shorter and simpler show than SpectroMagic, the Electrical Water Pageant is a charming progression of moving multicolor sea images whose sparkling lights are reflected in the dark water.

Downtown Disney

Downtown Disney keeps hopping long after the theme parks shut down. Some families wait to shop and eat late at night. Kids under 18 are allowed into most of the Pleasure Island venues if accompanied by an adult.

BoardWalk

Lively and gorgeous after dark, the BoardWalk is a hub of family-style activity. Eat dinner, then rent a surrey bike for a quick lap around the lagoon. There are also a few good clubs here, but they're strictly for the 21-and-over set.

Miniature Golf

Evening is often the most comfortable time to check out Fantasia Gardens or Winter Summerland, especially in summer.

Night Swimming

Blizzard Beach and Typhoon Lagoon run extended hours in summer, and evening swimming can be a delight during the hottest weeks of the year. You don't have to worry about sunburn, and the crowds are much lighter. Hotel pools stay open late as well, many until after midnight.

Disney World After Dark Without the Kids: Finding a Sitter

Why would any decent parent seek a sitter while on a family vacation? Consider this scenario: Meaghan's sucking the inside of her mouth. Loud. Mom keeps making everyone stop while she readjusts the strap of her shoe to accommodate the blister she picked up halfway around the World Showcase Lagoon. You spent $168 to get through the Magic Kingdom gates—and

Devin spends two hours feeding quarters into the same arcade game that's in the mall back home. Dad has been singing the first line—and only the first line—of "Zip-a-Dee-Doo-Dah" since Thursday. You've asked to see the kiddie menus from nine different restaurants in nine different Epcot countries, and you end up at the American pavilion fast-food joint because Kristy won't eat anything but a hot dog. It's 108 degrees, this trip is costing $108 an hour, and that infernal sucking sound is getting on your last nerve.

Helpful Hint

Although it may seem un-American to suggest building time apart into the middle of a family vacation, the truth is that everyone will have more fun if you occasionally break up the group for a while. Even the most devoted of families aren't accustomed to being together 24 hours a day—for every meal, every ride, every potty stop. Every minute.

Some of the hotels in Orlando have responded with programs designed to get the kids involved with other children while parents have a night on the town. The idea is that everyone returns refreshed and recharged, with some happy stories to tell, and you can start the next day actually glad to be together again.

Quite a few off-site hotels have their own kids' clubs. Visit and tour the club before you drop your children off and make sure that the place seems clean, safe, and has an appropriate child-to-caregiver ratio.

On-Site Kids' Clubs

The following on-site hotels have kids' clubs (all numbers begin with area code 407):

Animal Kingdom Lodge	938–3000
BoardWalk	939–5100
Polynesian	824–2000
Contemporary	824–1000
Wilderness Lodge	824–3200
Dolphin	934–4000
Yacht and Beach Clubs	934–8000
Grand Floridian	824–3000

The clubs generally run in the evening for kids ages 4 to 12—and children must be toilet trained. The clubhouses are well stocked with toys, computers, video games, and large-screen TVs. The cost is generally $8 an hour. Make reservations by calling Guest Services at the appropriate hotel; on-site guests get first crack at the available slots, but if the clubs don't fill up, space is available to off-site visitors.

Helpful Hint
Prices, policy, and planned entertainment change quickly at the kids' clubs, so confirm everything when you make your reservations.

The clubs usually open at 4 or 5 PM and closing time varies. Obviously, if you'll be dining at a Disney resort, it makes sense to try to book your kids into that hotel's child-care program so that you can just drop them off, go on to your restaurant, and return to pick them up later. Parents are given pagers in case of emergencies,

Insider's Secret
The Polynesian offers the most elaborate kids' program: the Never Land Club, with buffet food and entertainment for the youngsters. The cost is $10 an hour; call 407/939–3463 (407/WDW–DINE) for reservations.

so this is a relatively low-stress way of handling child care in a strange city.

In-Room Sitters

Kids' clubs aren't always the way to go. You'll need to arrange for an in-room sitter if any of the following conditions apply:

- @ You have a child under the age of 4. That's the cut-off point for most group programs.

- @ You plan to be out after midnight. Most kids' clubs close down before then, some as early as 10 PM.

- @ Your kids are exhausted. If you know in advance that you plan to employ an all-out touring schedule or your kids fall apart after 8 PM, hire an in-room sitter who can put them to bed at their usual time. Most of the kids' clubs try to put preschoolers down in sleeping bags by 9 PM but this involves moving them, and probably waking them, when parents return.

- @ You have a big family. Even with the add-on per-child rate, you can come out cheaper with an in-room sitter than you will if you book four kids into a group program.

If you decide you'll need an in-room sitter, begin by contacting your hotel. Many hotels are happy to arrange sitting for you through a licensed and bonded agency and this saves a bit of hassle. The person at the Guest Relations desk is also apt to give you a good recommendation for which service to try; if former guests haven't been pleased with a sitter or service, the hotel is undoubtedly the first to hear about it.

For those staying on-site, Kids' Night Out provides trained sitters for all the Disney hotels; call 407/207–1300 at least eight hours in advance. And prepare for sticker shock. The rate is $13.50 an hour for one child, plus $2 per hour for each additional child, with a four-hour minimum.

At least six independent agencies dispatch sitters to the off-site hotels, but the following two agencies have received especially high marks from our readers:

ABC Mothers	407/857–7447
Super Sitters	407/382–2558

Child-care services stay busy during the summer months, so it's not a bad idea to book them before you leave home. Rates are typically about $10 an hour with a four-hour minimum and an extra-child charge of $2 an hour per child. An $8 transportation fee is also common, meaning that in-room sitting for two kids for four hours runs close to $50. Not cheap, but for many parents it's well worth the cost.

Insider's Secret
No matter what child-care option you choose, the key point is to make your plans in advance. If you suddenly get an urge for fine dining at 4 PM on a Saturday in July, it will be hard to find a sitter or get into a kids' club. But if you've checked out your options and reserved space in advance, planning an adult night out is a breeze.

Dining Without the Kids
The following five restaurants are especially adult oriented and a good choice when the kids aren't along.

Victoria and Albert's
Where Disney has built a reputation on providing entertainment to the masses, this 60-seat, AAA five-diamond restaurant in the Grand Floridian proves that there's also room in Disney World for highly individual service. At Victoria and Albert's, harp music plays, candles flicker, menus are personalized, ladies are presented with roses, and people still dress up for dinner.

The six-course prix-fixe dinner presently costs $99 per person, or $150 if you have wine paired with each course, but it's an experience so elaborate that you'll be talking about it for years afterward. For example, on the evening we visited, the salad was a floral arrangement in a crouton vase—until our server, who called herself Victoria in keeping with the theme, tapped the side of the crouton with a spoon. It then broke, releasing the greens into a fan-shape pattern on the plate. We were nearly hypnotized by the ceremony. This is by far the most elegant and refined restaurant you'll find on Disney property.

Insider's Secret

What's more special than an evening at Victoria and Albert's? An evening at the chef's table. Visitors are seated inside the kitchen where Executive Chef Scott Hummel treats them as his private guests. The chef's table is the proverbial "once in a lifetime" gourmet experience and you need to reserve months in advance. Call 407/939–3463 (407/WDW–DINE) for details.

California Grill

Not only does the California Grill offer marvelous cuisine with stylish preparation, but the views from the top of the Contemporary are unparalleled. In terms of the quality and variety of the food, those in the know consider this the best restaurant on Disney property. A mom from New York agreed: "I'm a caterer so I know food, and I consider the California Grill to be by far the best restaurant in Disney World."

Bistro de Paris

The Bistro, upstairs from Les Chefs de France and accessible by a back staircase, is so lovely and secluded that you might forget you're in a theme park. The wine list is one of the best in Epcot, and the classic French fare is fabulous.

Citricos

Citricos, in the Grand Floridian, is the rising star of Disney fine dining. The menu features southern French cuisine, updated frequently to highlight seasonal ingredients, but Citricos is especially noteworthy for its wine selection, with many fine wines available by the glass.

Insider's Secret

Couples who are dining late may find themselves leaving a resort restaurant after the transportation system has closed down. You can either drive your own car or use Downtown Disney (whose buses run until 2 AM) as a transfer station. But if you've been making merry for several hours, driving yourself or attempting to negotiate a series of bus transfers is not a good idea. Instead, let the valets at the resort where you've been dining call you a cab. The cost from one end of Disney property to another is usually less than $10; fares to off-site locations average around $20.

Jiko

The "cooking place," as the name means in Swahili, serves truly innovative, sophisticated, well-spiced fare based on African cuisine. As an *amuse-bouche,* try the delicate pulled lamb in phyllo with onions and mint–cilantro chutney, or try the ahi tuna marinated in lemon and cumin. Your server will help you pair your main course (maize-crusted halibut, perhaps, or wood-grilled filet mignon) with a superb South African wine. Jiko has a refined look with roomy booths and a cooking island where chefs busily chop and prepare ingredients. Book well in advance.

CHAPTER

13

The Disney Cruise Line

The Cruise Vacation Package

Since debuting its first ship in 1998, the Disney Cruise Line (DCL) has made the idea of a cruise vacation much more appealing to families.

You have two ships and ergo two basic choices. The *Disney Wonder* makes three- and four-day runs to Nassau and Disney's private island, Castaway Cay. These shorter cruises can be combined with a three- or four-day stay at Walt Disney World as part of a land-and-sea package.

If you'd like to cruise for a whole week, the *Disney Magic* alternates between two seven-day itineraries. The Western Caribbean itinerary stops in Key West, Grand Cayman, Cozumel, and Castaway Cay. The Eastern Caribbean route stops in St. Maarten, St. Thomas, and St. John; some select Eastern Caribbean sailings include St. Lucia and Antigua.

Disney cruises are perfect for the family that needs a bit of everything in the course of a one-week vacation: time for the adults to relax alone and time together as a family. Families whose kids vary in ages are especially sold on the cruises. Because there are so many kids on board and the age categories in the youth programs are tight, it's equally likely that your 3-year-old and 13-year-old will each have found a friend by the end of the first day. Let's face it—nothing is more relaxing than a vacation where everyone is happy.

For more information, visit www.disneycruise.com or call 800/370–0097. You can also order a brochure and video through your travel agent. "We booked everything online but ordered the brochures just as a way to double-check everything," reported one father of three from New York. "We were glad we did because they're really cute and child-friendly and helped our kids visualize in advance what the ship would be like. The DVD is great too—almost like a free Disney movie."

The Land and Sea Package

Many first-time Disney cruisers opt for the Land and Sea package, which combines a stay at Walt Disney World with a three- or four-day cruise. (The only itinerary difference between the two is that the longer cruise has a full day at sea.) It's a good way to get the best of both worlds.

Most families begin their trip at Walt Disney World. You're met at the Orlando airport and escorted directly to your resort where you'll find all the documentation you need for the entire week. After the theme park segment of the trip is over, you're transported by a special DCL bus to the ship, which waits in Port Canaveral harbor, approximately 90 minutes from Orlando.

Disney does everything possible to make the transition "seamless"; the key to your Orlando hotel room is also the key to your stateroom on the ship and you can use it as a charge card both at Disney World and onboard the ship. Your bags are picked up from your hotel room and transferred directly to your room on the ship. In short, the logistics of checking in and checking out, arranging transportation, and lugging baggage are all handled for you.

Helpful Hint
Although it's possible to reverse the order, most families like touring first and cruising last. That way the relaxing cruise segment follows the more exhausting theme park segment of the week.

Cruise Only Packages

If you've already visited Disney World, you might want to opt for a cruise-only package. Both three- and four-day Bahamas cruises are available, as well as seven-day cruises to multiple Caribbean islands, such as St. Maarten and St. Thomas, or Grand Cayman and Cozumel. You can study the various ports of call at www.disneycruise.com.

The seven-day cruises have the same perks as the three- and four-day cruises, but since they include more time at sea, some extras have been added—more stage shows, a pirate-theme evening for the whole family, champagne brunches, and special parties for the kids.

Approximate Costs

Calculating the exact cost of your cruise depends on several key factors: the time of year, the size of your family, and the level of cabin or stateroom you choose. It's probably a little too late to do anything about the size of your family, but the other two factors are within your control.

If you look at the price charts in the brochure, it seems that off-season savings aren't very significant. But the brochure is deceptive because it doesn't list specials. And DCL actually offers some very interesting specials during the off-season. These deals are available via www.disneycruise.com, travel agents, organizations like AAA, and independent travel Web sites like www.mousesavers.com. In other words, if you're going in the middle of summer or Christmas week, you'll probably end up paying close to the amount listed in the brochure. If you're going the third week of October, you should be able to snag some sort of discount and it may well represent a significant savings over the prices listed in the brochure.

Lodging also affects the bottom line. All staterooms on board are nicely appointed, designed for families, and therefore 25% larger than standard cruise ship cabins, so it's really just a matter of how much space you're willing to pay for and how posh a resort you want in Orlando. Guests booking a suite on the ship will stay at the Grand Floridian during the Orlando part of their vacation; families in an ocean-view stateroom with veranda will stay at a deluxe resort like the Polynesian or Beach Club; if you choose an inside stateroom on the ship, you'll stay at one of the mid-price resorts like Port Orleans while in Orlando.

> ### Insider's Secret
> When shopping for discounts leave no stone unturned—and make no assumptions. Although some families report that travel agents found them the best deals, others say that agents quoted higher rates than those given when they called Disney directly.

Your selection of resort and room has a major impact on the final price. For example, a family of four taking the full seven-day vacation in summer, and staying in a deluxe ocean-view stateroom during their cruise and the Beach Club Resort during the land segment of their vacation, will pay about $6,000. If that same family going that same week is willing to book a regular-size stateroom and stay at Port Orleans, the price drops to the $4,500 range.

There are ways to knock the price down further. People who book early usually get a discount. You can opt to simply take the three- or four-day cruise without the time in Disney World. And if you drive to Orlando you save the cost of airfare.

The cost of the cruise-only packages is slightly less than the price of the land–sea packages. During the off-season a three-night cruise for a family of four might start as low as $1,700. A four-night cruise starts at $1,900, and a seven-night cruise at about $3,400. The prices climb if you upgrade your stateroom or if you cruise during the on-season.

To check out all your options and figure exact costs, call 800/370–0097, talk to your travel agent, or visit www .disneycruise.com.

Other Expenses

One of the beauties of cruising is that most of your expenses are included in your package price. Here's a list of what *isn't* included.

Alcoholic beverages

Arcade games

In-room babysitting

Medical services

Merchandise bought on board or at ports of call

Palo, the adults-only restaurant on both ships, which charges a $10 per person cover

Photography

Ship-to-shore phone calls

Shore excursions

Spa treatments

Tipping (Disney suggests $4 a day for both your dining-room server and cabin steward and $3 a day for your dining-room assistant)

Lodging

Lodging is all about location and size. Your cruise brochure contains sketches of all the different staterooms, from the basic inside stateroom designed for three people to a two-bedroom suite that can sleep as many as seven. The majority of the staterooms are in the deluxe ocean-view category, many of them with verandas and most about 200–250 square feet. (In fact, nearly 75% of the cabins are outside staterooms, so if you're planning to save a few bucks by booking an inside stateroom, call early.)

Cruise veterans recommend that if you're doing the Land and Sea package you should focus more on the resort you'll be staying at in Orlando; on the short cruises you're so busy that you're rarely in your stateroom so it's no big deal if you're a little cramped. In contrast, when you're taking the seven-day cruise you'll be at sea for three full days, so the size and location of your stateroom are more important.

Dining

Disney makes dining on board very special. For starters you don't dine in the same restaurant every night. "We figured that a family on vacation wouldn't ordinarily eat at the same restaurant three nights in a row," says Amy Foley of the DCL. "So why would a family on a cruise ship want to eat in the same dining room every night?"

Insider's Secret
When you book your cruise, you'll have to choose your meal times: either early or late. The early seating means you have dinner at 6 PM, while the late seating is at 8:30 PM. If you have young kids the early seating works best, although it does mean a crack-of-dawn breakfast time. But I've seen preschoolers literally fall asleep at the table at late seatings—active days bring about early bedtimes. Besides, if you want to sleep in, you can always skip the full breakfast and grab something light at the Topsider buffet.

Instead you experience "rotation dining," trying a different onboard restaurant each evening of your cruise. (Your server and tablemates rotate right along with you.) On *Disney Magic,* there's Lumiere's, which is decidedly French and the most elegant of the eateries, with a theme based on *Beauty and the Beast.* On *Disney Wonder,* you can find upscale dining at Triton's, named for the Little Mermaid's father.

On both ships there's Parrot Cay, where the mood and the food are Bahamian and casual, but Animator's Palate is the real showstopper, an interactive dining experience in which the restaurant transforms into a brilliant palette of color as you dine. The meal begins in a room that is utterly black and white, right down to the framed animation sketches on the wall and the servers' somber attire. With each course, more color is added to the artwork, the walls, the table settings, and the servers' costumes. By dessert the whole room is glowing.

On both *Disney Magic* and *Disney Wonder*, adults have a fourth dining option, Palo, an Italian restaurant perched high atop the ship, offering a sweeping view of the ocean. Excellent wine-tasting classes are held there as well.

Insider's Secret

Palo, the adults-only restaurant, serves the best food on both ships and is very popular. So popular, in fact, that if you want to book a table, you need to either do so via the Internet before you leave home or immediately upon boarding the ship.

Not all the dining is formal. A breakfast buffet is available daily on the pool level for families that want to get an early start on the morning. You can also find a casual buffet lunch daily, and, in case you don't want to take even a minute out of your fun, pizza, burgers, and ice cream are served all afternoon out by the pools.

Helpful Hint

So where do the kids eat on the night Mom and Dad dine at Palo? First of all, make sure you don't schedule your Palo date night on the evening when you're scheduled to dine at Animator's Palate. That's a major thrill for kids and even adults get caught up in the excitement. Once you do choose a night and make a reservation at Palo, you can arrange for the children to eat in one of two ways: either sign them up for one of the kids' programs that include dinner or escort them to the Topsider buffet or one of the fast-food restaurants for an early meal. Afterward, drop them off at the kids' center and head upstairs to Palo.

Ports of Call

The three- and four-day cruises spend one day in Nassau, giving guests a chance to shop, sightsee, or play the slot machines. There are shore excursions designed for families (and kids of all ages are apt to enjoy a horse-drawn carriage ride), but, frankly, the Nassau stop exists mostly to placate the adults on board who miss the presence of a casino. If you do want to try your luck at the slots, or if your children are too young to comfortably take along on a shopping trip to the straw market, you can always leave them on board to enjoy the kids' programs.

The seven-day cruises offer family-friendly shore excursions at every stop; kids especially enjoy the sailing lessons, and the snorkeling and submarine trips. A complete list of all shore excursions for every port of call can be found at www.disneycruise.com.

Castaway Cay

All the cruises stop at Castaway Cay, a private island where you disembark at the pier (cutting out the time-consuming tendering

Insider's Secret

The snorkeling is better on the shore excursions than it is on Castaway Cay, especially the snorkeling at Grand Cayman on the Western Caribbean itinerary and St. John on the Eastern Caribbean itinerary. Most kids 8 and older, assuming they're reasonably capable swimmers, can master the mask and tube. Everyone wears life jackets so you can periodically bob and rest.

process often required when a large ship stops at a small island) and stroll onto a beautiful beach. Once there you can snorkel, hike, bike, play volleyball, take a banana boat ride, rent sailboats or sea kayaks, or simply sun yourself. Organized excursions for families include a Kayak Nature Adventure (ages 10 and up) and a Personal Watercraft Eco Tour (ages 8 and up), where families can drive small speedboats into the natural waterways throughout the island.

Time-Saving Tip

Once you book your cruise, you can reserve shore excursions via www.disneycruise.com or your travel agent. Reserving in advance is a good idea because it guarantees you can get everything you want and also saves you from having to stand in line at the Shore Excursion Desk on the first day of your cruise.

The children's programs go full force on the island, so after you've played a while as a family, you can drop the kids off and have a little adult time. Counselors lead youngsters on scavenger hunts, "whale excavations," and sand castle–building

contests; older kids participate in boat races or bike
trips around the island with
the counselors; teens have
their own beach Olympics
and Survivor-style games.

Hidden Mickey
Going snorkeling?
Look for the cool
underwater Hidden
Mickey.

Meanwhile, adults can
escape to the separate mile-long quiet beach, sip a piña colada,
or have an open-air massage in a private cabana. Lunch is
cooked right on the island and there's a small shop in case you
find yourself in need of beach toys, towels, or sunscreen.

Helpful Hint
Castaway Cay is so popular that some itineraries
stop there twice. If you'd like a lot of beach time on
your cruise, consider one of those sailings.

Kids' Programs

Flounder's Reef is the nursery with play areas for children between 3 months and 3 years of age. It does not run the exten-
sive hours of the other children's programs, but is open daily to
give the parents of infants and toddlers time to relax together
or play with their older kids.

Disney's Oceaneer Club for kids ages 3 to 7 occupies a
huge play area complete with a re-creation of Captain Hook's
pirate ship. The well-trained and upbeat counselors lead the

Helpful Hint
In-room babysitting can be arranged if parents of
younger kids want to have a late night out without
worrying.

Insider's Secret

The *Disney Magic* offers a simulation game for kids 3 to 7 called Ocean Quest on its seven-night cruises. Kids enter a scaled-down replica of the ship with LCD screen "windows." They can sit in the captain's chair, look out over the bridge, and steer the ship into port. It's a fun little extra and a great photo op.

kids in games and crafts, including a Detective School and Ariel's Bubble Adventure, a fun outdoor "lab" where even little kids learn to make big bubbles. Highlights of the week include a tea party with Wendy of *Peter Pan* fame, and Pumbaa's PJ Party, a sleepover with games and storytelling.

Insider's Secret

Children, already overwhelmed by the size and newness of the ship, often suffer a bit of separation anxiety at the first drop-off. Try to persuade them to join the activities that first evening, when everyone is new and fast friendships are made. The counselors are trained to look out for shy or nervous children and help them make a smooth transition into the group activities.

Kids ages 8 to 12 hang out in the Oceaneer Lab where they can learn to make goop in the Apprentice Workshop, try out the ultimate belly flop in Goofy's World Records Pool Party, learn to draw animation cels, and pilot boats carved from soap. The activities run throughout the day and night, and whenever you drop them off, you are given a pager so that you can be reached at any time.

Teens ages 13 to 17 have their own space, a private haven called Aloft, which looks like a combination coffeehouse–dorm room, and they're also pretty much given the run of the ship. Counselors lead teens in ship-wide scavenger hunts, video game tournaments, karaoke contests, and pool parties. Glow Jam, a nighttime sport involving glow-in-the-dark balls, and the Teen Tribal Challenge, a Survivor-style contest on Castaway Cay, are especially popular.

On the first evening aboard the ship, counselors meet with the parents to explain the program and help ease the kids in.

Onboard Entertainment

There are three pools on board: one, shaped like Mickey, with a pint-size tube slide for little kids; a second "sports pool" for games and the rowdier activities of older children; and a third "quiet pool" for adults, complete with large, elevated hot tubs. In addition, the ship has a sports deck, a full-service spa, an exercise room, and several shops.

The cornerstone of onboard entertainment is the 975-seat Walt Disney Theater, one of the most technologically advanced theaters in the world and certainly the most remarkable on any cruise ship. Here DCL showcases live, Broadway-style shows, some of them new and some based on Disney classics. Must-see

Insider's Secret

The onboard spa offers a range of services, including some designed exclusively for couples. Just hanging out in the beautiful sauna and steam area is a great way to kill an afternoon. If you want to book a massage or facial, especially on a day when the ship is at sea, go immediately to the spa after boarding the ship to make an appointment. The best times get snatched up early.

productions include the new *Twice-Charmed,* based on the Cinderella story; the *Golden Mickeys,* a tribute to classic animated films; and the stunning *Disney Dreams,* which always seems to bring half the audience to tears.

Studio Sea, a family lounge, provides dance music, parties, and participatory game shows starring the audience. The Mickey Mania trivia game is a real blast. The Buena Vista Theater shows a variety of Disney movies daily, and a jumbo screen allows you to watch movies outdoors on the deck, a real thrill and a good way to coax wound-up kids to relax.

After the shows wind down, adults can congregate in the entertainment districts, dubbed Beat Street on *Disney Magic* and Route 66 on *Disney Wonder.* Expect a comedy club with an improv troupe, a dance club that alternates between rock and country music, a sports pub, and a piano bar. The seven-day cruises include some extra onboard treats, such as the infamous Pirates of the Caribbean deck party. This is a real extravaganza, starring Mickey, Captain Hook, and stunt performers who rappel down the ship. Fireworks, music, dancing, and bandannas for the partygoers round out the festivities.

More and more, large families are meeting up on cruises, where everyone can be together but still go off and do their own thing. Consider this report from a mother of three from Michigan: "My sisters and I have a family reunion at Disney World every other year. When we get all the kids and spouses together there are 14 of us, with a wide range of ages. Last year for the first time we took the cruise and found that worked great. Those with babies could go back to their cabins whenever someone got cranky or tired, those with school-age kids could just keep going, and those with older kids could let them go to the pools and arcades on their own."

CHAPTER

14

Universal
Orlando

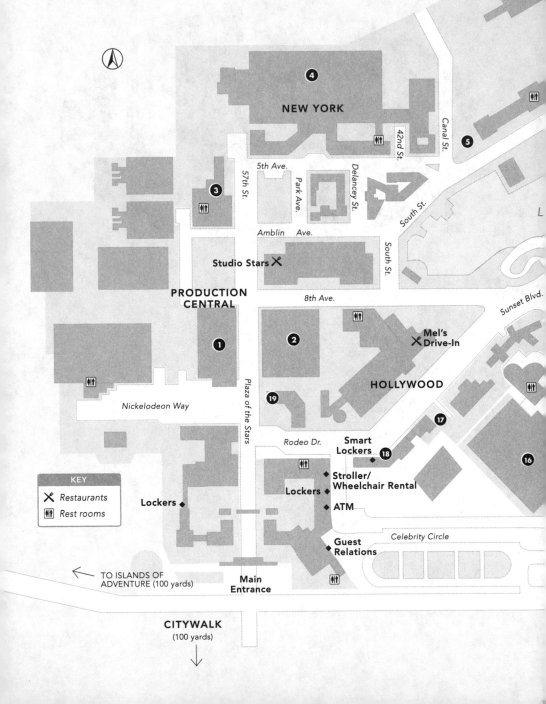

Universal Studios

NEW YORK

4

5

42nd St.

Canal St.

57th St.

5th Ave.

Park Ave.

Delancey St.

3

South St.

South St.

Amblin   Ave.

Studio Stars ✕

PRODUCTION CENTRAL

8th Ave.

Sunset Blvd.

2

Mel's
✕ Drive-In

1

HOLLYWOOD

Nickelodeon Way

19

17

Plaza of the Stars

Rodeo Dr.

**Smart
Lockers**

18

16

KEY

✕ *Restaurants*

🚹🚺 *Rest rooms*

◆ Stroller/
Wheelchair Rental

Lockers ◆

Lockers ◆

◆ **ATM**

Celebrity Circle

**Guest
Relations** ◆

← TO ISLANDS OF
ADVENTURE (100 yards)

**Main
Entrance**

CITYWALK
(100 yards)
↓

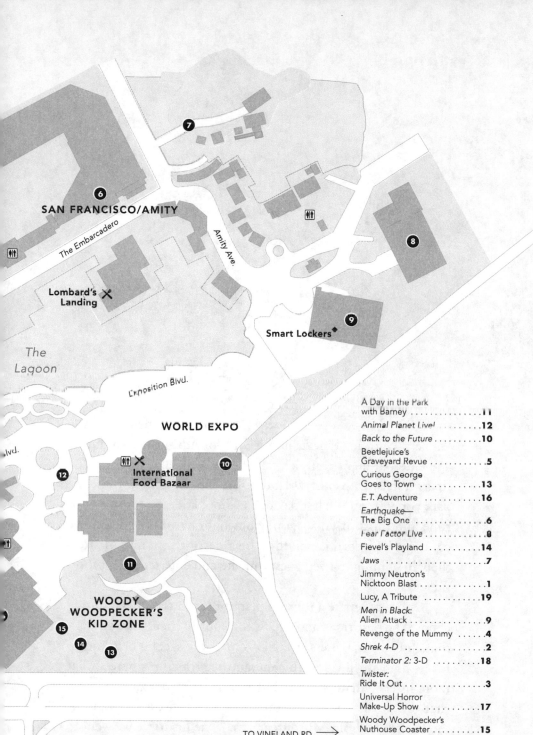

SAN FRANCISCO/AMITY

The Embarcadero

Amity Ave.

Lombard's
Landing ✕

The
Lagoon

Exposition Blvd.

Smart Lockers

WORLD EXPO

International
Food Bazaar ✕

Blvd.

WOODY
WOODPECKER'S
KID ZONE

TO VINELAND RD. →

With two full theme parks— Universal Studios Florida and Islands of Adventure—a dining and entertainment complex called CityWalk, and three on-site resort hotels, Universal Orlando is no longer content to be the park you visit on the last day of vacation, after the bulk of your time and most of your money have gone to Disney. On the contrary, Universal is poised to be a destination, not an afterthought, aiming to keep guests on-site and entertained for multiday stays.

As you prepare a touring plan for Universal, make sure to choose the best rides and shows for your particular family. Although Universal offers attractions for every age, it's best known for its high-thrill rides. In general, the attractions here are far more intense than those at Disney, so it's important to know that the shows and rides you choose are age appropriate. A mother of one from Missouri agrees: "The first time we went to Universal Studios our daughter was four and there wasn't too much she could ride or enjoy at such a young age. The next time we went back she was eight and she loved it. Kids really have to be a bit older to really get into the Universal Studios style of ride."

On the other hand, if you have teenagers, you may want to spend more time at Universal than at Disney. Consider this report from a father of three: "My children love roller coasters (the wilder the better) and prefer Universal to Disney. So we do the opposite of most families, staying at Universal and driving over for a day at Disney."

Universal Orlando is off Interstate 4 at Exits 74B and 75A. Road signs to the complex are clear and well marked. For more information visit www.universalorlando.com. To order a brochure or check hours of operation during the time you'll be visiting, call 407/363–8000.

Helpful Hint

Just as many people confuse Walt Disney World and the Magic Kingdom, Universal's expansion has led to some confusion regarding the names of its parks. The entire complex—two theme parks, three hotels, and CityWalk—is called Universal Orlando. Universal Studios Florida refers to the original theme park, which has attractions based on the movies that Universal Pictures has produced over the years. Islands of Adventure is the second theme park, with more thrill rides than any other in the Orlando area.

Should We Stay On-Site?

Whether you decide to stay at one of Universal Orlando's three on-site resorts—the Portofino Bay Hotel, the Hard Rock Hotel, and the Royal Pacific Resort—depends on how much you're willing to spend for certain conveniences and privileges extended only to on-site guests. The on-site resorts, managed by Loews

Hotels, are all luxurious, theme resorts with the ultimate in amenities, and price tags to match. Depending on the resort and the season, you can expect to pay from $199 to $369 a night.

There are plenty of expensive resorts on International Drive and other roads that flank the park, but Universal draws high-spending visitors by offering lots of perks for on-site guests.

Advantages of Staying On-Site

As you can see by the following list, staying on-site definitely makes your vacation more seamless.

- By far the biggest advantage is that resort guests can use the Express system on an unlimited basis. This means that you don't have to use the Express kiosks to make reservations to ride. Just show your resort ID, that is, your room key card, and you'll be admitted into the Express ticket line on any ride you choose at any time you choose. This virtually eliminates having to wait in line, and it's a huge, huge perk. It's also a $15 to $25 per person value—the cost of an Express PLUS pass.

- Resort guests can reserve 90 days in advance for selected shows within the theme parks and at the on-site, full-service restaurants.

- During holidays and in summer, resort guests are allowed into the theme parks an hour early on selected days.

- Special length-of-stay tickets are available to on-site guests, and hotel concierges can arrange ticket purchases and all dining reservations.

- Complimentary water taxi and bus transportation between your resort and the theme parks is included. (All three of the on-site hotels are linked to the two theme

Helpful Hint

For information about and reservations for all three of the on-site hotels, call 888/273–1311 or visit www.universalorlando.com.

parks and CityWalk by a series of scenic waterways.) Not only does the transportation system make it easier for you to return to your room for a midday break, but it saves you the time, effort, and expense of driving to the theme parks.

ⓔ Complimentary package delivery of in-park purchases to guest rooms.

ⓔ Resort IDs allow you to charge merchandise, food, and tickets to your hotel room. It's nice not to have to carry a lot of cash and to just have one bill at the end. (Note: You'll still need cash for snacks and souvenir stands.)

On-Site Hotels

Portofino Bay Hotel   **407/363–8000**

The Portofino Bay, Universal Orlando's first hotel, is modeled after the Italian seaside village of Portofino. From the outside you see quaint, colorful row houses that are actually all connected on the inside, housing 750 elegant rooms, including 18 children's suites.

Portofino Bay has eight restaurants and lounges, a full-service spa, three swimming pools, and the Campo Portofino, a supervised children's activity center that is open in the evenings.

Like all the on-site properties, this is a Loews resort, so the service is top-notch. Of the three resorts, Portofino Bay is the

Helpful Hint

All three of the Universal resorts are within walking distance of the Universal parks, about a 20-minute drive from Walt Disney World, and about a 10-minute drive from SeaWorld.

most posh with the most amenities geared to adults who want to relax in a beautiful environment. Rates for regular rooms range from $259 to $359 a night, while rooms that include kids' suites average about $500. For reservations or more information call 407/503–1000 or visit www.universalorlando.com.

Hard Rock Hotel   407/363–8000

Fun, flashy, and funky, the 650-room Hard Rock Hotel has a broad and eclectic collection of rock memorabilia. If you like the idea of a 7 AM serenade from Elvis, you can even ask for a rock star wake-up call in the morning. Music plays continually throughout the beautifully landscaped grounds and sophisticated lounges. The dramatic pool area has a 260-foot waterslide, plus a 12-speaker underwater sound system, so you can get your aural fix even while taking a swim. There are three bars and two restaurants, including an Orlando version of the well-known Palm Restaurant, as well as a gym and activity center with children's programs in the evenings.

The Hard Rock Hotel is the perfect choice for families with older kids and teens who can appreciate the hipper-than-thou ambience. Rates range from $229 to $359 per night, and if money isn't an object you can live like the King in the $1,350-per-night Graceland Suite. For more information or reservations call 407/503–7625 (407/503–ROCK) or visit www.universalorlando.com.

Royal Pacific Resort   407/503–3000

The Royal Pacific is the largest of the three Universal resorts, with 1,000 guest rooms on 53 acres. The lush grounds, thickly planted with tropical plants and trees, have a distinct South Pacific flair, and they're connected to CityWalk and the theme parks via water taxi and a series of winding, well-manicured pathways. There are two restaurants and two lounges, plus a luau party area, a fitness center, a children's activity center, and a massive pool area.

Perhaps most significant, the Royal Pacific is Universal's convention hotel, with 80,000 square feet of meeting space. This doesn't mean the resort won't be comfortable for families— the enormous pool and the children's center indicate that the resort is family friendly—but you may find a lot of businesspeople mixed in with the vacationing crowd.

Helpful Hint
To check out Universal packages, call 800/224–3838 or visit www.universalorlando.com. If none of the packages exactly suit your needs, you can type in the specifics you require, and the system will tally up the cost, in essence allowing you to create your own package.

Rates range from $199 to $299 a night, making the Royal Pacific the most affordable of the three on-site resorts. Reservations can be made at www.universalorlando.com or by calling 407/503–3000.

What Kind of Tickets Do We Need?

Universal offers several ticket options. Prices below do not include Florida's 6.5% sales tax.

One-Day, One-Park Ticket

Admits holders to either Universal Studios *or* Islands of Adventure for one day.

- Adults and children over 9: $63
- Children ages 3 to 9: $52

One-Day, Two-Park Ticket

Admits holders to Universal Studios *and* Islands of Adventure for one day.

- Adults and children over 9: $73
- Children ages 3 to 9: $63

Two-Day, Two-Park Ticket

Admits holders to both Islands of Adventure and Universal Studios for two days.

- All ages: $108

Four-Park Ticket

Admits holders to Universal Studios, Islands of Adventure, Wet 'n' Wild, and SeaWorld for 14 consecutive days.

- Adults and children over 9: $190
- Children ages 3 to 9: $156

Five-Park Ticket

Admits holders to Universal Studios, Islands of Adventure, Wet 'n' Wild, SeaWorld, and Busch Gardens for 14 consecutive days.

- Adults and children over 9: $235
- Children ages 3 to 9: $200

> ### Money-Saving Tip
> If you buy your tickets online, the savings can be significant. Specials vary with the season, but there's nearly always a reward for buying early, such as Universal's latest deal: three days' admission for the price of two.

Tips for Your First Hour at Universal Studios

- The parking garage is in New Jersey (it seems that way, anyhow), so arrive at least 30 minutes before the main gate opens. Parking costs $9 per car.

- If you arrive before the main turnstiles open, you'll have time to pose for pictures with and get the autographs of some of the Hanna-Barbera and Nickelodeon characters. This is your chance to meet SpongeBob SquarePants, the Wild Thornberrys, and the Rugrats.

- Guests are generally allowed through the main turnstiles and partway down Plaza of the Stars and Rodeo Drive about 20 minutes before the official opening time. If you want to ride *Back to the Future, Jaws, Men in Black,* or the E.T. Adventure first, go down Rodeo Drive as far as you're allowed. If you'd rather see Jimmy Neutron, *Shrek* 4-D, *Twister,* Revenge of the Mummy, or Earthquake first, go

> ### Time-Saving Tip
> Remember that the newer attractions draw the longest lines. As soon as you can in the morning, ride Revenge of the Mummy and Jimmy Neutron's Nicktoon Blast. Then head directly to *Shrek* 4-D.

down Plaza of the Stars until the ropes stop you. Families who haven't had breakfast may have time for a pastry at the Beverly Hills Boulangerie before the ropes drop.

@ If there's a show being taped on the day you're visiting, indicated on a sign as you enter the park, now is the time to get tickets. The attendant at the nearby Studio Audience window can tell you how to get tickets and the age limits for children. You can also call the general Universal number, 407/363–8000, for information on what shows, if any, are scheduled to tape during the times you'll be visiting.

@ In the off-season, some attractions open at 9, some at 10, and some (mainly the shows) start even later. Adjust your touring plan to take in the rides as they open.

Helpful Hint

Do you want to sleep in? Visit in the off-season when crowds are light and lines are short. You can arrive at the park at 10 AM and still comfortably do everything.

Universal Studios Touring Tips

@ If you're not an on-site resort guest and you didn't opt for the Express PLUS pass, try to visit the major attractions—Revenge of the Mummy, *Men in Black, Back to the Future, Twister, Jaws, Shrek,* E.T. Adventure, *Earthquake,* and Jimmy Neutron—in the morning or in the evening. Take in the theater-style attractions in the afternoon.

@ If you miss one of the major continuously loading attractions in the morning, hold off on it until two hours before the park closes. Midday waits of up to 60 minutes are common at popular attractions such as *Men in Black* and

Time-Saving Tip

Universal Studios offers Express passes that work like Disney's Fastpass.

The Express Distribution Centers are near each major ride. Go up to the kiosk, insert your admission ticket, and you'll get the admission ticket back along with an Express pass telling you when to return. When you do, you'll be allowed to enter a much shorter Express line. The anticipated wait time in an Express line is a mere 15 minutes.

Guests may only receive one Express pass at a time. You can get another Express pass after (1) you've used your existing one, (2) the one-hour time slot on your first pass has expired, or (3) two hours have passed from the time printed at the bottom of the Express pass.

For unlimited Express line access (no reservations required), consider buying an Express PLUS pass for $15 in the off-season or $25 in the on-season. Guests of on-site hotels can enter Express lines at any time by showing their hotel key cards.

Terminator 2: 3-D, but the crowds ease off a bit during the dinner hour.

If you plan to see Universal Studios in one day, it's unlikely you'll have time for an afternoon break. However, numerous theater-style attractions offer plenty of chances to rest up and let small kids nap. A lot of shows open around noon and begin a second performance around 2 PM. Ride in the morning and then catch a midday show, have lunch, and see a second show.

@ Most of the kiddie attractions—the Woody Woodpecker Nuthouse Coaster, A Day in the Park with Barney, Curious George Goes to Town, Fievel's Playland, the E.T. Adventure, and *Animal Planet Live!*—are in the same general area of the park. This means that you can park the strollers once, and then walk from attraction to attraction.

@ The theaters that hold the *Universal Horror Make-Up Show,* and *Terminator 2:* 3-D are high capacity, so even if the lines look discouraging, odds are you'll still be seated. Consult your entertainment schedule or check the board at the attraction entrance for showtimes, and then put one parent in line about 20 minutes before the show is due to start. The other can take the kids for a drink or bathroom break.

@ Headed to *Back to the Future, Men in Black,* or another intense attraction? Universal employees will help families traveling with a baby or toddler do a Baby Swap so that everyone can ride.

Helpful Hint

Few rides at Universal have height restrictions. You must be 48 inches tall to ride Revenge of the Mummy, 40 inches tall for *Back to the Future,* 36 inches tall for the Woody Woodpecker Nuthouse Coaster, and 42 inches tall for *Men in Black.* Just because your kids are big enough for *Jaws* and *Earthquake,* however, doesn't mean it's a good idea to let them into the attractions. Consult the ride descriptions for information about the scare factors.

Some attractions, such as E.T. Adventure and Jimmy Neutron, provide separate stationary seating for kids less than 40 inches, thus allowing families to go through the attraction as a group.

Money-Saving Tip

Try not to let the kids stop to shop in the morning; not only should you keep moving between rides while the park is relatively uncrowded, but each ride empties out through a shop that sells souvenirs related to that attraction. In other words, the shops encourage the ultimate in impulse buying, but you should try to hold off purchases until late in the day when you've seen it all.

The Scare Factor at Universal Studios

Some of the shows and tours are family oriented and fine for everyone, but several of the big name attractions are too frightening for preschoolers. The motion-simulation rides, especially *Back to the Future,* may induce queasiness, and be aware that in general the rides and shows are very loud. *Twister* and *Terminator* can practically jolt the fillings from your teeth.

Universal seems to set its age rules based on how physically wild the motion of a ride is and, except for Revenge of the Mummy, none of the rides at the Studios bounce you around too much. They're psychologically scary, however, and a few minutes inside *Twister* may lead to more bad dreams than the wildest of roller coasters. Indeed, *Twister, Terminator 2:* 3-D, and the *Universal Horror Make-Up Show* have PG-13 ratings, so they may be too violent and intense for younger children.

Helpful Hint

Because the rides are based on movies, how your child reacted to the movie is a good predictor of how well your child will handle the ride. If *The Mummy* movie scared him, it's a safe bet he's not going to like the ride any better.

Read the ride descriptions to help you decide what's right for your child.

The Universal Studios Don't-Miss List

Animal Planet Live!
Back to the Future
Curious George Goes to Town (for kids under 8)
A Day in the Park with Barney (for kids under 6)
E.T. Adventure
Jaws
Jimmy Neutron's Nicktoon Blast
Men in Black: Alien Attack
Revenge of the Mummy
Shrek 4-D
Terminator 2: 3-D
Twister: Ride It Out

Universal Studios Attractions

Jimmy Neutron's Nicktoon Blast
This motion-simulation ride stars Jimmy Neutron and plenty of other characters from the Nickelodeon lineup, including the Wild Thornberrys and SpongeBob SquarePants.

Time-Saving Tip
Because Jimmy Neutron is near the beginning of the Plaza of the Stars, lines form by 11 AM as late-arriving visitors walk through the front gate and simply queue up for the first attraction they see. Visit Jimmy Neutron first thing in the morning, both to avoid the crowds and to use the ride as a gauge for how well your kids will handle the more intense flight-simulation ride, *Back to the Future.*

The Scare Factor

The presence of familiar Nickelodeon heroes like Jimmy and SpongeBob will ensure that most kids, even many preschoolers, will be clamoring to ride. The action sequences shouldn't alarm kids raised on Saturday morning cartoons, but the motion simulation may be another matter. If you're prone to queasiness or think it might be too intense for your kids, ask for the stationary seating. If that goes well, you can always return and ride in the motion simulators on your second time through.

In the preshow you're introduced to Jimmy's latest invention, a spy camera, but then—as so often is the case in the world of theme park rides—something goes dreadfully awry. The audience is loaded into motion-simulation vehicles to help Jimmy defend the earth from an alien attack. The vehicles rise, tilt, and lurch in reaction to what's happening on the large screen in front of you, and while the actual movement of the "rocket" isn't much, the special effects combine to make you feel as if you're really hurtling through space.

Time-Saving Tip

Jimmy Neutron and *Shrek* will draw longer-than-average lines because they're relatively new and located close together near the park entrance. To reduce your wait time, get an Express pass for one attraction before lining up for the other. By the time you exit the first attraction, you should be able to use your Express pass to immediately board the second.

Quick Guide to

Attraction	Height Requirement
Animal Planet Live!	None
Back to the Future	40 inches
Beetlejuice's Graveyard Revue	None
A Day in the Park with Barney	None
Earthquake	None
E.T. Adventure	Separate seating for kids under 40 inches
Fear Factor Live	None
Fievel's Playland	None
Jaws	None
Jimmy Neutron's Nicktoon Blast	Separate seating for kids under 40 inches
Lucy, A Tribute	None
Men in Black: Alien Attack	42 inches
Revenge of the Mummy	48 inches
Shrek 4-D	None
Terminator 2: 3-D	None
Twister: Ride It Out	None
Universal Horror Make-Up Show	None
Woody Woodpecker's Nuthouse Coaster	36 inches

Scare Factor
0 = Unlikely to scare any child of any age.
! = Has dark or loud elements; might rattle some toddlers.
!! = A couple of gotcha! moments; should be fine for school-age kids.
!!! = You need to be pretty big and pretty brave to handle this ride.

Universal Studios Attractions

Speed of Line	Duration of Ride/Show	Scare Factor	Age Range
Fast	20 min.	0	All
Moderate	7 min.	!!	7 and up
Fast	25 min.	!	5 and up
Fast	15 min.	0	All
Moderate	20 min.	!	5 and up
Slow	15 min.	!	All
Fast	25 min.	!!!	7 and up
Moderate	n/a	0	All
Moderate	10 min.	!!	7 and up
Moderate	15 min.	!	5 and up
Fast	n/a	0	All
Fast	25 min.	!!	7 and up
Moderate	15 min.	!!!	7 and up
Moderate	30 min.	!!	4 and up
Slow	25 min.	!!!	7 and up
Moderate	15 min.	!!	7 and up
Fast	20 min.	!!	7 and up
Moderate	1½ min.	!	4 and up

Shrek 4-D

In the preshow you learn that vile little Lord Farquaad has plans to destroy Shrek from the great beyond. (Note the clever digs at Disney in the preshow area.) As you enter the main theater, you'll be given 3-D glasses, but what makes this show really special and different from the other 3-D attractions around town is that you're seated in special chairs that will make the experience tactile as well as visual. What does that mean? You'll not only see and hear the action happening on the screen, you'll feel and smell some of it, too. (Mercifully, taste is the one sense not engaged in the show.) And the adventures of Shrek and Donkey are predictably hilarious as they rescue the hapless Fiona.

The Scare Factor

While Lord Farquaad is not exactly the most intimidating movie villain of all time, the special effects are extremely convincing and the whole show is very loud, which may be too much for preschoolers. Consider having them wear earplugs to reduce the noise level. Kids ages 8 and older should do fine.

Revenge of the Mummy

Revenge of the Mummy combines a high-speed roller coaster with the latest technology in robotics and pyrotechnic effects—no wonder it's billed as a "psychological thrill ride."

Insider's Secret

Revenge of the Mummy is the hottest ride at Universal (literally) and often has lines to match. Be sure to use an Express pass and visit it as early in the day as possible.

As the story begins, you walk through shadowy Egyptian catacombs on a tour of the on-location set of the next *Mummy* movie. Once you're in the coaster, the ride's magnetic-propulsion launch system thrusts you forward, backward, and forward again as you dodge vengeful ghosts, mummies, and other monsters. The ride culminates with an overhead fire and a skeleton warrior who, in the midst of battle, leaps into your vehicle. Yowza!

The Scare Factor

The Mummy scares the willies out of preschoolers and some school-age kids as well. Your child must be 48 inches tall to ride.

Men in Black: Alien Attack

Remember the scene in *Men in Black* when Will Smith tries out for the force? Think you could do better?

The premise is that guests are rookie agents riding through the streets of New York and armed with laser guns called "alienators." Like in Disney's Buzz Lightyear ride, you're supposed to shoot the aliens, but *unlike* in the Buzz ride, these aliens can strike back, sending your vehicle into an out-of-control spin.

The Scare Factor

Most kids take the aliens in *Men in Black* in stride—especially if they've seen the movies and know what to expect.

Time-Saving Tip

Families with older kids should head for *Men in Black* directly after trying out Revenge of the Mummy. This attraction draws long lines by midmorning.

As you shoot at the 120 audio-animatronics aliens, the ride keeps track of your individual score and the collective score of the six people in your vehicle. You're not only fighting off aliens, but also competing against the team of rookies in the car beside you. Here's where it gets cute. Depending on how well you and your vehicle-mates shoot, there are alternate endings to the ride. Will you get a hero's welcome in Times Square or a loser's send-off?

Insider's Secret

Want to max your *Men in Black* score? Near the end of the ride (when you face the mega-alien in Times Square), you will hear Zed instructing you to push the red button on your control panel "*now!*" Whoever hits the button at this crucial point gets a whopping 100,000 bonus points. Take that, space aliens!

Because you're actually in a video game, it makes sense that video game rules apply—the more you play, the better you get. Can you spell addictive? Come early if you want to ride more than once.

Insider's Secret

If you're willing to split off from your party, the singles line moves much faster than the general line.

Helpful Hint

There are lockers outside *Men in Black* where you can store backpacks and large packages for free while you ride. The ride isn't that wild, but space in the training vehicles is very tight, so use the lockers if you're carrying anything bulky.

Back to the Future

Flight-simulation technology makes a quantum leap forward, and you make a quantum leap backward, in *Back to the Future*. In the preshow video, Doc Brown (played by Christopher Lloyd of the movie series) informs you that bad-boy Biff has sabotaged his time-travel experiments. Then, you're loaded into six-passenger DeLoreans.

Time-Saving Tip

Remember, you can cut down the amount of time you spend standing in line by using the Express system or using the single-rider lines.

What follows is a high-speed chase through the prehistoric era. The cars bounce around pretty violently, but it's the film that makes you feel like you're hurtling through time and space. *Back to the Future* is far more intense than Disney's Star Tours or Body Wars. Passengers who can bear to glance away from the screen will notice that as many as 12 DeLoreans, arranged in tiers, take the trip simultaneously, making Back to the Future a sort of ultimate drive-in movie.

The Scare Factor

At one point in your trip through the prehistoric era, you're swallowed by a dinosaur, making the ride much too much for most kids under 7, although technically anyone taller than 40 inches is allowed to board. If your child wants to try it, brief him or her that the majority of the effects can be erased simply by closing his or her eyes—and that's not a bad tip to keep in mind yourself if you're prone to queasiness.

Earthquake—The Big One

After a preshow hosted by Charlton Heston, you travel through two separate theaters to learn how special effects and stunts were used for *Earthquake,* the movie. The intricate models of San Francisco and the special effects are something of a revelation to most kids, because few have seen the original movie, made more than 20 years ago. In this second preshow, members of the audience can volunteer to play quake victims.

The Scare Factor

The final segment of *Earthquake,* in which you're trapped in a San Francisco subway station during the quake, is short but intense. Besides the rumbles, a water main will break, electrical fires will break out, and at one point a truck crashes through the pavement above you. It's dramatic, but most preschool kids—especially if they've been briefed about what to expect—aren't too frightened. The noise level may unnerve toddlers.

Next you are loaded onto your subway for the ride segment itself. *Earthquake* is a very short ride and less frightening than you may have been led to believe from the advertisements. Most kids hold up through the rumbles, fires, floods, and train wrecks just fine, and as one mother wrote, "It's fun to feel it really happen instead of watching it on a screen." It's even more fascinating to watch the water recede, the concrete mend itself, and the broken turnstiles arise when the ride is over!

Twister

After a taped intro by Bill Paxton and Helen Hunt, the stars of the film, you're led into the main show area. There, a five-story-high tornado is created right before your eyes. The tornado,

The Scare Factor

Twister is a dramatic experience and *extremely* loud. I recommend bringing earplugs along, but if you don't have them, try placing your hands over your kids' ears. They may fight you in the beginning, but they'll be looking for the comfort and protection when the show gets rolling. The experience is too frightening for small children, but most kids 7 and up will be fine.

along with accompanying fires and explosions, swirls through the building while you watch from two platforms. You'll feel the wind, the rain, and the rumbles, and yes, the flying cow from the movie comes along for the ride.

Terminator 2: 3-D

Universal's most high-tech action show combines 3-D effects, live actors, and movie clips. The best special effect is the way the live actors seem to emerge from the movie screen and then later run back "into" the movie. The show is fast and dramatic—just like the film series it's based on—and the ending is explosive.

The Scare Factor

Although not as violent as the film series, the show has some startling effects that may be too much for kids under 7. Again, it is *extremely* loud.

Because of the size of the theater, *Terminator 2:* 3-D is relatively easy to get into and best saved for the afternoon.

E.T. Adventure

The charming ride begins with a brief preshow featuring Steven Spielberg and E.T. Afterward you file through a holding area

where—and this seems rather mysterious at the time—you are
required to give your name in exchange for a small plastic "in-
terplanetary passport." Next you move on to the queue area,
which winds through the deep, dark woods—it even smells and
sounds like a forest. (As a rule, Universal does a bang-up job of
setting the mood in queue areas; E.T. is designed to make you
feel small and childlike.)

Helpful Hint

All the attractions for very young children are in the
same area of the park. If you have preschoolers,
hang an immediate right on Rodeo Drive after
you enter the park and follow the signs to
E.T. Adventure.

After handing "passports" to the attendant, children under
40 inches tall or anyone elderly, heavy, pregnant, or otherwise
unsteady is loaded into flying gondolas. Others ride bicycles,
and the lead bike in each group has E.T. in the front basket. You
rise up and fly over the forest in an effective simulation of the escape scene in *E.T.* the movie. After narrowly missing being captured by the police, you manage to return E.T. to his home
planet, a magical place populated by dozens of cuddly aliens.

The ride has a cute ending—as you sail past E.T. for the
final time, he bids you farewell by name. When you give your
name to the attendant before you enter the queue area, it's computer coded onto your plastic passport. As you give up the passport and join your group of bicycles, the cards are fed into the
computer, which enables E.T. to say, "Good-bye, Jordan.
Good-bye, Leigh. Good-bye, Kim . . ." and so on, as your family flies past.

Helpful Hint

Unfortunately, this "personal good-bye" system frequently malfunctions, so I wouldn't mention it to the kids at all. That way, if it works, everyone is extra delighted, and if it doesn't, the ride is still an upbeat experience.

Jaws

As the people of Amity Beach learned, that darn shark just won't stay away.

The ride carries you via boat through a big outdoor set. The shark rises from the water several times quite suddenly, the unseen boat before you "gets it" in a gruesome way, and there are also grenade launches, explosions, and a fuel spill. There's tremendous splashing, especially on the left side of the boat, and most of the boat captains throw themselves totally into the experience by shrieking, shouting, and firing guns on cue. It all adds up to one action-packed boat ride.

The Scare Factor

Kids 7 to 11 give *Jaws* a strong thumbs-up, and the ride is popular with many kids under 7. The fact that you're outdoors in the daylight dilutes the intensity. The really brave should wait until evening, when the "shark in the dark" effects are much scarier.

Fear Factor Live

Building on the merger between NBC and Universal in November 2004, this attraction is based on the popular television reality show of the same name. *Fear Factor Live* pits volunteers from the audience against each other in a series of extreme challenges designed to test the physical and emotional limits of the contestants. The audience gets into the act, too, by blasting contestants with water and controlling obstacles on stage. Some of the stunts and challenges are pretty creepy, and predictably, teens and preteens love it. But the show really isn't designed for young kids.

Helpful Hint

If you want to be a contestant in the physical challenges, head to the theater first thing in the morning; contestants for the gross-out challenges, such as eating bugs, are chosen from the studio audience. (Relax. They're not going to pull you out at random—you have to volunteer.)

Universal Horror Make-Up Show

A witty pair of young actors illustrates certain makeup effects on stage, and you'll also see clips from *The Mummy, The Fly,* and *An American Werewolf in London,* which has an astounding man-to-beast transformation scene. A lucky audience volunteer (an adult) is brought on stage to play victim.

The Scare Factor

Although the movie clips and general gore level are too intense for preschoolers, most kids over 7 can stomach the show. Better than adults, frankly. The show has a PG-13 rating because of the blood and a couple of mildly risqué jokes.

Animal Planet Live!

This is an appealing show for all age groups, but younger kids will be especially drawn to the animal stars. Kid volunteers from the audience join the fast-paced and funny performance. Showtimes are printed on your map; because of the large size of the theater, this is a great choice for the most crowded times of the afternoon.

Fievel's Playland

Fievel's Playland is cleverly designed and filled with Western-style props, including a harmonica that plays notes as kids slide down it; a giant, talking Tiger the cat; canteens to squirt; cowboy hats to bounce in; spiderwebs to climb; and a separate ball pit and slide area for toddlers.

The centerpiece of the playground is a 200-foot water ride in which kids and parents are loaded into two-person rafts and swept through a "sewer." The ride is zippier than it looks, will get you soaking wet, and is so addictive that most kids clamor to get back on again immediately. The water ride loads slowly, so by afternoon the waits are prohibitive. If you come in the morning, it's possible to ride several times with minimal waits, but by afternoon one ride is all you can reasonably expect.

Time-Saving Tip

Fievel's Playland often opens an hour or two after the general park opening. If you ride the big-deal rides and then show up at the playground at the opening time indicated on your map, you'll be able to try the water ride without much of a wait.

A Day in the Park with Barney

Designed to appeal to Universal's youngest guests, A Day in the Park with Barney is actually an enclosed parklike setting with pop-art-style, colorful flowers and trees. Barney appears several times a day in a song-and-dance show, and there's also an interactive indoor play area for toddlers. This play area is far cooler and calmer than Fievel's next door, and the nearby shop and food stand are never crowded. "The highlight of my two-year-old daughter's day was the Barney show," a mother of two from Illinois wrote to us. "The kids sit so close to him and his friends, and the setting is beautiful. I loved watching my little girl sing along during the 'I Love You' song at the end."

Woody Woodpecker's Nuthouse Coaster

Somewhat like Goofy's Barnstormer at Disney, the Nuthouse Coaster is scarier than you'd guess and kids must be 36 inches tall to ride. Watch it make a couple of runs before you line up with your 4-year-old.

Curious George Goes to Town

Perhaps a better name for this attraction would have been "Curious George Goes to the Car Wash." This large interactive play area is a simulated city that includes climbing areas, ball pits, and lots of chances to get very, very wet. There are fountains in the center and water cannons up above; many parents let their kids wear bathing suits under their clothing so they can strip down and really get into the spirit of the place. It's a great way to cool off in summer, but if you're going in the off-season, save it for the warmest part of the afternoon or keep walking.

Helpful Hint

In chilly weather the water is shut off and Curious George Goes to Town becomes a dry play area. The water ride in Fievel's Playground is closed on cold days.

Helpful Hint

At Curious George Goes to Town, you can attempt to follow the footprints in order to stay dry as you maze your way through the town—but what kid is going to do that? The footprints do cut down a bit on parental drenching.

On the other hand, if you're up for a maximum splash, a clanging bell over the Fire Department indicates that a big wave of water is under way. On a hot summer day, this may be the highlight of the park for young kids.

Insider's Secret

Check your entertainment schedule and, if time permits, stop to watch some of the street entertainers that play around the park throughout the day. The Blues Brothers, featuring Jake, Elroy, and a talented singer named Mabel, play in the New York section and offer one of the liveliest shows in the park.

Beetlejuice's Graveyard Revue

This rock and rap show starring Dracula, the Wolfman, and Frankenstein and his bride is primarily aimed at preteens and teens. Beetlejuice is the host and he offsets the ghoulishness with plenty of goofy humor. Younger kids won't be too frightened of the monsters themselves, but the extremely high volume of the music coupled with pyrotechnics might upset preschoolers. The show plays several times in the afternoon so getting in isn't hard; arrive about 15 minutes before showtime for good seats.

Insider's Secret

Universal can really throw a party. The park is festively decorated for Christmas, and a special parade runs for the weeks around Mardi Gras.

But the best holiday celebration of the year is Halloween. Halloween Horror Nights are a time-honored tradition at Universal and very popular with Orlando locals. All the movie bad guys are out in full force. Teenagers will love this ultimate spook house, and kids under 7 definitely won't. If you have kids ages 7 to 11, just make sure to stay close to them.

Lucy, A Tribute

Fans of *I Love Lucy* should take a few minutes to walk through this exhibit, which houses memorabilia from the famous TV show, including scale models of the Tropicana and the Ricardos' apartment; clothes and jewelry worn on the show; personal pictures and letters from Lucy and Desi's home life; and the numerous Emmys that Lucille Ball won throughout the years.

The "California Here We Come Game" is a treat for hardcore trivia buffs. By answering questions about episodes of *I Love Lucy*, game participants get to travel with the Mertzes and Ricardos on their first trip to California. They lost me somewhere in the desert, but perhaps you'll do better.

Tips for Your Last Hour at Universal Studios

Crowds thin at night so it's a good time to revisit favorite attractions or drop by anything you missed earlier in the day. If you want to have dinner at CityWalk, leave Universal about an hour before the official closing time to avoid the mad rush of exiting guests.

CHAPTER

15

Islands of Adventure

Islands of Adventure

Smart Lockers

JURASSIC PARK

TOON LAGOON

THE LOST CONTINENT

MARVEL SUPER HERO ISLAND

SEUSS LANDING

PORT OF ENTRY

Smart Lockers

Lockers

First Aid

KEY
🚻 Rest rooms

Islands of Adventure is all about rides: full sensory-immersion 3-D experiences, state-of-the-art coasters, watery descents that'll leave you dripping, and kiddie rides so cleverly designed that even the most cynical adults get totally into the spirit.

A one-day ticket to Islands of Adventure costs $59.75, $48 for children ages 3 to 9, excluding sales tax. For information on multiday passes that include Universal Studios, see Chapter 14. Check for any price changes by calling 407/363–8000 or visiting www.universalorlando.com.

Money-Saving Tip

If you're in one Universal park and decide you'd like to visit the other, it's easy to upgrade to a two-day pass. Just stop by Guest Services.

Getting Around Islands of Adventure

The layout of Islands of Adventure (IOA) is like a big lollipop, and you enter through the stick—the Port of Entry, which has shops, restaurants, and service areas. Port of Entry ends at the lagoon, and around the water are clustered the five islands of the theme park: Marvel Super Hero Island, Toon Lagoon, Jurassic Park, the Lost Continent, and Seuss Landing.

Because of IOA's essentially circular design, it's an easy park to tour. The sidewalks naturally lead you from one attraction to the next, with no crossroads or choices, and bridges connect each of the islands. The moods of the separate lands are quite distinct. As you walk into the mysterious and mythic Lost Continent, for example, you're greeted by the gentle tinkling of wind chimes; and to enter Jurassic Park, you walk through an enormous stone gate flanked with torches. Below your feet you'll see fossil prints in the sidewalk; and if you listen closely, you'll hear the rumbles and calls of dinos in the bushes.

We advise an early morning lap of the park to ride the big-deal attractions; an afternoon lap to check out the shows, play areas, water rides, and minor attractions; then a final circle in early evening to ride anything you missed—or revisit favorites. Sounds like a lot of walking, but in this user-friendly theme park, touring is a snap.

How Scary Is "Scary"?
As Dr. Seuss Would Say, "Very!"

Nine of the 12 major attractions at Islands of Adventure have height restrictions—your first clue that this park is loaded with physically wild rides. Measure your kids before you leave home; there's no point in promising your kindergarten-age coaster warrior a trip on the Incredible Hulk if he's less than 54 inches tall. Here are the specific height restrictions:

Dueling Dragons	54 inches
Jurassic Park River Adventure	42 inches
Dudley Do-Right's Ripsaw Falls	44 inches
The Incredible Hulk Coaster	54 inches
The Amazing Adventures of Spider-Man	40 inches
Popeye & Bluto's Bilge-Rat Barges	42 inches
Dr. Doom's Fearfall	52 inches
Pteranodon Flyers	36 inches
Flying Unicorns	36 inches

In addition, a couple of the shows are atmospherically scary; *Poseidon's Fury* and the *Eighth Voyage of Sindbad* have frightened some preschoolers.

The bottom line? Read the ride descriptions carefully before you board. If the ride is outside (and many IOA attractions are), watch it make a couple of cycles before you decide. And if someone in your family panics while in line, inform the attendant you'll need to do a Baby Swap (or husband swap, as the case may be).

The Islands of Adventure Don't-Miss List for Kids 2 to 6

Camp Jurassic

Caro-Seuss-el

The Cat in the Hat

Flying Unicorn

If I Ran the Zoo

Me Ship, the *Olive*

One Fish, Two Fish, Red Fish, Blue Fish

Popeye & Bluto's Bilge-Rat Barges (for older kids)

The Islands of Adventure Don't-Miss List for Kids 7 to 11

The Amazing Adventures Spider-Man

Camp Jurassic

The Cat in the Hat

Dudley Do-Right's Ripsaw Falls

Dueling Dragons (older kids)

The Incredible Hulk Coaster (older kids)

Jurassic Park River Adventure

Popeye & Bluto's Bilge-Rat Barges

Poseidon's Fury

The Islands of Adventure Don't-Miss List for Kids 12 and Up

The Amazing Adventures of Spider-Man

Dudley Do-Right's Ripsaw Falls

Dueling Dragons

Dr. Doom's Fearfall

The Incredible Hulk Coaster

Jurassic Park River Adventure

Popeye & Bluto's Bilge-Rat Barges

Poseidon's Fury

Helpful Hint

Confirm hours of operation by checking with your hotel or calling 407/363–8000.

Tips for Your First Hour at Islands of Adventure

@ Arrive 30 minutes before the stated opening time, which is generally 9 AM. (If you're staying on-site and visiting on an early-entry day, be there 10 minutes before the gates open to on-site guests.) Get tickets, maps, and take care of any business, such as locker or stroller rental.

@ Sometimes Port of Entry is open before the rest of the park. If so, browse the shops or have a quick breakfast at Croissant Moon Bakery, but be sure to be at the end of the street by the time the ropes drop.

@ The tip board will tell you which rides are running. During the on-season, most rides will open immediately; on less-crowded days, the rides may come online section by section. Either way, Marvel Super Hero Island and Seuss Landing, the two islands adjoining Port of Entry, will be open.

Insider's Secret

Perhaps because most guests stay off-site and must rise, eat, drive, park, and undertake the substantial trek from the parking garage, Islands of Adventure is relatively empty in the morning and grows more crowded in the afternoon. The first two hours after opening are definitely your best chance to ride Spider-Man and other big-deal attractions.

Quick Guide to

Attraction	Location	Height Requirement
The Amazing Adventures of Spider-Man	Super Hero Island	40 inches
Camp Jurassic	Jurassic Park	None
Caro-Seuss-el	Seuss Landing	None
The Cat in the Hat	Seuss Landing	None
Discovery Center	Jurassic Park	None
Dr. Doom's Fearfall	Super Hero Island	52 inches
Dudley Do-Right's Ripsaw Falls	Toon Lagoon	44 inches
Dueling Dragons	Lost Continent	54 inches
Eighth Voyage of Sindbad	Lost Continent	None
Flying Unicorn	Lost Continent	36 inches
If I Ran the Zoo	Seuss Landing	None
Incredible Hulk Coaster	Super Hero Island	54 inches
Me Ship, the *Olive*	Toon Lagoon	None
One Fish, Two Fish Red Fish, Blue Fish	Seuss Landing	None
Popeye & Bluto's Bilge-Rat Barges	Toon Lagoon	42 inches
Poseidon's Fury	Lost Continent	None
Pteranodon Flyers	Jurassic Park	36 inches
River Adventure	Jurassic Park	42 inches
Storm Force Accelatron	Super Hero Island	None

Scare Factor
0 = Unlikely to scare any child of any age.
! = Has dark or loud elements; might rattle some toddlers.
!! = A couple of gotcha! moments; should be fine for school-age kids.
!!! = You need to be pretty big and pretty brave to handle this ride.

Islands of Adventure Attractions

Speed of Line	Duration of Ride/Show	Scare Factor	Age Range
Moderate	15 min.	!!	7 and up
n/a	n/a	0	All
Slow	3 min.	0	All
Moderate	6 min.	0	All
n/a	n/a	0	All
Slow	2 min.	!!	7 and up
Moderate	8 min.	!!	7 and up
Moderate	7 min.	!!!	7 and up
n/a	25 min.	!!	8 and up
Moderate	1 min.	!!	All
n/a	n/a	0	All
Moderate	4 min.	!!!	8 and up
n/a	n/a	0	All
Slow	4 min.	0	All
Moderate	12 min.	!	4 and up
n/a	20 min.	!!	7 and up
Slow	80 sec.	!	4 and up
Slow	n/a	!!	7 and up
Slow	3 min.	!!	All

- If your kids are old enough to enjoy intense rides, veer left to Marvel Super Hero Island. Ride the Incredible Hulk Coaster, Spider-Man, and Dr. Doom's Fearfall in that order.

- If your kids are younger, veer right to Seuss Landing and start with One Fish, Two Fish and the Cat in the Hat.

Helpful Hint

Rides are most likely to be closed for maintenance in winter. Check www.universalorlando.com to see if any attractions are scheduled for refurbishment during your visit.

Port of Entry

As the name implies, Port of Entry is where you enter Islands of Adventure. It's a visually charming area, meant to resemble an exotic Middle Eastern seaport; the elaborately decorated bicycles (like the one marked "Fire Brigade") and other wacky forms of transportation make great places for a group snapshot.

Time-Saving Tip

Don't spend too much time shopping in the morning. The park is at its least crowded then, and you need to hurry on to the rides. You can always return to shop in the afternoon or evening.

Many of the park services are in Port of Entry: locker rentals ($8), Guest Services, film developing stands, the lost and found, and an ATM are all here. You can rent a stroller ($10, $16 for a double) or a wheelchair ($12, $40 for an electric convenience vehicle).

In addition, there are shops and restaurants. The Universal Studios Islands of Adventure Trading Company is a store that's almost as big as its name, and, because it has merchandise from all five islands, it's a good place for wrap-up shopping on your way out of the park.

Pause for a second as you near the end of Port of Entry. There's a great view of the Jurassic Park Visitor Center across the water, and if you've seen the movie, the authenticity of the structure, especially from this vantage point, will get you reaching for the camera. To your left is the tip board, which gives you information on the opening sequence of the rides, approximate wait times, and upcoming showtimes. The tip board is staffed by an Islands of Adventure employee who can answer any questions.

Helpful Hint

Some IOA restaurants, including the Confisco Grille, close in the off-season. But Universal does a good job of estimating crowd flow, so there are always enough places open to serve everyone in the park.

Port of Entry also has several dining options. Confisco Grille, the only full-service restaurant in Port of Entry, offers pasta, fish, and steak as well as lighter fare such as salads and sandwiches. Adjacent to the Confisco is the Backwater Bar, which serves half-price drinks during the 3-to-6 PM happy hour.

The Confisco hosts character meals during the on-season, and a table is set up across from the restaurant where you can

Time-Saving Tip

Islands of Adventure has plenty of quick-service restaurants scattered throughout the park, so finding food usually isn't a problem. But if you're visiting on a busy day, consider returning to Port of Entry for lunch. Crowds are usually lighter there.

make reservations for either character dining or a meal at the park's other full-service restaurant, the excellent and elegant Mythos, in the Lost Continent section of the park.

Fast-food choices include the Croissant Moon Bakery, which offers bagels, pastries, and a variety of coffees—it's a great place for a quick breakfast as you enter the park. Later in the day sandwiches and first-rate desserts are added to the menu. The Arctic Express offers funnel cakes and ice cream, while the Cinnabon next door offers the same gooey treats you find in malls and airports. Looking for something lighter? The Last Chance Fruit Stand has water, juice, and fresh fruit.

Time-Saving Tip

Express and Express PLUS passes are the way to go on crowded days. For $15 in the off-season or $25 in the on-season, the PLUS pass lets you into every Express line all over the park on an unlimited basis. Guests of on-site hotels get this perk without having to pay for the PLUS pass—just show your resort ID.

The basic Express pass is free with admission, and it lets you use Express lines on a reservation basis, much like the Fastpass system at Disney. You simply insert your theme park ticket into a kiosk near the ride and you'll get the ticket back along with a second ticket printed with an hour-long time frame in which you should return for Express-line access.

Unlike the Express PLUS pass, which lets you into any Express line whenever you like, you can only use basic Express passes one at a time, so make sure to use it for attractions that draw really big lines. You can get a second Express pass after (1) you have used your existing Express pass, (2) the one-hour time slot to experience the attraction has expired, or (3) two hours have passed from the transaction time at the bottom of the Express pass.

Marvel Super Hero Island

This is by far the wildest section of IOA, the island where super heroes fight bad guys, and theme park guests test their mettle on three high-thrill attractions. Most people are so busy dashing to the rides that they don't take the time to appreciate how well this section visually duplicates a comic book world. Signs are intentionally generic as in "Store," "Arcade," or "Café"; and colors are chosen to give everything a flat, grainy appearance.

The Amazing Adventures of Spider-Man

Spider-Man, the world's first 3-D, simulator thrill ride, is the most technologically advanced attraction in all of Islands of Adventure. The ride combines actual movement on a track, motion simulation, and 3-D effects. Unlike most 3-D shows, where you're sitting still and the action is coming toward you, in Spider-Man you're moving from scene to scene through a comic book story. It feels as if everything is really happening, especially the 400-foot simulated drop at the end, yet the actual ride movement is very mild. In other words, young kids or people who freak out on coasters can enjoy the ride.

The concept is that the Sinister Syndicate, made up of such comic book villains as Doctor Octopus, Electro, Hobgoblin, and Hydro Man, have taken over New York (wonder why the bad guys never nab Boston or Omaha?) and stolen the Statue of Liberty. Reporter Peter Parker, alias Spider-Man, is nowhere to be found and the city is in a panic. Chief Jamison, the bombastic newspaper editor, is "so desperate for the

Insider's Secret

The first row of the Scoop-Mobile has the best 3-D effects. The back row feels more of the spinning motion, and the middle row probably offers the most balanced experience.

story that I might have to send a bunch of tourists out in the ScoopMobile." That's your cue.

Stay alert while you wait in line; the queue area effectively sets up the story and the posters help you keep your bad guys straight. Thanks to Chief Jamison's utter disregard for the welfare of his cub reporters, even the instructional tape on how to load the ScoopMobile is hilarious.

The Scare Factor

Spider-Man has a 40-inch height requirement, which means quite a few preschoolers qualify to ride.

The actual ride movement has plenty of spins and bumps, but the infamous "drop" at the end is totally simulated, making it far more fun than scary. The real issue is the villains. The Sinister Syndicate throws everything it has at you, and the characters often appear very abruptly. If the in-your-face bad guys are too much for your kids, tell them to shut their eyes.

Once you're loaded in, you'll be immediately stunned by the quality of the 3-D effects, which make you feel as if Spider-Man is on the hood of your car and that bricks are flying toward your face. The ending of the ride, in which you're "thrown" off the top of a New York skyscraper and caught in Spider-Man's net, is the biggest thrill of all.

The first time through the ride you're focused on sheer survival, but Spider-Man is an attraction that holds up through return trips. Pay close attention to detail. For example, when Hobgoblin throws his fiery pumpkins at you, Spider-Man snares the first one in his net, but the second one goes awry and crashes through the wall and into the next scene.

Insider's Secret

The first time you ride Spider-Man, skip the Express and single-rider lines, and enter through the main entrance. The reason is that the walk-through to the ride is basically the preshow that tells you who you're fighting and why. Without it, you'll probably be wondering "Why are all these pieces of the Statue of Liberty lying around?"

Money-Saving Tip

As you exit Spider-Man, you'll notice how Universal Orlando cleverly encourages souvenir shopping. While you're still excited about the ride, you exit through a shop full of Spider-Man merchandise. Remember this rule: No souvenir shopping until the afternoon, when you've tried out lots of rides and know what you really want.

Once you know a happy ending is guaranteed, a return trip through is a blast. Consider what this mother of two from California wrote to us: "Spider-Man is a wonderful ride and my husband's favorite. The first time we rode it with our kids (ages 9 and 11) the younger one was terrified, not by the movement of the car but by the fact that the bad guys land on the hood of the car and it really feels like they're reaching out for you. But once she got off it and walked around a while, she wanted to ride it again."

Time-Saving Tip

Long lines? There are three ways to cut down on your wait:

- Use your Express PLUS pass or make a basic Express pass reservation to access the Express line.
- Stay at an on-site resort. Guests of Universal hotels are allowed Express-line access simply by showing their resort ID.
- Use the single-rider line. After you've gone through an attraction like Spider-Man at least once as a family, older kids might want to ride again on their own. The single-rider line moves much faster than the general-admission line.

The Incredible Hulk Coaster

This is not your mother's roller coaster, on which you slowly crank up a hill getting ready for your first plunge. The Incredible Hulk Coaster is big, green, and mean—just like David Banner after he played around once too often with those gamma rays.

The Scare Factor

The 54-inch height requirement eliminates many young kids, and Hulk is a pretty heart-thumping experience—probably too intense for any child under 10. Watch it make a few laps before you decide to ride.

The ride opens with a "cannon" shot from a 150-foot tube, zooming from 0 to 40 mph during the first two seconds of motion, then immediately flipping over to give riders the

Helpful Hint

Those lockers at the Hulk entrance are there for a reason, and they're free to use. Store everything you can because seven big flips can send car keys and sunglasses sailing.

sensation of going weightless. You'll make seven different inversions during the course of your ride, and twice disappear into a subterranean trench. Although the ride is wild, it's smooth, with very few jerky movements, and many coaster warriors swear that despite its awesome appearance, Hulk is the most user-friendly coaster in the park.

Insider's Secret

There's a separate line for those who want to sit in the front row, which has the best views, but the longest wait. The movement is wilder in the back of the car.

Dr. Doom's Fearfall

Dr. Victor von Doom is trying to defeat the Fantastic Four by sucking all the fear out of innocent citizens like you and using this collective fear to take over the world. (OK, so logic isn't the strong point of these rides.) The point is that you're strapped into outdoor seats, and shot 180 feet into the air. There's a bit of a yo-yo effect—you're raised and lowered several times—but the first five seconds of the ride are by far the scariest. Most riders report that once you're launched, you're fine.

Time-Saving Tip

On a tight touring schedule? Spider-Man and Hulk are must-sees, but you can skip Dr. Doom.

Insider's Secret

If you like Dr. Doom in the morning, you'll love it at night when you have the added thrill of looking down at the glowing theme park lights and CityWalk.

The Scare Factor

The height requirement is 52 inches for Dr. Doom's Fearfall, and whether your child should ride boils down to one question: How does he feel about heights? Most riders, including kids, think this ride is over too quickly to get scary.

Storm Force Accelatron

This simple spinning ride—the cups spin individually and the discs that they're mounted on also move—is a cranked-up version of the Mad Tea Party at Disney World. It's a good way to entertain younger siblings while older kids tackle the nearby Hulk.

The Scare Factor

Storm Force isn't scary, but like all spinning rides it can produce motion sickness. Riders control how fast the individual cars twirl (although there's nothing you can do about the circulating discs you're mounted on), so if you're feeling queasy, just back off a bit.

Toon Lagoon

Like Marvel Super Hero Island, Toon Lagoon is also devoted to comic strip characters, but these are the stars of the Sunday funnies—such as Beetle Bailey, Cathy, Dagwood, and the kids of the Family Circus. The focus of the island isn't the toon, it's the lagoon, and the attractions here are designed to splash you silly.

Dudley Do-Right's Ripsaw Falls

This log flume ride, in which you're helping Dudley and Horse save the perpetually pitiful Nell from Snidely Whiplash, culminates in a breathtaking 75-foot drop. The ride façade is so enormous that it serves as a park icon, and hardly anyone can walk by without stopping to gawk. The actual fall is even more dramatic than it looks; there's an explosion of light when the log enters the TNT shack at the bottom of the flume, followed by a second descent, in which you drop an additional 15 feet below the water level.

Needless to say, a descent of this magnitude isn't accomplished without a lot of splash. The water not only flies back in your face, but also sloshes into the log, puddling around your hips and feet. You'll enjoy the ride a lot more

Insider's Secret

The ride façade obviously spoofs Mount Rushmore, but also keep your eye out for a clever jab at Disney's Pirates of the Caribbean near the end of the ride.

The Scare Factor

Kids ages 7 and up name Dudley Do-Right as one of their favorites. The last drop is a definite squealer, so anyone with a fear of heights should think twice before getting in line.

when you're ready to get wet—in other words, in the hottest part of the afternoon—when you're also likely to encounter long lines. Dudley Do-Right's Ripsaw Falls boards slowly and hour-long waits are not uncommon.

Popeye & Bluto's Bilge-Rat Barges

If Dudley Do-Right is all about splashing, Popeye is about getting drenched straight through to your underwear. Parties of eight are loaded into circular rafts and sent on a wild and winding water journey. If through some miracle you manage to avoid the waves, the boat wash at the end of the ride spares no one. To add insult to injury, you're squirted with water guns by the kids aboard the nearby play area, Me Ship, the *Olive*.

For this reason, riding Popeye requires a bit of planning. Families in the know wear lightweight soccer-style shorts, don ponchos or plastic bags, or perhaps even bring a whole change of clothes. (If you were planning on buying a souvenir T-shirt anyway, hold off until after you ride, when fresh, dry clothes are bound to feel great!) Leave cameras and valuables inside the nearby lockers and stow everything else that you can in the central pouch, including shoes and socks. A wet fanny can lead to momentary discomfort, but wet socks can lead to blisters and ruin your whole day.

The Scare Factor

Popeye & Bluto's Bilge-Rat Barges is one of the best big-deal rides for young kids, and parents with kids as young as age 5 report that they loved it.

Although there are some sizable dips and drops along the way, the fact that the whole family rides together in a circular raft somewhat dilutes the intensity, making this ride a good choice for kids who are not quite up to Dudley Do-Right's megadrop but still want to try a water ride. And because the rafts hold a fair number of people and load quickly, Popeye never seems to have the daunting lines that are standard at Dudley. All in all, it's a good choice for the afternoon.

Insider's Secret

The three major water rides—Dudley Do-Right and Popeye in Toon Lagoon, and the River Adventure in Jurassic Park—are fairly close together. Ride them all in a row, and you'll only have to dry off once.

Me Ship, the Olive

This is a compact play area designed like a ship, with slides, climbing webs, and buttons that make tooting and beeping noises. Swee' Pea's Playpen is a separate play area for toddlers.

By far the most enjoyable feature of Me Ship, the *Olive,* are the water guns that allow you to take aim at the occupants of Popeye & Bluto's Bilge-Rat Barges below. If you have a child too young to ride Popeye, take him

Insider's Secret

Watch out—the squirt guns can squirt back!

aboard the *Olive* while you wait for the rest of the family to ride; he can seek revenge on his siblings as they pass.

Pandemonium Circus

A cartoon-character live show whose theme changes from time to time plays several times a day in the Pandemonium Circus Theater during the on-season. Showtimes are marked on your map. Although young kids enjoy these lighthearted shows, they're pretty simple, so check them out only if you have preschoolers in tow. The characters pose for pictures with the kids afterward.

Insider's Secret

Toon Lagoon is full of great photo ops. You can pose beneath the giant word bubbles, so that it appears you're saying or thinking such phrases as "It must be Sunday—we're in color!" and "I have the feeling people can read my thoughts!" The fountain on Comic Strip Lane is the hangout place for every cartoon dog you can think of and another fun place for a group snapshot.

Jurassic Park

As you walk through the high stone entryway with its torches, note the distant rumbling of unseen beasts, and look down at the fossilized leaves and footprints in the sidewalk before you. The Canadian pines around Dudley Do-Right's Ripsaw Falls have given way to lush tropical vegetation, and the merry beat of Toon Lagoon slows to an ominous jungle rhythm. Is there any doubt you've entered Jurassic Park?

River Adventure

One of Islands of Adventure's premier attractions, the River Adventure starts out with a mild cruise through the habitats of gentle vegetarian dinosaurs. Hmm, do you think we'll stay on course? If you don't know the answer to that, you have to go back to Theme Park 101.

Helpful Hint

Is there a gap in the ages of your kids? Or are some members of the family more risk-tolerant than others? You can always take the younger children to play areas while the older kids ride the scarier attractions. For example, Camp Jurassic is a good place for young kids to hang out while their older siblings try River Adventure.

The Scare Factor

Eighty-five feet may sound like a T-Rex-size drop, especially in contrast to the 75-foot drop next door at Dudley, but because you're loaded into much larger boats, the fall doesn't feel that intense. Most families report that they found the River Adventure plunge less frightening than the one at Dudley Do-Right. There is some atmospheric scariness, however, in the form of some very real-looking dinos. I think it's key to let nervous youngsters know what to expect in advance—that is, you'll get pushed in with the raptors. If it's any consolation, this part of the ride is very short—less than two minutes from the beginning of the climb to the final plunge. Our surveys indicate that most kids 7 and up love the ride.

Sure enough, a playful dino bangs your boat, sending you drifting into a restricted zone, and once you're inside the dangerous containment area, your boat is pulled up a long ramp past vicious little raptors that leap around spitting at you. When the T-Rex at the top decides you'll make a good snack, you escape via an 85-foot plunge—the longest, fastest, and steepest descent ever built on a theme park water ride.

Camp Jurassic

Of the three play areas in Islands of Adventure, this is the best one for kids 6 to 10. The setting is a group of posteruption volcanoes, with caves for hiding, and a multilevel, fairly rough terrain perfect for jumping, climbing, and exploring. There are slides, plenty of netting, and some take-no-prisoners water cannons. Because the Camp Jurassic play area is bigger and more spread out than Me Ship, the *Olive,* in Toon Lagoon and If I

Ran the Zoo in Seuss Landing, it's easy for kids to get lost. Unless you're sure they can find their way back to one of the benches where Mom and Dad sit waiting, you may need to go with them.

Pteranodon Flyers

This aerial ride, in which children dangle beneath the wide wings of a gentle flying dinosaur, is the first thing you see when you enter Jurassic Park. Ergo, most kids insist on making a beeline there. It is indeed a pleasant 80-second flight around lushly landscaped Camp Jurassic, offering you great views of Islands of Adventure. The catch is that only three birds, each holding two riders, are on the track at a time. That adds up to lines that stretch all the way back to the Cretaceous period, even on days when the park isn't crowded. On busy days, you can wait more than an hour, and there's no Express line. "It was so not worth it," a dad from Florida confided to us. "We waited longer for Pteranodon Flyers than anything else in IOA and the ride doesn't last but about a minute."

In an effort to cut down on the line, Islands of Adventure has limited the ride to kids 36 to 56 inches tall, allowing one adult to ride with each child. In fact, the entrance signs almost try to talk you out of riding, telling you that there are height requirements on both sides of the ruler and the ride lasts only 80 seconds. People flock to it anyway. Try to talk the kids out of riding unless you're there on a quiet day when the wait is less than 20 minutes.

The Scare Factor

Pteranodon Flyers is fine for anyone who doesn't have a fear of heights, although there's a bit more swing to the Pteranodons than you'd guess.

Insider's Secret

Pteranodon Flyers generally opens around 10 AM. The tip board will give you exact times. If your kids are determined to ride, be at the entrance to Camp Jurassic as close to opening time as possible. Once Camp Jurassic is open, the line at Pteranodon Flyers can jump to a 20-minute wait within seconds.

Discovery Center

The Discovery Center is like a small, very hip museum. Little kids can make dinosaur sounds while the older ones X-ray eggs and guess which species is inside. The Dino DNA sequencing profile lets you superimpose your face onto a dinosaur or you can test your scientific knowledge against two other contestants in my personal favorite, a raucous game show called *You Bet Jurassic.*

The biggest kick is when a raptor hatches from an egg, a wonderful little treat in which an authentic-looking audio-animatronics baby pecks his way through the shell. The kids in the crowd get to name it. Being in the Discovery Center for a birth is a bit of a hit-or-miss proposition, but a honking noise alerts you that one of the eggs is getting ready to crack.

The center is cool and relatively uncrowded, making it a good place to drop by in the afternoon, when everyone's energy is flagging.

The Lost Continent

The Lost Continent is probably the most thematically complex island in the park, encompassing three distinct sections. You begin in Merlinwood, which is based on the stories of Camelot and echoes medieval England with thatch-roof houses and Celtic music. This is where you can find Dueling Dragons, a

Insider's Secret

Speaking of afternoon, successful touring depends on getting a midday rest. If you're visiting in summer, when the parks run long hours, you may want to return to your hotel for a swim and a nap after lunch, returning to the park in late afternoon. This is a snap if you're staying on Universal property and can take the boat back to your hotel. Families with a car may want to try it as well, especially if the commute between their hotel and Islands of Adventure is 20 minutes or less. Just save your parking receipt for reentry, and keep in mind that it's a pretty good hike to the parking garage.

roller coaster based on a legend so rich it takes Merlin himself to narrate the tale.

Within a few steps, the music and the mood change to indicate you're now in the Arabic section, home to the *Eighth Voyage of Sindbad,* and a jumble of tented, Middle Eastern shops in the marketplace known as Sindbad Village. There are fortune-tellers and you can get your hair wrapped, your face painted, or your arm temporarily tattooed.

The last section of the Lost Continent is based on Atlantis. Here you can find the amazing-looking theater where *Poseidon's Fury* plays, and IOA's most elegant restaurant, Mythos.

Helpful Hint

Feeling queasy from your trip on Dueling Dragons? A first aid station where you can sit and recover is among the shops of Sindbad Village.

Dueling Dragons

This double roller coaster, meant to emulate the bat-

The Scare Factor

Dueling Dragons is hands down the scariest ride in the park, as the 54-inch height requirement indicates. Children under 7 aren't allowed to ride, and it may even be too much for many kids 7 to 11.

tling Fire and Ice dragons, is the fiercest in the park, running at speeds of 55 to 60 mph. Two suspension-style coasters (that is, they hang beneath the track) operate at once, coming so close—within 12 inches of each other—in their mock battle, that riders have the distinct impression they're going to crash.

The walkway to the ride is a long one, so there's plenty of time to establish the premise of how the Fire Dragon and the Ice Dragon have been fighting each other since time immemorial. As you wind through Merlinwood Castle, stained-glass windows tell the grim story of the demise of all who have approached the fierce dragons, and the muffled sound of their roars can be heard in the background. Merlin repeatedly advises you to turn back, but as you get closer to the ride, he accepts your determination and casts a spell to protect you.

You're gonna need it. Dueling Dragons is a technologically complex ride; once you're loaded into one of the coasters, computers calculate the weight of your group of riders and make minute adjustments in speed to assure that the two dragons do

Insider's Secret

Seeking the ultimate thrill? Dueling Dragons veterans say that riders in the outside seats are far more aware of how close the "close calls" really are. Or, if you want to have a good view of all the impending danger, queue up in the separate, longer line to wait for front-row seats.

Time-Saving Tip

If you want to ride Dueling Dragons twice to try out both Fire and Ice, try to ride once in the morning, and then get an Express pass for the afternoon, when lines can be monstrously long.

indeed come within inches of each other at various points along the track. The red Fire Dragon goes about 5 mph faster, but most of the survivors we surveyed felt the blue Ice Dragon, which has plenty of side-to-side movement, was the wilder ride.

The Eighth Voyage of Sindbad

This stunt show usually plays four to six times daily in the early afternoon and evening. (Showtimes are listed on your map.) The 25-minute show has everything you'd expect—fights, falls, drops, daring escapes, and comedy in the form of an inept sidekick whose pratfalls are a lot more dangerous than they look. The theater is large, so you shouldn't have any trouble being seated as long as you show up 15 minutes before showtime. *Sindbad* is a good choice for afternoon, when you'll welcome the chance to sit down and rest for a while.

The Scare Factor

Sindbad is another loud performance with lots of pyrotechnics. In fact, there's so much fire on stage that those in the first three rows of the audience will feel the heat on their skin. If your kids are easily frightened and sensitive to loud noises, sit farther back.

The Mystic Fountain

As you enter the theater where *Sindbad* plays, pause for a minute at the fountain in the courtyard. At various times throughout the day—including the periods just before and after a show—the mysterious spirit trapped within the Fountain of Knowledge will talk to you. The result is pretty funny as the spirit loves riddles, jokes, and questions, and will gently tease any kids willing to step forward and enter the game. Encourage the kids to ask a question and be prepared for lots of punk attitude, as well as an occasional blast of water.

Poseidon's Fury: Escape from the Lost City

This 20-minute walk-through show takes place in one of the most impressive buildings in the whole theme park, a crum-

Helpful Hint

You either walk or stand during *Poseidon's Fury*, so young kids in the back won't see much (this may be a blessing—see the Scare Factor). If you want a good view of the action, be sure to be among the first in your tour group to exit every room so that you can be in the front row in the next room.

bling castle from the lost underwater city ruled by the water god Poseidon. The story line is established in the long, dark (and somewhat scary for kids) queue area, where we learn that we're on an archaeological dig at the ancient temple of Poseidon. But there's trouble—the power keeps flickering on and off, a professor is missing, and the sleep of an evil priest has been disturbed. He wants to find a powerful trident and it's up to you, as the new archaeological team, to find the trident and restore it to its rightful owner, Poseidon.

The Scare Factor

Poseidon's Fury is a walk-through show, not a ride, but the special effects are intense and the noise level is very high in places. Once you enter the castle, you're literally a captive audience; there are a couple of exit points along the way if children become frightened, but for most of the show you're in a series of darkened rooms. If your children are nervous, stand near the back, especially in the final room where the battle reaches its peak; viewers in the front will feel the fire-and-water effects more intensely than those in the rear.

You move from room to room, and there are some great special effects along the way. At one point you walk through a swirling tunnel of water. The final scene is a battle between fire and water, with plenty of splashing and pyrotechnics.

Flying Unicorn

This is billed as a "kiddie coaster," but it has plenty of zip. Although it's a very simple ride, your coaster car is, as the name of the attraction implies, a unicorn that flies. Flying Unicorn is a good warm-up for more intense coasters, and even older kids love it.

The Scare Factor

Although the low (36-inch) height requirement means most preschool-age children are allowed to ride, the Flying Unicorn goes pretty fast and has a couple of steep drops. If you have any doubt the kids are up to it, watch it go through a few revolutions, and if you decide to ride, sit in the middle of the beast, where the ride is the least intense.

Seuss Landing

You'll find nothing but pastel colors and curved lines—even the trees are bent!—on this dreamlike island, where everything looks like it popped out of a Dr. Seuss book. Almost everyone stops in their tracks at the sight of the amazing Caro-Seuss-el and the bright flying beasties of One Fish, Two Fish. But take your time strolling through—some of the best visual treats aren't so obvious.

One Fish, Two Fish, Red Fish, Blue Fish

One Fish, Two Fish is an innovative circular thrill ride designed for young kids. Each fish has a joystick that controls the height of his flight, and throughout the ride you're given instructions such as "Red Fish fly high." If you opt to follow the instructions, that is, go "with

Money-Saving Tip

Are you a member of AAA? If so, you'll get a 10% price break on food and shopping throughout both IOA and Universal Studios.

Helpful Hint

Due to a relatively low rider capacity, One Fish, Two Fish can draw long lines in the afternoon. Come in the morning if you can.

The Scare Factor

One Fish, Two Fish is okay for any age. The joystick allows you to keep it low for kids who dislike heights. Everyone flies high at the end of the ride for a few seconds, but by that time nervous kids have been aboard long enough to get used to the idea. The two-fish cars are big enough to let several family members ride together.

the book," you stay dry. But if you disobey and go "against the book," one of the "bad fish" will spit on you. The idea is that this teaches kids to follow directions—I suspect it really shows them how much fun it can be to rebel—but either way it's a terrific ride, and in the finale everyone aboard gets a spritz.

The Cat in the Hat

This is a kiddie ride that's not just for the kiddies. My own 15-year-old and 11-year-old rode it several times on our last trip to Islands of Adventure, and a surprising number of kids from age 7 to 15 ranked Cat in the Hat as one of their favorite rides.

You board adorable couch-style cars to ride through 18 scenes taken straight from the well-loved book. The basic plot: Mom leaves and the Cat in the Hat shows up with those well-known literary rowdies, Thing 1 and Thing 2. All sorts of mayhem results, sometimes enough to send your couch spinning wildly, and through it all the poor goldfish frantically tries to maintain order. The effects are so funny that any rider, no matter what the age, will exit with a grin on her face.

Insider's Secret

The Cat in the Hat is like Spider-Man for the younger set. A lot goes on in a short time frame, and if you ride a second time you'll notice even more cute details.

The Scare Factor

Expect some bumping and a few fast, tight spins of the car. The ride is designed to appeal to any age, however, and most kids love it.

Helpful Hint

Preschoolers will enjoy the Cat in the Hat ride, as well as the other Seuss Landing attractions, much more if they're familiar with the Dr. Seuss books. Read them on the trip to Orlando.

Caro-Seuss-el

The 54 mounts of this ultimate merry-go-round are all lifted directly from the stories of Dr. Seuss. While the up-and-down and round-and-round motion is familiar to any kid who has ever been on a carousel, the real kick is that you can make the beasties blink, flick their tails, and turn their heads.

Helpful Hint

Snapping the kids aboard the colorful Caro-Seuss-el is one of the best photo ops in the whole park.

If I Ran the Zoo

IOA's third interactive play area was designed with preschoolers in mind, although older kids enjoy it, too. You can jump, climb, and squirt, as well as play tic-tac-toe with a Gak. Trap your friends in a cage of water or wait for the scraggle-foot Mulligatawny to sneeze—there's a silly surprise around every corner.

Insider's Secret

The emphasis on the big-deal rides makes many families automatically assume that Islands of Adventure is only for older kids. But the three play areas, and the attention to detail in all of Seuss Landing, show that Islands of Adventure has plenty to offer younger siblings as well.

Afternoon Resting Places

Families who'll be staying in the park all day need to build in afternoon rest stops to give everyone a chance to regroup. You basically have three options:

@ *Restaurants.* Consider making lunch your big meal of the day. A sit-down meal, either at Confisco Grille, Mythos, or CityWalk is a chance to get off your feet and relax.

@ *Shows. The Eighth Voyage of Sindbad* and the Pandemonium Circus show give you a chance to sit down in a theater for a while. The Jurassic Park Discovery Center, although a museum-style attraction, is a quiet, calm, and cool place to catch your breath.

@ *Play areas.* Sometimes kids just need to burn off their pent-up energy. If you suspect they need to climb, run, and play for a half hour, head for one of the three play areas.

Meeting the Characters

The times and places for character meetings are well marked on your map. The superheroes, including Spider-Man, appear in

Helpful Hint

Sometimes kids are overwhelmed by the characters, especially the Masked Marvels who show up on Marvel Super Hero Island, and the villains, such as Snidely Whiplash in Toon Lagoon and that nasty green Grinch in Seuss Landing. If your child appears nervous, don't push her forward; let her watch other kids pose for pictures for a while and she may loosen up. Asking for an autograph is a great way to break the ice.

Marvel Super Hero Island; cartoon characters make the scene in Toon Lagoon; and the Seuss characters can be found, logically, in Seuss Landing. If you want to be guaranteed autographs and pictures without the elbow of some stranger from Michigan in each shot, make reservations for the character lunch at Confisco Grille.

Tips for Your Last Hour at Islands of Adventure

If you plan to have dinner at CityWalk, rest assured that 10,000 other people have the same good idea. Make advance reservations as you enter in the morning, if possible, or at least try to be sure you're out of the park at least an hour before it closes. If you're not planning to eat at CityWalk, it's still a good idea to be on your way 30 minutes before closing time, when a wave of people hits the turnstiles at once, clogging the streets of City-Walk, and making the exit from the parking garage the scariest ride you've been on all day.

CityWalk

CityWalk is the dining, shopping, and entertainment complex that links Universal Studios with Islands of Adventure. A fun destination in its own right, CityWalk also provides theme park guests more dining options than what's in the parks. If you'd like a break from touring, just have your hand stamped, exit the

Helpful Hint
If you're staying on-site, make CityWalk dining reservations through Guest Services at your hotel. If you're staying off-site you can make reservations at a well-marked booth as you enter CityWalk from the parking deck in the morning.

park, and head for lunch at CityWalk. Or stop there for dinner on your way home in the evening.

Good choices for family dining include:

- *NBA City.* A basketball-theme restaurant that serves Shaq-size servings of steak, pasta, and sandwiches, as well as hearty appetizers such as buffalo wings and quesadillas. Basketball games, both current and classic, play on giant screens throughout the sports bar and restaurant.

- *Hard Rock Cafe.* You can enter this restaurant through either CityWalk or Universal Studios (the gate is near the Nickelodeon Tour). The Hard Rock is munchie central, with indulgent snacks like potato skins, nachos, and the signature Pig Sandwich. The gift shop always manages to have some of the coolest T-shirts around.

Money-Saving Tip
You can shop and dine at CityWalk without buying a ticket or paying a cover charge until around 8 PM when the club-hopping starts.

- *Jimmy Buffett's Margaritaville.* The menu focuses on southern Florida and Caribbean foods, but you can also find Cheeseburgers in Paradise. The Volcano Bar erupts margaritas on a regular basis, and entertainment consists of Buffett concerts on big-screen TVs and sometimes live music on the pleasant porch.

- *NASCAR Café.* Expect good ol' boy cuisine such as ribs, steaks, and fried chicken at this restaurant. Race fans will enjoy the memorabilia scattered around the restaurant, the servers dressed like a pit crew, the rumble of race broadcasts on overhead TVs, and the NASCAR-theme games in the dedicated play area.

◎ *Pastamore.* This Italian restaurant doesn't offer much entertainment, but the food is good and the lack of glitz makes it the easiest to slip into when CityWalk is crowded. Specialties include oven-roasted pizzas and excellent gelato.

Some CityWalk restaurants are more suitable for adults:

◎ *Emeril's.* The most upscale and expensive option at CityWalk, Emeril's offers amazing food, such as crabmeat-crusted tournedos of beef, citrus-glaze duck, and Maine-lobster cheesecake. The restaurant is never stuffy or overly formal and is, in fact, the perfect spot for a parents' night out.

Insider's Secret

Emeril's is a popular restaurant, so you need reservations, at least for dinner, and it never hurts to make them before you leave home. Call 407/224–2424 to get your name on the list. It's easier to find a table without a reservation at lunch.

◎ *Pat O'Brien's.* This New Orleans import serves gumbo, jambalaya, and po'boys, but is really known for its huge fruit drinks—especially the Hurricane, so named because it's rumored to knock you level in two-minutes flat. Enjoy your two minutes in the piano bar.

Helpful Hint

If you want to visit several CityWalk clubs on a parents' night out, you can buy a one-price, all-clubs Party Pass for about $10. The cover charge for one club is $2 to $3. The price of tickets for Hard Rock Live shows varies depending on the act.

Money-Saving Tip
During the off-season, when CityWalk is less crowded, holders of a multiday Universal pass are sometimes allowed into the clubs for free. Check when you buy your ticket.

@ *Bob Marley's.* Modeled after Marley's home in Kingston, Jamaica, this restaurant serves island-influenced dishes like jerk chicken, plantains, and tropical fruit salads. The outdoor patio is the perfect spot for casual eating and drinking, especially at night when live reggae bands play.

@ *Latin Quarter.* Some of the best food in CityWalk is served at Latin Quarter; examples of dinners include pork loin marinated in orange and cilantro, and broiled red snapper on yellow rice. Musicians play salsa and merengue music, while professional dancers and vacationing wannabes dance far into the night.

@ *CityJazz.* Intimate and low-key, CityJazz offers live jazz music and a limited menu of tapas-style appetizers, as well as a martini bar and a wide selection of wines by the glass.

@ *The Groove.* The most high-energy dance club at City-Walk, the "groove" hosts a variety of theme parties, including hip-hop, trance, retro, progressive, Top 40, and alcohol-free teen-oriented nights. To see what's playing the night you're planning to visit, check out www.universalorlando.com.

@ *Hard Rock Live.* A 2,500-seat auditorium adjacent to the Hard Rock Cafe, Hard Rock Live has a "state of the future" sound system and offers an impressive roster of musical acts. To check out who's playing while you're in town, visit www.universalorlando.com.

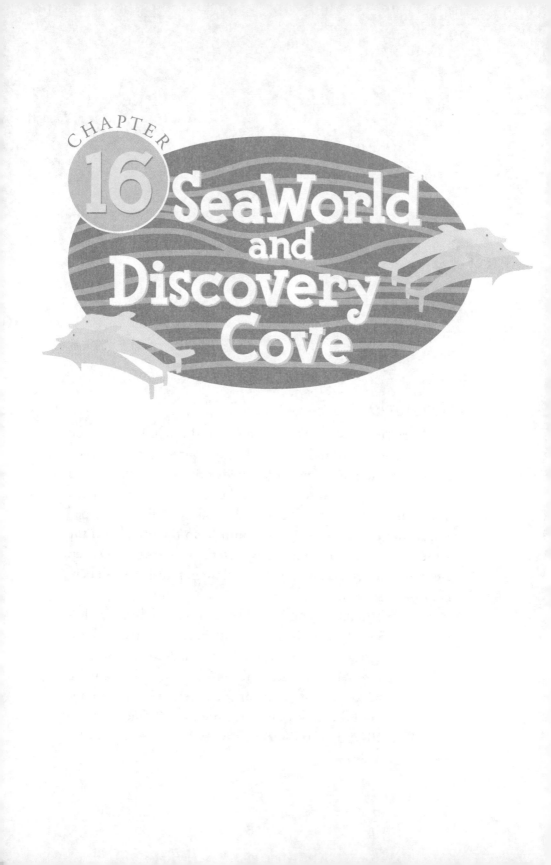

CHAPTER

16 SeaWorld and Discovery Cove

SeaWorld

SeaWorld is a low-stress experience, and much less frenzied than the other Orlando parks. Easily toured in six or seven hours, it's laid out so that the crowds pretty much flow from one scheduled animal show to another, working in the smaller attractions along the way. SeaWorld is so beautifully landscaped that you often can't see one stadium from the other, and the sense of space is a welcome change after a week spent at Disney. But the openness also means that children up to age 5 will benefit from a stroller.

SeaWorld admission is $62 for adults and $48 for children ages 3 to 9, excluding tax, but there's an incentive for buying your tickets online at least seven days in advance: the price drops to $56 for adults and $44 for kids. You can also find discount coupons at many off-site hotels or in local tourist magazines, and the park is also included in FlexTicket packages. Call 407/351–3600 or visit www.4adventure.com for more information.

Shows

For years SeaWorld's claim to fame has been its animal shows, especially those that feature the dolphins, the sea lions, and the park icon, Shamu. Although there are other shows with other featured animals, these three classics are the funniest and the most fascinating. See them if you do nothing else.

The dolphin show, the sea lion show, and the Shamu show all take place in enormous open-air theaters, so touring SeaWorld is as simple as consulting your map for showtimes and being at the theater about 15 minutes early. Clever preshows make the waits not only bearable, but also fun.

Other shows, such as waterskiing and acrobatics performances, are updated on a rolling basis. Pets Ahoy! features the comic talents of a group of dogs, cats, potbellied pigs, and other pets that were rescued from animal shelters. It's a favorite of young kids. Work in these shows as your schedule permits; they're well done but not as essential as the classic three—the sea lions, the dolphins, and Shamu.

Insider's Secret

Be forewarned that if you opt to sit in the "splash zone"—the first 10 rows of the stadium— Shamu's good-bye wave will leave you drenched straight through to your underwear. Kids enjoy the blast of saltwater, at least on a summer day, but if you're touring off-season or catching a nighttime show, it's wiser to sit farther back and laugh at the unwary tourists down by the tank.

Rides

There are only two, but they pack quite a punch. Plus, since the shows are the main attraction, the lines for the rides are shorter than at Disney and Universal. A mother of three from Michigan visited SeaWorld in the off-season and reported, "After all the time we spent waiting in line for rides at Disney and Universal, we were stunned to find that the rides at SeaWorld had practically no waits at all. There aren't that many of them, but the kids loved Kraken and were able to ride it several times with no wait."

Journey to Atlantis

On the Journey to Atlantis, guests are transported back to the lost city of Atlantis, and the ride combines the excitement of a water flume with a high-speed coaster. Designers call this hybrid a water coaster, and it's a thrilling, splashy ride.

Helpful Hint

If you have a rain poncho, bring it. This one's a soaker.

Guests board Greek fishing boats and are promptly lured by sirens into the depths of the lost city. The tiny boats twist, dodge, and dive at near-highway speeds through the water. For the first drop, the tracks come out of the front of the building, but the sirens pull you back for the second, unseen, 60-foot, S-shape drop.

Scare Factor

The height requirement is 42 inches and the descents are similar in intensity to the final drop on Splash Mountain. Kids 7 and up should be okay.

Kraken

Kraken is the fastest, tallest, and longest roller coaster in Orlando, and that's high praise in a town that takes its fun seriously.

Kraken reaches speeds of 65 mph with seven loops and three different points where it plunges underground into misty tunnels. We're talking major intensity. When I first read about Kraken, I suspected the name referred to the sounds your back and neck made as you rode. Not so. The motion of the ride is surprisingly smooth and the name actually refers to the great underwater dragon-monster of ancient Norse mythology.

Scare Factor

The height requirement is 54 inches. Needless to say, kids under 8 should not ride.

Standing Exhibits

SeaWorld is also known for its fascinating standing exhibits, such as the Penguin Encounter, where you can observe the tuxedoed charmers both above and below the ice floe, and witness their startling transformation from awkward walkers to sleek swimmers. Check your map, which is also your entertainment schedule, for feeding times, when the trainers slip about on the iceberg with buckets of fish and the penguins waddle determinedly behind them. The birds ingest the fish in one gulp and you can stand on the top observation level and watch for as long as you like.

If your kids are too cool to like cute, try the Terrors of the Deep exhibit, where you'll encounter sharks, moray eels, and barracudas up close.

The California sea lions live at Pacific Point Preserve, and in the Key West section, you can find the endangered manatee, as well as dolphins, stingrays, sea turtles, and other species indigenous to the Florida Keys. There are underwater viewing

Insider's Secret

At both the dolphin and sea lion exhibits you can buy fish and feed the animals. This is exciting for the kids and the ultimate photo op.

tanks where you can observe many of the animals from a different perspective. These continuous-viewing exhibits do not have special showtimes and can be visited at your leisure as you circle the park.

Wild Arctic is dedicated to polar bears. You can opt to ascend to the top of the exhibit either via a simulated helicopter ride or by walking. (Kids must be 42 inches tall to take the simulator ride.) The ride is a total snooze in comparison to the Disney and Universal simulator rides so you may as well save yourself the time and just walk to the top of the exhibit. The fun part is seeing the bears anyway, especially watching them from the underwater tanks.

Finally, the Budweiser Clydesdales are also part of the SeaWorld family and kids enjoy meeting these gentle creatures in their pretty stable. The nearby Anheuser-Busch Hospitality center is a quiet, cool escape from the rest of the park; beer samples are given out to adults and the deli inside is never as crowded as other SeaWorld restaurants.

Insider's Secret

At certain times of the day, noted on your park map, one of the Clydesdales is taken out into a paddock and children are allowed to get close enough to have their pictures taken. The horses are so enormous that it makes a memorable snapshot.

Preschoolers and Toddlers

Small children at SeaWorld welcome the numerous chances to get close to the animals, so save plenty of time for the standing exhibits where you can feed a sea lion or reach over to touch a dolphin or stingray. At theme parks it's easy to get caught up in dashing from show to show but, especially with preschoolers, it's essential to slow down and savor the small moments of animal interaction.

Another kick for kids is Shamu's Happy Harbor, a play area that's not only happy but huge, with an elaborate web of climbing nets, a ship with water-firing muskets, a splashy climb-through area, ball pits to sink into, and padded pyramids to climb. After a few hours spent in shows or exhibits, drop by and let the kids just play for a while.

A separate play area for smaller kids ensures that they don't get tangled up in the webs, whacked by an older kid on a tire swing, or, worst of all, lost. Because several of the play areas involve water, some parents let kids wear their bathing suits under their shorts and totally cool off. There's a midway and arcade next door where older kids can hang out while the younger ones play.

Helpful Hint

Appropriately, the crowd at SeaWorld moves in waves. The shows are timed so that you can move around the park in a circular fashion, taking in one show after another.

This also means, however, that if you want to visit standing exhibits, feed the animals, or play in Shamu's Happy Harbor, some times are far more crowded than others. For example, Shamu's Happy Harbor is virtually empty while the nearby Shamu show is going on, but the minute the show is over a flood of people stream out and head for the playground.

The solution? If you have young kids and would like to be able to play in the Harbor undisturbed or interact with the animals in a calm, unrushed manner, make note of when the shows are in session and visit the play area or standing exhibits then.

Educational Tours

If you're feeling guilty about taking the kids out of school, Sea-World offers educational tours. (Quick—can you tell the difference between a sea lion and seal?) The tours are reasonably priced ($16 for adults, $12 for kids), and reservations are not necessary. There's a booth near the park entrance where you can buy your tickets.

Sharks Deep Dive Program

If the opening bars of *Jaws* never fail to get your pulse rumbling, consider signing up for Sharks Deep Dive. Guests ages 10 and up can participate in the two-hour program that begins with a presentation on basic shark information, including the "myths about these misunderstood animals." (In other words, sharks are our friends.) Then guests don wet suits and either scuba or snorkel in a shark cage through a 125-foot-long habitat with more than 50 sharks. The dive isn't too long and the sharks in question are among the more harmless species, but it can still be a real thrill for preteens and teens.

The Sharks Deep Dive programs cost $150 per person. Call 800/406–2244 to reserve a spot in advance or visit the tour counter inside SeaWorld.

If all this is just a little too much excitement, you can still get a great view of the sharks by dining at the Sharks Underwater Grill, a full-service restaurant adjacent to the exhibit. The same 50 sharks, as well as colorful tropical fish, swim by while you dine on Caribbean specialties.

Camp SeaWorld

SeaWorld hosts a variety of camps for all age groups. Preschoolers (with a parent along) can participate in morning camps that explore how the animals are fed or how they play hide-and-seek in their environments. Grade-school-level children have lots of choices; there are weeklong camps that study dolphins, manatees, sharks, and other SeaWorld residents. Teenagers can participate in weeklong resident camps where they go behind the scenes of the park and assist the trainers in caring for the animals.

In addition there are family sleepovers where you can all actually spend the night inside the dolphin, polar bear, or penguin exhibit.

Most of the day camps take place in summer, although the sleepovers occur periodically throughout the year. For information on all your options, call 866/479–3267 (866/4SW–CAMP) or visit www.seaworld.org. The wonderful brochure describes all the classes for every age group and gets you so fired up that you want to register for everything.

Discovery Cove

Discovery Cove offers its guests a chance to actually have up-close encounters with dolphins and other sea life. Visitors swim and play with bottlenose dolphins, and then snorkel through clouds of fish in a coral reef lagoon. Or you can just enjoy the tropical island ambience of beach chairs, hammocks, swaying palm trees, cooing birds—and hardly any people.

That's right. The most unique thing about Discovery Cove is what it doesn't have. Crowds. This is a reservations-only park that admits a mere 1,000 people per day. With such a low number of guests, you truly have the personal attention of the staff, which includes expert trainers (many of them drafted from SeaWorld, Discovery Cove's sister park).

You check in at a concierge desk (!) and from there a guide takes you on a walking tour of the park, explaining all the activities. A swim in the dolphin lagoon is the undeniable highlight of the day, but reserved for guests 6 or older. The trainers teach you about dolphin behaviors and then lead you out into the water where you play with the dolphin and learn how to communicate basic commands. Once you and the animal get used to each other, you can end the session by grasping onto his dorsal fin and going on a wild ride across the bay.

The saltwater coral lagoon offers a variety of experiences, including the chance to snorkel among tropical fish. Since the water is calm, clear, and warm, and there are thousands of fish, this is a great first snorkeling experience for young kids. In the ray lagoon, you can play with gentle stingrays, some as big as 4 feet in diameter, whose barbs have been removed, or you can swim alongside barracuda and sharks kept behind Plexiglas.

Helpful Hint
Bring beach shoes. The pools are quite rocky.

A freshwater tropical river meanders its way through the park. As you float along you pass through several different settings, including a tropical fishing village, an underwater cave, and an immense aviary that houses 300 birds from all over the world.

When you've explored to your heart's content, there's no better way to end the day than by snoozing in your hammock on a white-sand beach.

So what do you pay for this bliss? Prices are $279 per person if you opt for the dolphin swim. If you're willing to forgo the swim with the dolphins, the price is $179, but you'll be missing the major thrill of the park. (Since kids under 6 aren't allowed to participate in the dolphin program, the price is automatically $179 for children 3 to 5.) The price includes wet suits, beach umbrellas, lounge chairs, towels, a locker, swim and snorkel gear, and lunch, plus seven-day admission to SeaWorld. When you factor in the SeaWorld tickets, the prices begin to seem a little more reasonable. For details and reservations (remember, they're a must), call 877/434–7268 (877/4–DIS-COVERY) or visit www.discoverycove.com.

Index